# Finding a Job Worth Having
for creatives & people who want to make a difference

## Fourth Edition

Vicki Lind, M.S.
Cynthia Dettman, J.D., M.S.W.

**Copyright© 2012, Portland, OR**
**Fourth Edition**
You may share a few copies of a few pages with friends and colleagues without permission. If you would like to reproduce more pages or a larger quantity, please contact us and we can work out an equitable fee.

**Career Services**
To learn more about Vicki Lind's career services, job clubs and workshops, see her website at www.vlind.com; email her at vlind@teleport.com; or, give her a call at 503-284-1115.

To learn more about Cynthia Dettman's individual and group coaching services, see her website at www.cynthiadettman.com; send her an email at cyndettman@msn.com; or call her at 503-754-0972.

**Editing and Production**
Sande Corbett
Ursala Garbrecht
Emmy Ageros
Erin Butler

**Graphic Design**
Angela Reat (www.linkedin.com/in/angreat)
Marianna Crawford (marianna@mcrawfordart.com)

**Ordering**
Each handbook is $17.95. For ordering more copies of the handbook, visit either of our websites at www.vlind.com or www.cynthiadettman.com.

ISBN **978-1-105-90655-8**

*You must be the change you wish to see in the world.*

Mahatma Gandhi

# Table of Contents

**INTRODUCTION** ...... 1
About the Authors ...... 3
About This Handbook ...... 6
Four-Phase Model of Career Transition ...... 8
Four-Phase Career Transition Checklist ...... 9
Ten Most Common Mistakes ...... 10
Surviving and Thriving ...... 12
Tools for the Journey ...... 13
Gifts to Give Yourself During Career Transition Stress ...... 14

**SELF-ASSESSMENT—PHASE I** ...... 15
Phase I: Self-Assessment: What's Inside? ...... 17
*Self-Assessment Tools*
Discerning Your Interests and Passions ...... 19
Jobs, Careers and Callings ...... 20
Your Personality Type ...... 21
Values Checklist ...... 22
Exploring Your Values ...... 24
Your Occupational Themes ...... 25
Skills Checklist ...... 26
Exploring Your Skills ...... 27
Technology and Social Media Self Assessment ...... 28
Technology and Social Media Skills Checklist ...... 29
Employer Characteristics Checklist ...... 30
Feedback Sheet: Instructions ...... 32
Feedback Sheet ...... 32
Self-Assessment Profile Summary ...... 33
Recommended Reading for Self-Assessment ...... 34
*Resources and Barriers*
Identifying Resources and Barriers ...... 36
Resources and Barriers Grid ...... 37
Families and Friends as Resources and Barriers ...... 38
How Long Will it Take? ...... 40
Reducing Negative Self-Talk ...... 43
Income for the Transition ...... 45
Ten Strategies to Simplify for the Transition ...... 47
Faith ...... 48

**RESEARCH AND NETWORKING FOR CAREER EXPLORATION—PHASE II** ...... 51
Phase II: Career Exploration: What's Out There? ...... 53
Career Exploration Checklist: What's Out There? ...... 55
*Researching Job Titles*
Brainstorming Possible Job Titles, Organizations and Career Arenas ...... 56
Short List of Possible Jobs ...... 57
Researching Job Titles ...... 58
*Researching Trends*
National Career Trends ...... 59
Oregon Career Trends ...... 60
Portland Career Trends ...... 61

iii

Portland for Creatives .................................................................................... 63
Careers in Fundraising and Development ...................................................... 66
Going to School ............................................................................................. 68
*Networking for Career Exploration*
Crafting Your Initial Basic Message ............................................................. 72
Your Approach to Social Media ..................................................................... 74
LinkedIn: Profiles and Inviting Connections ................................................ 76
Informational Interviews ............................................................................... 79
Requesting Informational Interviews ............................................................ 81
LinkedIn: Expanding Your Network .............................................................. 82
Networking SOBIN Style .............................................................................. 87
Staying in Touch with Your Network ............................................................ 88
Social Media: Twitter, Facebook, Virtual CV's, Websites, Blogging .......... 90
Strategic Volunteering ................................................................................... 94
Sample Request for Strategic Volunteering ................................................... 97
Deciding on a Career Objective ..................................................................... 98
Post Assessment Career Exploration Checklist: What's Out There? ............ 100

**FINDING THE JOB—PHASE III** ........................................................... 101
Phase III: Finding the Job .............................................................................. 105
*Job Search Strategies*
Pre-Assessment Job Search Plan Checklist: Finding the Job ........................ 106
Finding Job Openings on the Internet ........................................................... 107
Social Media: Finding Position Openings and Getting Insider Help ............ 110
Internships: Posted or Self-Designed ............................................................ 111
Sample Request for Internship ....................................................................... 112
Job Search for the Older Candidate ............................................................... 113
Telecommuting and Working at Home ........................................................... 114
The Spirit of Networking ............................................................................... 116
Networking by Email ..................................................................................... 119
Your Networking Contact List ...................................................................... 120
*Resumes and Cover Letters*
Resumes .......................................................................................................... 121
Accomplishments for Resumes ...................................................................... 122
Accomplishments for Creatives ..................................................................... 123
Accomplishments for People Who Want to Make a Difference .................... 124
Sample Resumes ............................................................................................. 125
Resume Checklist ........................................................................................... 133
Cover Letter Formats: Letter Style ............................................................... 134
Cover Letter Formats: Memo Style ............................................................... 135
Sample Cover Letters ..................................................................................... 137
*The Interview*
Preparing for an Interview ............................................................................. 141
Common Interview Questions ........................................................................ 143
Telling a Story in PAR (Problem, Action, Results) Format .......................... 144
Interviewing for the "Older" Candidate ........................................................ 146
Interviewing for the "Overqualified" Candidate ........................................... 147
What Should I Wear? ..................................................................................... 148
Interview "Thank You" Letter ........................................................................ 149
References ....................................................................................................... 150
Bad or "Iffy" References ................................................................................ 151

Post Assessment Job Search Plan Checklist: Finding the Job.........................................................152
Gifts to Give Yourself Before Starting Your New Job .................................................................153

**ACCEPTING THE JOB—PHASE IV** .......................................................................................155
Phase IV: Accepting the Job..........................................................................................................157
Mind Your "P"s: Is This the Right Job for You?..........................................................................158
How to Negotiate...........................................................................................................................159
Salary Research .............................................................................................................................160
Salary Surveys ..............................................................................................................................161
Conclusion: Saying Yes ...............................................................................................................162

**APPENDIX A—RESOURCES FOR CULTURAL CREATIVES** .............................................163
Books for Creatives ......................................................................................................................163
Websites for Creatives...................................................................................................................164
Professional Associations for Creatives .......................................................................................165

**APPENDIX B—RESOURCES FOR CAREERS IN SUSTAINABILITY** ...............................166
Explore Local Green Resources ....................................................................................................166
Websites for Local Sustainability Job Positions............................................................................167
National Websites: Job Postings and Career Information in Sustainability ...................................168
Green Occupations ........................................................................................................................169

**APPENDIX C—RESOURCES FOR SOCIAL JUSTICE**.........................................................173
Social Justice Websites and Books................................................................................................173

**APPENDIX D—RESOURCES FOR MAKE-A-DIFFERENCE TYPES** .................................175
Books for People Who Want to Make a Difference........................................................................175
Websites for People Who Want to Make a Difference ...................................................................176

**APPENDIX E—FUNDRAISING RESOURCES** .....................................................................178
Resources for Fundraising and Development Careers ...................................................................178

**APPENDIX F**
Community Resources for Your Transition ...................................................................................180

**APPENDIX G**
Funding for School........................................................................................................................181
How to Find, Organize and Win Scholarships ..............................................................................183

**APPENDIX H—CAREER SERVICES** ....................................................................................184
Vicki Lind: Career Counselor and Marketing Coach....................................................................184
Cynthia Dettman: Life and Career Coach .....................................................................................185

v

# Introduction

# About the Authors

*The only joy in the world is to begin.*

– Cesare Pavese

We can help you find a job that speaks to your triple bottom line: your values, your soul and your bank account. We have helped more than 250 kindred spirits in their career quests over the past 10 years. Most, like you and each of us, want to stay in the beautiful, yet economically challenged Portland area. We want to work for employers who share our commitment to helping individuals, our community and the planet. We sometimes are saddened and discouraged by the upside-down values of the dominant economy.

Career Counselors and Coaches find that our clients are stuck in one of two broad areas. Either they do not have a clear vision of what they want, or they do not know how to translate their vision into a job with adequate compensation.

Most people find career transition and job searching painful. They would rather have an epiphany, a fully formed career calling and clear direction to its door. You may have waited for the sparks and fanfare. However, you may now have run out of money or patience or both – and you're still waiting. There is a saying, "When one door closes, another opens," but no one tells you that it can be "hell in the hallway." We have both the formal education and the life experience to provide light in the hallway.

### Vicki's Formal Qualifications

I'm a Nationally Certified Counselor (NCC) with a master's degree in education from Portland State University, Oregon, and a master's degree in counseling psychology from the University of Oregon. A life-long learner, I later completed the coursework for a certificate in human resource management from Linfield College, Oregon.

### Vicki's Colorful Career Path

One of my greatest interests in life has been learning about the stages of human development throughout the lifespan. I believe that our twenties are a time for getting a broad education through both study and bold exploration – from studying poetry to traveling to India to playing in a band. Clients in their early thirties often tell me that they feel "behind" their friends who went straight through medical school, law school, etc. They can take heart from my own colorful, varied twenties. Before I was 30, I had the following jobs:

- Picked strawberries, babysat and was a camp counselor (Portland, OR)
- Created a neighborhood newspaper, *The Taylor's Ferry Herald* (Portland, OR)
- Sold overpriced alligator purses on Fifth Avenue (New York, NY)
- Planned programs in a camp for Hispanic mothers and children (Chicago, IL)
- Picked peaches (Israel)
- Helped in a camp for homeless people (France)
- Assisted in day treatment for the mentally ill (San Francisco, CA)
- Temped (San Francisco, CA)
- Taught at a day care center for African American children (Oakland, CA)
- Mothered Jessica and Miriam; lived on a commune (Mist, OR)
- Worked as a Fire Watch (Mist OR)
- Sold crafts at craft fairs (Portland, OR)
- Finished my first master's degree in education, putting down my first serious career roots.
- Became Head Start Education Coordinator (Clatskanie and Astoria, OR)
- Taught parenting classes at Clatsop County Mental Health (Astoria, OR)

- Taught Early Childhood Education and Psychology at Clatsop Community College (Astoria, O). After six years, I became more interested in how adults grow and transform themselves, using education as a tool. I admired the bravery and tenacity I saw in adults who decided to open new doors by finishing their education. I also woke up to the merits of health insurance and retirement planning and plunged seriously into a commitment to the following long-term positions:
    - Student Advisor for Linfield College (Albany, OR and Astoria, OR)
    - Director of Adult Degree Program, Linfield College (McMinnville, OR)

I was very successful for the first decade or more, followed by a few years of searing burnout, which culminated in being asked to resign. I insisted that they throw me a big celebratory good-bye party. I enjoyed the validation, but my leaving was followed by a period of pain and confusion. I share this because I have found that doing so has helped scores of talented professionals who have also had a mixed bag of successful and painful career experiences.

I wanted to get it right for my third career, and I followed a rough version of the process I outline in this book and use with my clients. I read career books and identified my top skills as facilitating groups, connecting people with resources and coaching/counseling individuals. I clarified what I valued: variety, autonomy, creativity and time flexibility to garden and make art. Then, I identified three options that seemed to match: diversity trainer, mediator and career counselor. I took six months to try out what I now label "strategic volunteering." And, Career Counseling won handily!

**Cynthia's Formal Qualifications**
Cynthia Dettman, J.D., M.S.W., is a Life and Career Coach with fifteen years experience teaching and coaching students in the community college environment. Earlier in life, she was a legal aid attorney advocating for the rights of battered women, minorities and low-income people.

**Cynthia's "Making a Difference" Journey**
My life journey has been blessed with colorful adventures, amazing people, educational opportunities, and career transitions galore. Throughout, I have been dedicated to advocating for the needs of women, minorities and those who lack voice and power. Here's a sampling:
- **Growing up:** Grew up in Tamil Nadu, South India, during the 1950s and 1960s, the daughter of liberal American missionary educators. I worked as a waitress and secretary after college; the BA in Sociology didn't get me anywhere! (***Moral of the story: develop marketable skills before you finish college!***)
- **Being a Poor People's Lawyer:** I attended a progressive law school that enrolled 50% women as early as 1974. I worked with miners in the mountains of Kentucky; helped farm workers in the melon fields of South Texas (even went to jail for being on a picket line!); argued a case before the West Virginia Supreme Court that resulted in the release of two African American women wrongly imprisoned with 25 year sentences; and started a battered women's hotline.
- **Dabbling in Journalism**: I left law after 11 years and jumped into Journalism School and had internships at the *Corvallis Gazette Times* and *The Oregonian*. I loved writing but decided against journalism. (***Moral of the story: get some career counseling and do informational interviews before going back to school and changing careers!***)

- **Finally got my dream job:** I earned my Master's in Social Work, and after an eight-year, zigzag series of temporary jobs, landed a position coordinating the Transitions Program at Mt. Hood Community College. There I provided Life and Career Coaching Services for diverse, low income women for fourteen years, and then partially retired in 2010 after earning good wages thanks to a strong faculty union and a powerful collective bargaining agreement. *(**Morals of the story:** explore public employment for good wages and benefits; AND career change takes time. Be patient; allow for serendipity.)*
- **Student Loans:** Eventually paid off all undergraduate, law school and grad school loans! In this case, it was worth the ride.
- **Adventures in retirement**: My novel, *The Fragrance of Skin*, is set in India and the South Carolina Sea Islands and will be completed in July 2012. I hope to be in Madurai, South India, from July-December 2012 teaching at a women's college on a Fulbright Grant.
- **Life as a Career Coach**: My eclectic journey and years as a Career Counselor have now joyfully culminated in a private Career Coaching practice. Based on my past career mistakes and successes, combined with extensive professional training and experience, I am blessed to be offering state-of-the-art coaching services to help others blossom into their dream jobs and careers!

**Moral of the story**: Do research before you change careers or go to school. Be adventuresome. Make a difference in the world. Be grateful. Enjoy our glorious, multicultural world and your freedoms, whatever they may be. Hang out with all sorts of people, including rich people and poor and oppressed people. See the world and have fun!

# About This Handbook

The four-phase model of career transition presented here is not special – it's pretty similar in sequence to what's presented by most career counselors and in career books. What is special is the process has largely worked for many, many people in the Portland scene. Because Portland's progressive community seems, at times, like a village, we have chosen to ask the people who have found a career that fits to share their stories. They have often shared their names. Each of these people began with only bits and pieces of a career picture. You may want to flip to **Conclusion: Saying Yes** to see how they ultimately emerged from the hallway, finding a "room of their own." Perhaps you know one of them; perhaps you feel like a kindred spirit.

- **Susan Gilson** knew that 20 years' work with budgets and policy, as a behind-the-scenes administrator in one organization, was more than enough. She knew that being around seniors made her happy and that she was ready to use her counseling/coordination skills with clients.
- **Alison Wiley** knew that she liked leadership and had skills in speaking, writing and relationship building. She wanted to reduce the carbon emissions that drive global warming.
- **Owen Wozniak** knew that he loved the outdoors and that getting a PhD in History no longer spoke to his greater calling to do work with an impact on the environment.
- **Cyd Cannizzaro** knew that her corporate job was bad for her soul and bad for the planet. Her first clue to her future was noting how much she loved to take out the recycling. As she says, I began "talkin' trash" to anyone who would listen.
- **Jennifer Bloeser** wanted to use her Masters in natural resource management to preserve the health of waters; however, funding for the Pacific Marine Conservation Council was simply no longer available.
- **Salvador Del Cid** knew that being a realtor was no longer rewarding, and he began to resent the constant interruptions to his weekend time with his family.
- **Laura Belson** loved her volunteer experiences. Now she needed to generate an income.
- **Lynn Welch** was worn out from the ups and downs of being a freelance creative.
- **Carla Ingrando** knew that she cared deeply about civic engagement and wanted to work for a foundation that gives money to worthy civic projects. She had a long talk with her husband, and they decided that it was worth it to move out of state, but only for the perfect opportunity.
- **Nancy Kramer** knew that she wanted out of low-paying, arts management non-profits. She craved to use her talent for organization and her commitment to diversity.
- **Kristine Mugot** just graduated, with a bachelor's in interior design, when the bottom fell out of that industry. She knew that she would need to choose a new direction.

**New Edition: Updates and Expansions to Reflect our Times**

Many of the career transition ideas and job search tips in this handbook are longstanding: you can pick up the first 1972 edition of Richard Bolles' *What Color is Your Parachute* and find similar encouragement to carry out a self-assessment and make networking a priority in your exploration and job search strategies.

Beginning in 2001, *Finding a Job Worth Having* brought Portland job seekers a unique emphasis on building careers in our local creative, nonprofit, educational, healthcare, and sustainable communities. This emphasis continues, and with the participation of new co-author, Cynthia Dettman, resources have been added related to social service and social justice careers.

In addition, significant revision and expansion has gone into addressing two influences that are now dramatically impacting local career transition and job search. **Technology and Social Media** now impact all stages of job search, career development, and job success. **The Slow Economic Recovery** has limited some options and sharpened the need to balance career realism with career optimism.

**Technology and Social Media**

Staying or getting up to date on technical skills presents something between a welcomed challenge and a nightmare to "technophobes." Since use of the web and other technology is now key in most professional jobs, employers expect you to come with skills commensurate with the proficient current college graduate. This includes proficiency in the most widely used tools such as web research and Office Suite (Word, Excel, Access, PowerPoint), as well as those specialized to different industries.

We have included a new section on Technology Self-Assessment to help you assess your starting point, set goals, and track progress. After you have selected a career objective and researched needed technical skills, you will be able to review and update this technology self-assessment.

Social media, especially LinkedIn, now plays a powerful role in a robust networking and job search plan. Begin or update your LinkedIn and Internet presence with the most open and curious attitude you can muster. Say to yourself: "Hmm. I want to find out what all the fuss is about."

If you hear yourself groaning, you may need to try a few tactics to get an "attitude adjustment." Try engaging friends, relatives (such as teens who grew up with computers as toys) or workshops that help you tackle one growth step at a time. We'll give you encouragement, tips, and guidance throughout the new edition of the handbook.

**The Slow Economic Recovery**

Every headline and every political candidate remind us that unemployment rates remain high and that job growth is improving slowly, particularly in sectors hit the hardest by the recession. Those of you in building-related fields or government/social programs still see very few position openings. Yet, you can't stop and freeze your career development until things pick up. You must do thorough research, make a decision, and offset inertia with step-by-step action. Decisions such as whether to invest in more education or to relocate to follow potentially rewarding jobs take serious reflection and analysis. This handbook includes expanded information about education and funding for school.

To offset this weak economic picture, you can derive strength and grounding from the huge wave of kindred spirits committed to sustainability, social justice, and work/life balance. Portland's Five Year Economic Development Plan emphasizes bringing in clean industry, and the 2011 report lists major accomplishments of bringing to Portland industry-leading companies including Vestas North America headquarters, SoloPower, a maker of thin solar cells, and ReVolt Technology, a leader in energy storage. We have also developed the wind energy supply chain; this effort led to a two million dollar increase in sales for local producers of turbine parts and service providers assisting with ongoing maintenance. On the smaller scale, it is encouraging to see expansion of Portland favorites such as New Seasons Markets, bike shops, and the explosion of small, creative, entrepreneurial, and solo businesses.

We believe that the best antidote to barriers is the following brew:
- One part: driving commitment to making a better community and world.
- One part: strong personal and professional support system.
- One part: knowledge of tactics and information to separate fear from fact.
- One part: ability to break things down into manageable steps, following the phases and suggestions we present in this handbook.
- Stir and repeat as needed.

# Four-Phase Model of Career Transition

**Phase I. Self-Assessment: What's Inside?**

An introspective examination of your self as a professional is the core of the first phase. This is the time to clarify what you really want in a new career or job, and a time to identify your key **interests, personality type, values, skills** and **the characteristics of your ideal employer**. It's also critical to assess both your **computer and social media skills** and identify those that will boost your career. It's a time to reflect on who or what in your life will provide meaningful support during the stressors of a career change. As an outcome, you will create a one-page **Self-Assessment Profile Summary** of five key interests, passions, values, skills and employer characteristics.

**Phase II. Career Exploration: What's Out There?**

You will go through the process of **examining your various career choices**, eventually narrowing them down to the two to four possibilities that best match your interests, personality, values and skills. You will begin by brainstorming as **many options as possible** (fifteen or more) that could match your Profile Summary without worrying about practicality. Then select the **top contenders and systematically research** each one, using a combination of electronic and print resources as well as discussions (i.e., informational interviews) with people who work in those fields.

**Phase III. Focused Job Search: Making the Match**

Make a **commitment to one or two career destinations** and follow a multi-part action plan that will get you hired. You begin by crafting a heartfelt "basic message" that summarizes your strengths and specifies job titles and/or organizations. You then identify and develop **job leads** through networking and print and Web-based resources. You will tailor your resume, cover letter and interview strategies to those jobs. Finally, you will draw on the skills honed during your research and **interview practice** sessions to win a job offer. The door, at last, has opened.

**Phase IV. Winning and Accepting the Job**

In today's tight job market, you need to be systematically upbeat and positive throughout the interview, even if you do have concerns. Once you have been offered a position, you may ask for another face-to-face meeting to candidly discuss those concerns. Before you say "yes" and go through the door, it is advisable to reflect again on your values and skills. Will you really be satisfied in this new environment? Once you have garnered the offer and decided to accept, it is the time to see if you can **negotiate the offer** for compensation and/or ask for any other changes such as working hours, vacation time, title or location to maximize your job satisfaction.

# Four-Phase Career Transition Checklist

**Phase I. Self-Assessment: What's Inside?**

- What social/environmental/aesthetic issues **interest** you?
- What is your **personality type**?
- What are your **values**?
- What **skills** do you want to use?
- What **technology skills** do you need?
- What **characteristics** do you **need from your employer?**

**Phase II. Career Exploration: What's Out There?**

Define Career/Job Title Options

- Obtain business cards with contact information
- Create an initial LinkedIn Profile and invite connections
- Brainstorm 15+ job titles/organizations
- Select two to four job titles/organizations to research

Research

- Carry out informational interviews
- Use web sites to research career responsibilities, salaries, training needed and outlook
- Explore LinkedIn groups and ask questions to others in your field

**Phase III. Focused Job Search: Making the Match**

- Commit to a specific **career objective** (and, possibly, an alternative)
- Refine your **basic message** and LinkedIn Profile to fit your career objective(s)
- **Target your resume** to your career objective(s)
- Identify three to six **job search sites** or listservs and select best key words
- Follow ten to twenty **target employers** on their websites and/or on LinkedIn
- Connect with resources and **professional organizations** that can provide job leads
- Consider **strategic volunteering,** internships, or entry-level positions in targeted organizations to build skills and contacts needed for your career objective(s)

**Phase IV. Winning and Accepting the Job**

- Develop an interview strategy and practice examples of your strengths in action (PAR statement); research each organization prior to an interview
- Discuss any areas of concern with the potential employer
- Research appropriate salary ranges and negotiate

# Ten Most Common Mistakes

### Mistake #1: Having Too Many Career Options

Most of you are divergent, creative thinkers with many skills and interests in multiple environmental, social and aesthetic issues. We salute you; we join you. But you need to focus your search on one or two arenas, because you will need a separate networking strategy and knowledge base for each career target. After an initial broad exploration, narrow down to one or two arenas such as housing, natural resources, Web design, landscape architecture, green building, public relations, etc.

### Mistake #2: Thinking with Your Heart

You do start with your heart to determine your values and passions that will drive your career decision. However, once you have some options to explore, you will need to shift to your brain to analyze marketplace need. If you are really passionate about growing gardens with low-income people, you may find that there are less than a handful of positions in Portland. After you thoroughly analyze your odds, your time frame and your financial needs, you may need to simultaneously follow the trends, including legislative changes, to see where more plentiful options are emerging.

### Mistake #3: Expecting It to Happen Quickly

The stark reality is that it often takes two or more years to transition into a new, crowded field. This is particularly true if you want to change both your job function and the type of organization. Many people spend a year or more volunteering or in entry jobs to position themselves for meaningful and well-compensated professional positions.

### Mistake #4: Less Time Online, More Time Networking

Reviewing job postings online can be mesmerizing. There are lots and lots of horrible jobs listed there and only a few that match your skill set. It is better to limit your time online, and read this handbook to flesh out a networking style that works for you. Plan on looking for jobs online up to two times per week for one to 1 ½ hours (or until your eyes get blurry).

### Mistake #5: Failing to Broadcast Your Skills and Needs

You need a basic message that clearly states what you are looking for so that others can more readily help you. Then you need to actually use your message – a lot. For example, Lori B. found a lead that unexpectedly resulted in a job at Parametrics by broadcasting, "I want to meet people who work on air or water quality compliance issues. I want to use my eight years of business background along with my degree in Environmental Science. My strengths include being organized, a good writer and passionate about creating a healthier environment."

### Mistake #6: Indiscriminate Volunteering

Strategic volunteering can be one of the most potent job search tools; indiscriminate volunteering may waste your time even if it promotes wonderful causes. Strategic volunteering means selecting volunteer activities in an organization that might hire you, or where you can meet many people who might hire you, or where you can learn a desired skill to get hired.

### Mistake #7: Expecting to Date the Prom Queen

In every worthwhile field, there are a few "prom queens" that draw a large volume of applicants. In the creative world, Weiden+Kennedy is our local queen with high-end design firms such as Zeba and Second Story sharing the spotlight. Many sustainability-oriented people cite The City of Portland's Bureau of Planning and Sustainability as their ideal career mate. Unless you have the exact qualifications, including those preferred or known to the decision makers, it's best to focus elsewhere. There are more options and better odds when you target less visible organizations, especially those that are growing in their commitment to creativity and making a difference.

**Mistake #8: Hiding Volunteer Activities on the Second Page**
If your volunteer work is relevant and includes professional-level activities, a description should be included in the first page of your resume. This can be done if you label the section with your job history as "Professional Experience." If it was a significant activity and extended over time, you should mix it into the chronological section along with your paid positions. In this case, you would note "volunteer" in parentheses after the position title. Stuffing envelopes, no! Chairing the fund-raising committee for the symphony, yes!

**Mistake #9: Submitting a One-Size-Fits-All Resume**
Your resume needs to be targeted to each position or type of position. Readers don't have time to read through extraneous material that detracts from their focus on how you match their needs. Start with a summary of qualifications that match those identified in their position announcement. Purely chronological formats work if your most recent job (appearing on the first page) is the most relevant. If not, start with a summary of qualifications or a few functional areas that match the qualifications listed in the announcement. Using vocabulary directly from their listed responsibilities or qualifications may seem uncreative, but it can be the most effective because it is easiest for the person sorting the resumes to see that you meet the requirements in the few seconds of the first scan of the stack. The purely functional resume without descriptions under the jobs in chronological order leave the hiring managers wondering, "Exactly where did he/she do what?"

**Mistake #10: Doing it on Your Own**
It helps to work with a career counselor, participate in a job club and/or find a job search buddy. Career development and job hunting are emotionally draining – they require commitment to an ongoing process rather than fits and starts. For more **Career Services** information, please see **Appendix F**.

# Surviving and Thriving

The career transition process is deeply personal and challenging for most people. You probably will experience periods of emotional upheaval and doubts. Job seekers rarely talk about these feelings publicly since it is important to show a positive face during networking. If you are employed unsatisfactorily, you may have to pretend that you still find selling socks meaningful. Or, if you're unemployed, you may hate being continually asked how the search is going. You may say, breezily, "I'm enjoying spending quality time with the kids, and there are several interesting options that I am exploring." You wish you could groan lavishly and say frankly, "I feel like last year's style that you find in the Goodwill sale bin."

To offset the emotional challenges, it is important to assess your resources; review your emotional needs; and stay in contact with people who provide positive support – or fun respite when you feel worn down. Some experts claim that job seeking is a full-time job. We don't agree. We think it is an excellent time to develop a schedule that balances job-seeking tasks at the computer, enjoyable networking, skill building, self-care and pleasure. It is also a wonderful time to engage in physical, spiritual and social play that won't fit as easily into your schedule after you have a job.

Career and personal counselor, Gail Nicholson, and Vicki Lind created the following checklist, **Tools for the Journey** to help start your transition with a positive mindset. The checklist has three categories of activities: practical elements that support your journey, elements of spiritual/emotional support and means for engagement in community. These are discussed briefly below.

### Practical Elements

We start the checklist with practical tools, particularly the importance of creating and stocking an attractive area in which to work. Vicki's father, a small business consultant, advised, "You'll work best with a clean desk that only includes three items: your immediate task, a picture of someone you love and something living, like a plant or goldfish."

### Spiritual/Emotional Support

We next turn to tools that will strengthen you internally and help you invite joy, peace and meaning into your process. It is a time to review the tools that have helped you through other life challenges, from journaling to golf. It is a time to find and strengthen your connections to people who can both share the inside journey and support the outward tasks of the search. In addition to supportive family and friends, you might consider working with a career counselor. We can help you clarify a career goal, overcome doubts and fears, and/or provide practical tools such as resume and interview help. Almost all of us provide at least a free 20-minute phone consultation and have personal Websites. In short, the time to call is when you have tried your other resources and feel stuck.

### Community Engagement

If you are unemployed, you have probably lost the community of co-workers that you engaged with on a daily basis. Belonging to communities, even taking time to meet your neighbors, provides personal support at a challenging time; and, it provides networking opportunities that are integral to the successful job search.

# Tools for the Journey

| | I=Important<br>D=Desirable<br>N=Not Important | Action Step | Date to Schedule |
|---|---|---|---|
| **1. Practical Elements** | | | |
| Attractive work area | | | |
| Day-Timer | | | |
| *Do Not Disturb* sign | | | |
| Organize files | | | |
| Update e-mail address book | | | |
| Money/ temporary income for transition | | | |
| Dedicated work space | | | |
| Improve computer skills, including LinkedIn | | | |
| Other: | | | |
| **2. Spiritual/Emotional Support** | | | |
| Inspirational reading/music/film | | | |
| Journaling | | | |
| Supportive family & friends | | | |
| Career counselor | | | |
| Getaways | | | |
| Reflection time | | | |
| Creative expression | | | |
| Small daily gifts of self-care and fun | | | |
| Other: | | | |
| **3. Community Engagement** | | | |
| Professional association | | | |
| Neighborhood involvement | | | |
| Strategic volunteering | | | |
| Church/spiritual affiliation | | | |
| Other: | | | |

By Gail Nicholson and Vicki Lind

# Gifts to Give Yourself During Career Transition Stress

Perhaps the list of most common mistakes for those in career transition was discouraging, and you realized that there is a lot to learn. Throughout the process, we encourage to you to take out time for pleasure and exploration. To help you get started, we've placed 25 ideas below.

- Visit Portland's Japanese or Chinese Garden
- Search out a long-lost friend
- Walk instead of ride
- Look at the stars
- Use a new word
- Open up to the person nearest to you
- Veg out in front of your favorite television program
- Go to the downtown library and admire the steps
- Browse in a bookstore
- Be thankful
- Go to an arts festival
- People watch at a public place and make up stories about their lives
- Hug a tree
- Tell someone that you love him or her
- Snuggle in bed with a good book
- Take a rainy-day nap
- Sign up for a class or workshop
- Do something that you have always wanted to do
- Meditate
- Surprise a child
- Relax in a hot tub
- Go the next step with technology
- Take a vacation from your job search
- Read about someone whose life had purpose
- Draw a picture, even if you can't draw
- Add your own:

- _____
- _____
- _____

# Self-Assessment
## phase I

# Phase I. Self-Assessment: What's Inside?

Begin by looking inward and identifying your interests, personality type, values and skills. In addition, it helps to specify what criteria your future employer would need to meet, from location to compensation. For your new career to be deeply satisfying, it is necessary to understand your authentic self. In our first jobs, it is common to "fall into" something that crosses our path. Serendipity leads to a door that is ajar. The task of the young adult is to find out who he or she is by hanging out in some interesting, diverse rooms. Before Vicki reached 25, she had been a fruit picker in Israel; a rural preschool teacher; an advisor for developmentally delayed men; a children's crafts teacher; a camp director for Hispanic women; and a seller of alligator purses on Fifth Avenue in New York City.

As we mature, we learn to reflect on these diverse experiences and reject the rooms that do not feel right for us. This process of becoming oneself is captured by May Sarton, a writer who came fully into her own self in her 70s and 80s.

> *Now I become myself*
> *It's taken time, many years and places*
> *I have been dissolved and shaken*
> *Worn other people's faces*
> – May Sarton
> "Now I Become Myself" in *Collected Poems*,
> 1930-1973. New York: Norton. 1974. p. 150.

### Interests and Passions

The first part of self-assessment is a reflection on sustaining interests and passions. Our souls shrivel if we do not follow their lead, either vocationally or avocationally. Most career counselors stress interest as the greatest predictor of career success because interest sustains the drive to succeed through challenging times. Some Creatives and social activists are driven by such a compelling passion that they are certain only one room is for them. Practical concerns may fade next to the intensity of such a passion. For such a person, the room that says "Actor" may seem to have such magnetism that the excitement quells the voice of practical concerns. Another career seeker with a passion for acting may be more inclined to value financial stability and take performance into more prosaic arenas, such as becoming a teacher or theater promoter.

### Psychological Type

Jung coined the term "psychological type" as a way for people to look at their natural, healthy preferences in four areas: introversion/extroversion, sensing/intuition, thinking/feeling and judging/perceiving. Career counselors often use the Myers-Briggs Assessment to help career changers look at their type and the careers that tend to fit each type.

### Skills and Expertise

We generally are happy in careers in which we can use skills for which we have a natural aptitude and/or which we have honed through practice. Therefore, the next step is to review a range of widely applicable skills and rate both your enjoyment in using them and your level of competence.

It is important to be honest about the limits of your competence, as well as your strengths. As an adult, you have tried out many skills with uneven results. Let both the negative and the positive feedback you have received be your teacher. Successful career dreams evolve if they are consistent with your skills and nature. "Everything in the universe has a nature, which means limits as well as potentials," says Parker Palmer in *Let Your Life Speak*. He goes on to say, "Making pottery, for example, involves more than telling the clay what you dream it can become. The clay presses back on the potter's hands, telling her what it can and cannot do – and if she fails to listen, the outcome will be both frail and ungainly" (Ref. Parker Palmer. *Let Your Life Speak*, V: Amazon States. 2000. p. 16.).

Therefore, the purpose of the skills exercises is to eliminate areas where your results have been ungainly. For example, facing reality, for Vicki, is acknowledging that she has some passion for rock and roll, but being tone deaf for a few decades limits her access to most musical careers. The final step is to narrow the field and identify approximately five top skills that use your talent and bring you enjoyment.

### Technology and Social Media Skills
In this day and age, analyzing your competency with a variety of technology skills and comfort with social media is key. Notice as you are dealing with the challenges of learning new technology how you relate to learning it. We are happier when we are challenged in ways that excite rather than frustrate us. While some of these skills are basic for almost any career, the growing number of technology focused employment opportunities may help us decide how important this is for our career exploration and decision.

### Characteristics of Employer
After you identify your passions/interests, values and skills, and decide which ones you want to bring to your next job, you need to identify what the employer must offer you in order for the position to be a fit. Since you have already identified key values, focus on the practical concerns, such as minimum salary and compensation, purpose of organization, geographic locations, etc. It is also a good time to commit to characteristics of the employer that are non-negotiable, such as fair-trade practices, inclusive management style and family-friendly policies.

### Summary
As an outcome of self-assessment activities, complete the **Self-Assessment Profile Summary (p. 33)**. Many creative and socially committed people have numerous and varied skills and values. (On a good day you may feel like a Renaissance person; on a bad day like a dilettante.) In order to focus your career search, it will be necessary to prioritize and limit yourself to five top interests/passions, values, skills and employer characteristics. The **Self-Assessment Profile Summary (p. 33)** will become a guide to the next, more concrete step: the identification of possible job titles.

*Feel yourself drawn*
*by the deeper pull*
*of what you truly love.*
– Rumi

# Discerning Your Interests and Passions

Reflect on several of the following questions. You may find it helpful to write about them and/or discuss them with someone who knows you well and is a good (i.e., non-judgmental) listener. We suggest answering the questions twice. The first time, do it without restrictions, straight from the heart. Then, if your answers are all about jazz and poetry and dogs and talks with friends, this is invaluable to know. If so, do the list a second time, removing those passions that you are content to keep in the non-career part of your life. If your remaining list is very small, look for additional answers that tend to intersect more with the world of work. Aim for keen interest as a criterion, and save time for your deepest passions in your free time.

What do you love to do when you have spare time?

What social and/or environmental/creative concerns are most important to you?

What groups do you most enjoy interacting with? (Examples: children, teens, professionals, elders, people from other cultures, Creatives.)

What are the recurrent topics in books and magazines that you enjoy reading?

What are your recurrent work-related daydreams and fantasies?

Where have you been the most successful (in your eyes) in doing something that matters?

What are some passions and interests that you had as a young person that are still important to you?

What topics do others tire of hearing you talk about?

Which courses or fields did you enjoy most in school?

Who are your heroes and heroines, and what were they passionate about?

Reflect on those that are most important to you in your next job. Select five to transfer to the **Self-Assessment Profile Summary (p. 33)**.

# Jobs, Careers and Callings

Martin Seligman studies the art of happiness in love and work in his book, *Learned Optimism*. We were interested in the following observations he made about satisfaction on the job, published in *Newsweek* (September 16, 2002):

> Scholars distinguish three kinds of 'work orientation': a job, a career and a calling. You do a job for the paycheck at the end of the week, and when the wage stops, you quit. A career entails a deeper personal investment in work. You mark your achievements through money, prestige and power, and you move on when the promotions stop. Unlike a job or a career, a calling is a passionate commitment to work for its own sake. The effort you expend becomes its own reward, regardless of the money or status it brings. People with callings are consistently happier than those with mere jobs or careers.
>
> And if you think callings are only for artists and healers, think again. Recent studies suggest that any line of work can rise to that level. In one seminal study, researchers led by Amy Qrzesniewski of New York University studied 28 hospital cleaners. Some viewed their work as drudgery, but others had found ways to make it meaningful. The cleaners with a calling believed strongly that they were helping patients get better, and they approached their work accordingly. They timed themselves for efficiency. They prided themselves on anticipating the doctors' and nurses' needs. And they took interest in brightening the patients' days, whether by rearranging furniture or decorating the walls. Researchers have seen the same phenomenon among secretaries, engineers, nurses, kitchen workers and haircutters. The key to contentment, their studies suggest, is not getting the perfect job but finding one you can make perfect (or at least better) through the use of your own strengths.
>
> Part of what turns a job into a calling is the state known as flow. My colleague Mihaly Csikszentmihalyi (Mike for short) defines flow as complete absorption in an activity whose challenges mesh perfectly with your abilities. Flow is not the pleasure you derive from a warm shower or a cold beer but the loss of self-consciousness you experience while engrossed in a task that calls on your strengths. People who experience it are not only happier, but more productive, for they stop thanking God that it's Friday. "I have always subscribed to the expression," the historian John Hope Franklin once said, "because to me Friday means I can work for two days without interruption."

The definitions of these three categories are more simplistic than our experience leads us to conclude. There are many people who have careers that may not be their ultimate calling, who find a lot of meaning in their work. They are not, as Seligman claims, motivated only by prestige and financial goals. We agree with Seligman, however, that people with callings are internally driven to show up for their work, regardless of the compensation. Yet, we find that as we move past our young adult years, true career happiness often occurs when responding to a calling that also meets important financial goals.

Even a true calling can grow faint when the voice of unmet financial needs fills the mind. It is most helpful to move beyond dividing jobs into two stereotypical factions: those with no soul that pay well versus those with a lot of soul that pay poorly. The work of work is actually much more nuanced.

# Your Personality Type

This worksheet will allow you to do a quick self-assessment of your personality type. Read each description and put check in the box next to the item that sounds most like you. After you have finished, circle the letters of each section that has the most checkmarks below. This is your four (4) letter code, or personality type. We encourage you to work with a career services expert to take the official Myers-Briggs Personality Inventory, which has been researched for greater validity.

| Extroversion (E) | Introversion (I) |
| --- | --- |
| □ Energized by the outer world of people and things | □ Energized by the inner world of thoughts, feeling, ideas |
| □ Want to be with others | □ Want time to be alone |
| □ Like a variety of activities with lots of action | □ Like solitude and time for concentration |
| ☑ Prefer to work with other people | □ Prefer to work alone |
| □ Develop ideas by brainstorming/discussing with others | ☑ Develop ideas by contemplation and reflection |
| **Sensing (S)** | **intuition (N)** |
| □ Oriented toward present realities | □ Oriented toward future possibilities |
| ☑ Want information to be practical and realistic | □ Want information to be imaginative and innovative |
| □ Focus on specifics and details | ☑ Focus on the "big picture" |
| □ Notice things that need to be done now | □ Envision future priorities |
| □ Pay careful attention to details | □ Look for new problems to be solved |
| **Thinking (T)** | **Feeling (F)** |
| □ Decide based on objectivity and logic | □ Decide based on individual values and needs |
| □ Focus on things, truth, principles | □ Focus on people, tact, harmony |
| □ Interact with other in a businesslike way | □ Interact with others in a personal way |
| □ Use logical analysis to make decision | ☑ Use personal values to make decisions |
| ☑ Consider the principles of the situation | □ Consider the underlying values in a situation |
| **Judging (J)** | **Perceiving (P)** |
| □ Are decisive and self-regimented | □ Are curious, flexible, and adaptive |
| □ Focus on completing tasks and coming to closure quickly | □ Focus on starting tasks and enjoying the process |
| □ Feel comfortable with system and order | ☑ Feel comfortable adapting to change |
| □ Produce best with structure and schedules | □ Adapt well to changing situations |
| ☑ Focus on completion | □ Focus on process |
| □ Is punctual and prefers clearly defined work hours | □ Is not a slave to the clock, enjoys coming and going freely |

**Where do you have the most checkmarks?**
Extroversion (E) or Introversion (I)
Sensing (S) or iNtuition (N)
Thinking (T) or Feeling (F)
Judging (J) or Perceiving (P)

Write your four-letter code or type below and on the **Self-Assessment Profile Summary (p. 33).**

# Values Checklist

| | Always Important | Usually Important | Somewhat Important | Rarely Important | Not Important |
|---|---|---|---|---|---|
| Accomplishment | ✔ | | | | |
| Adventure | | | ✔ | | |
| Balance in work & personal life | | ✔ | | | |
| Beautiful work environment | | | | | |
| Challenge | | ✔ | | | |
| Competition | | | | | |
| Contribution | | | | | |
| Cooperation | | | | | |
| Community | | ✔ | | | |
| Competence | | | | | |
| Courage | | | | | |
| Creative expression | | ✔ | | | |
| Egalitarian relationships | | | | | |
| Ethnic & gender diversity | | | | | |
| Ethics | | ✔ | | | |
| Family | | ✔ | | | |
| Financial prosperity | | ✔ | | | |
| Flexible hours | | | | | |
| Friendship | | | | | |
| Helpful | | | | | |
| Honesty | | | | | |
| Independence | | | | | |
| Influence/ persuasion | | | | | |
| Inner harmony | | | | | |
| Job security | | | | | |
| Justice | | | | | |

| Leadership | | | | | |
|---|---|---|---|---|---|
| Learning | | | | | |
| Love | | | | | |
| Loyalty | | | | | |
| Mental health | | | | | |
| Nature | | | | | |
| Pleasure | | | | | |
| Recognition | | | | | |
| Respect | | | | | |
| Spirituality | | | | | |
| Tranquility | | | | | |
| Social justice | | | | | |
| Stability | | | | | |
| Structure | | | | | |
| Sustainable practices | | | | | |
| Variety | | | | | |
| Wisdom | | | | | |
| Other: | | | | | |

# Exploring Your Values

List your top ten values. You may include any that did not appear on the values list. Write your own definition of each value. What does each mean to you regarding your career?

1. _____

_____

_____

2. _____

_____

_____

3. _____

_____

_____

4. _____

_____

_____

5. _____

_____

_____

6. _____

_____

_____

7. _____

_____

_____

8. _____

_____

_____

9. _____

_____

_____

10. _____

_____

_____

Reflect on those that are most important to you in your next job. Select five to transfer to the **Self-Assessment Profile Summary (p. 33)**.

# Your Occupational Themes

John Holland, a leading career planning theorist, created a personality type system using six type letters. These letters represent "occupational themes," or general categories of work activities that people enjoy. We encourage you to work with a career services expert to take and interpret the **Strong Interest Inventory**. The extensive resulting report will rank your themes and assign you a "Holland Code" (the top 3 letters that best suit your work interests and style). If you aren't working with a coach or counselor, this assessment can help you narrow and summarize your work interests.

- Prioritize the following letters in order of preference.
- Rank the categories from 1-6 according to which work activities you would find most attractive, interesting, and satisfying in your future job or career.
- Your top three are your top "occupational themes."

| Realistic | You like to work with things you can see and touch. You prefer things that seem real rather than ideas or concepts. You enjoy mechanical and/or physical tasks. |
|---|---|
| Investigative | You enjoy logical thinking and like to understand how things work. You like scientific and mathematical tasks. You are good at solving problems, doing research, and understanding data. |
| Artistic | You enjoy expressing yourself creatively, possibly in art, dancing, acting, music writing, or other arts. You like to express yourself freely and enjoy variety and creativity. |
| Social | You like to work with people. You enjoy solving problems by talking about them. You like helping, understanding, and teaching others. You are friendly, and you care about other's feelings. |
| Enterprising | You like to lead others or be in charge of your own work. You may enjoy competition and like to be in control. You are willing to be responsible for getting work done and for supervising others. |
| Conventional | You like to keep things in order. You like clear rules and instructions and enjoy producing detailed, precise work. You are good at handling data and very careful to do things the right way. |

R
I
A
S
E
C

25

# Skills Checklist

Rank each of the following skills and select those that you would find most satisfying to use in your next career. Rank each of them on a scale of 1-3. Don't rate skills you would prefer not to use.

1. Very Satisfying: skills that you would enjoy using fifty percent of your time or more.
2. Moderately Satisfying: skills that you would like to use 25 to 50 percent of your time.
3. Somewhat Satisfying: skills you would like to use ten to 25 percent of your time

### Communication
__ Explain
__ Influence/persuade
__ Facilitate groups
__ Speak before groups
__ Promote
__ Meeting the public
__ Consult
__ Interview
__ Generate enthusiasm
__ Write
__ Sell quality products & services
__ Serve as a liaison
__ Edit
__ Use social media

### Social
__ Counsel
__ Provide hospitality
__ Listen
__ Teach/help children
__ Teach adults
__ Help ill people &/or seniors
__ Coach
__ Train/instruct
__ Advocate
__ Build collaborative teams

### Leadership/Management
__ Negotiate
__ Make decisions
__ Project management
__ Mediate conflict
__ Coordinate
__ Initiate
__ Organize
__ Supervise
__ Strategic planning
__ Determine policy
__ Carry out follow-through

### Creative Thinking
__ Visualize
__ Generate options
__ Playful
__ Conceptualize
__ Improvise
__ Use intuitions
__ Generate creative ideas

### Physical
__ Build/construct
__ Work outdoors
__ Use body movement
__ Make tangible products
__ Demonstrate physical skills (yoga/woodwork)

### Creative & Expressive Arts
__ Produce events
__ Creative writing
__ Write and/or play music
__ Make crafts
__ Cook
__ Give speeches and presentations
__ Create visual environments
__ Create images
__ Perform/act
__ Use creative software

### Analytical
__ Calculate
__ Research
__ Manage information
__ Budget
__ Use computer applications
__ Observe
__ Analyze
__ Decipher technical material
__ Monitor and evaluate

---

Use the **Oregon Career Information System** (http://oregoncis.uoregon.edu/home/) online program to sort 72 skills into three categories in descending order of importance. With this sort, you can select your skills online. You may choose to either visit the Career Center at PCC Sylvania for free and full use of the program or purchase Internet access to this system for up to a year for $60 if you are working with a coach who has purchased a CIS license. (Note: as of June, 2012, CIS has not yet publicized this private license option, but we anticipate coaches will get on board by 2013.)

**Why purchase personal access to CIS?** This is an excellent program, which includes assessments related to interests, values and skills. AND it matches your profile to Oregon-specific occupations.

# Exploring Your Skills

Reflect on the skills that you selected as "very satisfying." This exercise will help you explore their meaning to you as well as clarify your top choices. You will also gain insight into why you enjoyed and/or were recognized for these skills. By answering the questions below, you will also build your ability to present your skills in networking, the resume, cover letter and interview.

For each of your "very satisfying" skills, think of a time that you used that skill successfully. Did you receive positive feedback? Why was using this skill rewarding? Some more detailed examples follow:

- **Speak before groups**. I explained how the new recycling program would work to small groups of skeptical business owners. They commented on how clear I was about the benefits, and they liked my diagrams and humor.
- **Use computer applications.** I created a new database for a youth agency to track intakes, services and outcomes. I really enjoyed interviewing both clients and staff and analyzing their needs. It excites me to know that the system is still being used for grant applications.

**Skill:** _____
**Example:**_____
_____
_____
_____

**Skill:** _____
**Example:**_____
_____
_____
_____

**Skill:** _____
**Example:**_____
_____
_____
_____

**Skill:** _____
**Example:**_____
_____
_____
_____

**Skill:** _____
**Example:**_____
_____
_____
_____

Now, add your top five skills to the **Self-Assessment Profile Summary (p.33).** If you have more than five, for the purposes of the summary, you can combine two that are natural partners, such as "writing and editing" or "teach and train."

# Technology and Social Media Skills Self-Assessment

We encourage you to do this technology self-assessment once when you launch your career transition and a second time after you have completed your research and know more specifically which skills are ideal for your job target. Necessary computer skills will continue to expand at a dizzying rate, and now is the time to assess the skills you will need as well as the way to grapple with this fact. During **Phase II, Career Exploration**, you can return to this self assessment after you determine the level of competency you will need to compete well. Inquire during informational interviews and carefully note the vocabulary indicated in position announcements qualifications: basic, intermediate, or advanced.

You may be hesitant to spend time on building technology skills in your job search calendar, believing that you are a fast learner able to master these skills after you are hired. This belief may be buoyed by managers who say that communication skills and critical thinking abilities play a larger role in their hiring decisions than specific technical skills that can be learned.

Such comments can mislead job applicants to apply to jobs for which they do not have the required technical skills. The resume screeners are the gatekeepers and they tend to be more concrete and literal than the managers. HR is usually tasked to present the hiring manager with a small subset of the resumes—those with the best match on years of experience and technical skill. The person in HR is usually a recruiter or software-scanning device; even mid-sized companies are using computer-scanning software, which is designed to select for keywords and skills. The manager will receive only the resumes of those who meet the experience and technical requirements and then make his or her more holistic assessment based on interpersonal and other soft skills. In sum, unless you have some well-developed pipelines to hiring managers, you will be best to use time during career transition to upgrade these skills.

Begin by reflecting on what kind of environment will help you achieve optimal mental clarity and the ability to stick to it. If you have experienced resistance in the past, explore this task as a learning experiment. Try something new, like inviting your techno-nephew over to help you navigate and understand social networking, and notice if this process was enjoyable and productive to you. If not, try something else, like a workshop.

| Factors that Increase Success | Helpful | Somewhat Helpful | Not needed or Not helpful |
|---|---|---|---|
| Working at home | | | |
| Working at a coffee shop | | | |
| Working alongside a friend | | | |
| On-line self-study courses | | | |
| Classes/workshops (in person) | | | |
| Help from techno-friend or relative | | | |
| Putting in day timer for AM hours | | | |
| Other: | | | |

# Technology and Social Media Skills Checklist

If you need help in assessing your level of competency and creating a structure for training, Vicki has found these two sites extremely friendly, affordable, and effective.

- www.Lynda.com has 63,000 video tutorials, from basic to advanced. Topics include audio, business, design, photography, video, web + interactive and more. For the basic fee of $25 per month, you can determine your current level, and use as many tutorials as you like. Training is broken down into micro-lessons so you can learn in ten-minute bites or focus on a course for several hours.
- http://office.microsoft.com/en-us/training is a free service offering tutorials for all Microsoft products (2003, 2007, 2010).

| Basic Technology Skills | Basic | Intermediate | Advanced |
|---|---|---|---|
| Word Processing | | | |
| Excel Spread Sheet | | | |
| Database (Access or Other) | | | |
| PowerPoint* | | | |
| LinkedIn | | | |
| Outlook/scheduling programs | | | |
| Web research | | | |

*Normally, Basic PowerPoint to make presentations is sufficient

The following section can only be filled out after you have selected and researched a career/job objective. For example, if you want to become a graphic designer, it would include intermediate level Dreamweaver, Illustrator, Photoshop, and InDesign.

| Specialized Technology Skills | Basic | Intermediate | Advanced |
|---|---|---|---|
| | | | |
| | | | |
| | | | |
| | | | |
| | | | |
| | | | |

**Technology and Social Media Skills Summary**

**Summary Strengths**
    1.
    2.
    3.
**Needs Improvement**
    1.
    2.
    3.

After identifying your top 3 computer strengths that will be applicable for your future career, them on the **Self-Assessment Profile Summary (p. 33).**

# Employer Characteristics Checklist

| Employment Characteristics | Required | Very Desirable | Desirable | Acceptable | Not Desirable |
|---|---|---|---|---|---|
| **Compensation** | | | | | |
| $20 K-$29 K | | | | | |
| $30 K-$49 K | | | | | |
| $50 K-$69 K | | | | | |
| $70 K-$89 K | | | | | |
| $90 K-$110 K | | | | | |
| $110 K or more | | | | | |
| Bonus or commission | | | | | |
| **Benefits** | | | | | |
| Health insurance | | | | | |
| Paid time off | | | | | |
| Dental and/or mental health insurance | | | | | |
| Day care assistance | | | | | |
| Employer retirement contribution | | | | | |
| Other: | | | | | |
| **Schedule** | | | | | |
| Flexible work schedule | | | | | |
| Full-time | | | | | |
| Part-time | | | | | |
| No weekend work | | | | | |
| Rare overtime | | | | | |
| **Physical Location** | | | | | |
| In Portland/Metro Area | | | | | |
| Close-in Portland | | | | | |
| Convenient for public transportation | | | | | |
| Office is in a physically attractive space | | | | | |
| **Purpose** | | | | | |

| | | | | | |
|---|---|---|---|---|---|
| Organization's mission matches my values | | | | | |
| Department I work in matches my values | | | | | |
| **Career Development Opportunities** | | | | | |
| Step to career advancement | | | | | |
| Learn new on-the-job skills | | | | | |
| Provides professional development opportunities | | | | | |
| Other: | | | | | |
| **Respectful Job Environment** | | | | | |
| Provides clear expectations | | | | | |
| Provides positive support | | | | | |
| Provides opportunities to work in team | | | | | |
| Provides independence in how I perform the job | | | | | |
| Considers my feedback and input | | | | | |
| Other: | | | | | |
| **Social & Environmental Contribution** | | | | | |
| Organization contributes to community | | | | | |
| Organization has good sustainability practices | | | | | |
| Other: | | | | | |

After you have completed this checklist, review those selected as "required." Choose the five most important to list on the **Self-Assessment Profile Summary (p. 33)**.

# Feedback Sheet: Instructions

This feedback sheet adds the perspective of others who know you well. We all have some blind spots to both our strengths and limitations. We suggest that you select three to six people among your family, colleagues and friends whose perspectives you trust. Explain that you are in the process of career planning and development. As part of deciding on a satisfying career direction, you are reflecting on your values and skills and would appreciate their feedback. Ask them to fill this sheet out honestly and objectively.

Make three to six copies of the letter below, or send an email to three to six people. Make sure you do not include this instruction section on the copy that you give your friends and family.

# Feedback Sheet

**Dear Friends and Family,**

As part of deciding on a satisfying career direction, I have been meeting with Vicki Lind, a career counselor. I have completed a series of exercises and discussions to clarify my interests, values and skills (attached). We have begun listing career directions that match what I have learned. You know me well, and I would appreciate your ideas and job suggestions—practical or not. Please get this back to me in one week.

Have I missed any important skills?

Do you see additional values as key to my career happiness?

What kind of work environment do you think suits me best?

What do you see in me that I might not see in myself?

List any job titles or employers that might be a fit for me, whether practical or not.

# Self-Assessment Profile Summary

**Interests/Passions** (Examples: sustainability, pottery, poverty relief)
1.
2.
3.
4.
5.

**Personality Type** Use your self-assessment from the **Your Personality Type** article, or if you were able to complete the Myers-Briggs assessment, use those results.

1._____ (Extroverted, Introverted, Not sure)
2._____ (Sensing, Intuitive, Not sure)
3._____ (Thinking, Feeling, Not sure)
4._____ (Judging, Perceiving, Not sure)

**Values** (Examples: autonomy, creativity, justice)

1.
2.
3.
4.
5.

**Occupational Themes** Write down your top three Occupational Theme letters derived from **Your Occupational Themes**, or if you were able to take the Strong Interest Inventory, write down your Holland Code.

Occupational Themes: ____ ____ ____

**Skills** (Examples: write clearly, motivate others, organize details)

1.
2.
3.
4.
5.

**Technology and Social Media Skills** (Examples:  Excel, PowerPoint, Dreamweaver, Photoshop)

1.
2.
3.

**Employment/ Employer Characteristics** (Examples: 20-minute commute, $45K with benefits, socially responsible purpose)

1.
2.
3.
4.
5.

# Recommended Reading for Self-Assessment

**Beck, Martha**. *Finding Your Own North Star: Claiming the Life You Were Meant to Live.* New York: Three Rivers Press, 2002, 2008. In this absorbing combination of detailed self-awareness exercises and true stories from her own counseling experience, Harvard-trained sociologist, Martha Beck, walks readers through a thorough exercise to evaluate their current lifestyle's pleasures and pains; teaches the process of listening to the body for directional cues; describes how to heal all those self-defeating emotional wounds; and provides an intriguing "Map of Change" to achieve an authentic life.

**Beck, Martha**. *Finding Your Way in a Wild New World.* New York: Free Press, 2012. This is a remarkable path to the most important discovery you can make: the knowledge of what you should be doing with your one wild and precious life. Beck guides you to find out how you got to where you are now and what you should do next with clear, concrete instructions on tapping into the deep, wordless knowledge you carry in your body and soul. This is the book that will lead you to unleash your incredible creative energy—and fulfill your life's purpose.

**Boldt, Laurence**. *Zen and the Art of Making a Living: A Practical Guide to Creative Career Design.* New York: Penguin, 2009. This 600-page resource guide for creative career changers integrates Eastern principles about Zen and mythic archetypes and Western conventional materials like writing a resume. Boldt's premise is that everyone is an artist in his or her own life. He offers thought provoking exercises to help you discover work that will be deeply satisfying. A 2010 edition features expanded Web and book resources at empoweryou.com.

**Bronson, Po**. *What Should I Do with My Life?* New York: Random House, 2005. Bronson carried out in-depth interviews with hundreds of people who had successfully grappled with what he calls "life's ultimate question: What Should I Do with My Life?" While most of the interviews are with 30-something professionals, Bronson values very diverse people who make wide-ranging choices. Bronson's book was a run-away success on the *New York Times* bestseller list. He has also been featured on Oprah and NPR.

**Bridges, William**. *Making Sense of Life's Changes, Revised.* Da Capo Press, 2004. This brief book, a newly revised 25th Anniversary Edition, has helped a generation of people understand the three-part process that accompanies change. Bridges describes the emotional landscape of loss, followed by a confusing neutral zone. When an individual goes through significant losses, divorce, loss of health, or loss of job, these stages need to precede the final, more enjoyable stage of engaging in a new beginning.

**Brown, Sara and Joan Malling**. *How to Create the Life You Want After 50.* Ashland, OR: Savvy Sisters Press, 2004, 2008. Starting in 1989 Vicki met with her colleague, Joan Malling, to ponder what they wanted for themselves after they turned fifty. They knew that they would not want to continue their high-demand, long-hour positions as continuing educators for another decade. Joan created a life for herself where she lives half of the year on a boat in France and, for the other half of the year, teaches others about life choices after fifty. This book offers a three step planning process to midlife readers.

**Clifton, Donald**. *Clifton StrengthFinder.* Gallup Organization, 1998. The book has a code to access the assessment test online, and it says our greatest growth happens around developing strengths more than focusing on improving weaknesses. Clifton talks about how we are each unique, and when we develop skills we are already confident in, we tend to be much happier.

**Kalil, Carolyn.** *Follow your True Colors to the Work You Love: The Popular Method for Matching Your Personality to Your Career.* True Colors, 1998, 2011. Kalil takes a look at self-esteem through personality types: Blue–to love and be loved, Green–knowledge is power, Gold–plan it, and Orange–where the action is. Through assessment, readers determine which colors match their personalities and replace career transition fears with confidence from self-knowledge.

**Keirsey, David.** *Please Understand Me II: Temperament, Character, Intelligence.* Prometheus Nemesis Book Co., 1998. This book is based on the theory of the Myers-Briggs Type Indicator, and provides a simple way to assess your own personality type/temperament. Each temperament is described in terms of language, intellect, interest, orientation, self-image, values and social role. Having given a basic description of each temperament, the book then devotes a chapter to the three main areas of life: mating, parenting and leading.

**Levoy, Gregg.** *Callings: Finding and Following an Authentic Life.* New York: Three Rivers Press, 1997. *Callings* is a jewel for career changers who want to probe deeper questions of their life's purpose. Levoy draws on literary images and spiritual thinkers to help the reader examine the clues they receive through dreams, art and synchronistic events. Levoy addresses the following introspective questions: How do we recognize a true calling? How do we handle our resistance to a call? What happens when we say yes?

**Palmer, Parker.** *Let Your Life Speak: Listening for the Voice of Vocation.* Jossey-Bass, 2000. With wisdom, compassion and gentle humor, Parker J. Palmer invites us to listen to the inner teacher and follow its lead toward a sense of meaning and purpose. Telling stories from his own life and the lives of others who have made a difference, he shares insights gained from darkness and depression as well as fulfillment and jobs, illuminating a pathway toward vocation for all who seek the true calling of their lives.

**Sher, Barbara**. *It's Only Too Late If You Don't Start Now: How to Create Your Second Life at Any Age.* New York: Dell, 1998. Sher is a tell-it-like-it-is Jewish grandma who didn't write her first famous book until she was in her 60s. She challenges the career changer's inner foot-dragger that says, "It is too late to follow my creative dream." Sher uses humor to motivate the creative midlife career changer.

**Waldman, Joshua.** *Job Searching with Social Media for Dummies*. For Dummies, 2011. Waldman covers everything from the strategy of using social media, to personal branding, etiquette, and avoiding pitfalls. Useful for those in their first job search, those changing careers, and people who have been out of the work force for a while. He guides you through all of the main social media sites: Google, Twitter, Facebook, LinkedIn and more. Waldman also has a blog called Joshua Waldman's Career Enlightenment, which can be found at http://careerenlightenment.com/.

**Bolles, Richard.** *What Color Is Your Parachute? Guide to Job-Hunting Online.* Berkley: Ten Speed Press, 2008. As a job-hunter, you need to understand the Internet and know how to use it effectively in your job-hunt. If you can do that—learn how the Internet can help you find work, how it cannot, and even learn how the Internet will likely be harmful to your job-hunt—then you are no longer the average job-hunter. Bolles shows you how to cut the access and save time in your job hunt.

*The privilege of a lifetime is being who you are.*
– Joseph Campbell

# Identifying Resources and Barriers

Now that you're coming to the end of your self-assessment phase, it's useful to predict what barriers you might face and the resources you bring to overcoming these barriers. As you read the next few pages, jot notes on the **Resources and Barriers Grid**. The goal of identifying barriers is to bring them into awareness so that they will not subconsciously sabotage your journey; the goal of naming resources is to create your winning team for the journey.

First, consider **INTERNAL BARRIERS** such as self-defeating beliefs and thoughts. Some anxiety about career transition is natural, particularly if you had a negative work experience in the recent past. These feelings need to be named and addressed so that they do not undermine your career search. If you have incessant nightmares about your old boss or are continually plagued by coulda-shoulda thoughts, some therapy may be needed. If your negative thoughts are intermittent and you function reasonably well on most days, you can increase your equilibrium with **Reducing Negative Self-Talk**.

*A day spent judging another is a painful day.*
*A day spent judging yourself is a painful day.*
*You don't have to believe your judgments:*
*they're simply an old habit.*
– The Buddha

Second, turn to **INTERNAL RESOURCES**, which are usually personal qualities and beliefs, such as persistence or confidence in your intelligence. Spiritual beliefs and practices can be a powerful internal resource during times of transition as well.

Next, we explore **EXTERNAL BARRIERS** such as the inability to relocate, an unsupportive spouse, or the need for a short-term subsistence job. It is critical to be bold and honest as you assess the size and veracity of these barriers. Family, friends and others in your life may criticize your drive to excel in a new career arena, thus becoming one of your external barriers. Because this is both commonplace and disruptive, we've included **Families and Friends as Resources and Barriers**.

Last, we identify **EXTERNAL RESOURCES** such as memberships in professional associations, a savings account, fellow jobseekers, or an active university alumni association. As the Beatles sang, "we get along with a little help from our friends." This is the time to identify the family and friends that do a little or a lot to energize our transition.

# Resources and Barriers Grid

| INTERNAL BARRIERS | INTERNAL RESOURCES |
|---|---|
| **EXTERNAL BARRIERS** | **EXTERNAL RESOURCES** |

# Families and Friends as Resources and Barriers

Family members and friends can be resources or barriers. Our goal is to maximize contact with those who are a resource and minimize contact with those whose attitudes pose a barrier to our progress. On occasion, you can teach people who are not helpful how to be more supportive allies. Start by dividing the people in your life into three categories relevant to the career process: toxic, supportive, or teachable.

## Toxic

Even people who care about you deeply can be toxic to your highest career goal. For example, Mike S., in his early thirties, found his father toxic to his career independence since dad was invested in having his only son join him in the construction business. When his dad started lecturing on the topic, Mike would become triggered and raise his voice, which sometimes led to a fight. After these conversations Mike found himself procrastinating on his next career transition tasks. Vicki first helped him practice techniques to avoid such emotional triggers by calmly asserting his own preferences. During this time he also minimized contact with his dad. Second, he had to turn off the part of himself that had internalized his father's sentiments. He learned to notice and reject the messages that his career choice needed to make his father happy. When his own feet were clearly committed to his path as a green entrepreneur, he could resume more frequent conversations with his dad—staying on safer, less loaded topics like sports.

When you want to leave one career that you studied to find something more creative and meaningful, it might be hard for the older generation to understand that security is not tantamount to career happiness. Having alternative role models in your family makes it easier to ignore the people who say, "But it's such a good company! The job is so secure!"

It is particularly hard for people to understand when your career dream pulls you into a different geographic or cultural sphere. For example, Mary P., a bright and creative 30-something client came from a small town near Salem, Oregon, where her father worked for state government. Whenever she took a creative risk, like creating a band with other young women, it exacerbated the family fear that she would become unemployable. She lacked role models with unconventional careers, and her family had a strong scripting that "our clan does not leave Oregon." These were palpable, but unexpressed barriers, that needed to be articulated and discussed before she could make a career choice truly congruent with her skills and vitality.

If you relate to these stories, we encourage you to find a few inspiring biographies of people whose commitment and verve catapulted them beyond their familial expectations. One of our favorites is the autobiography of Elizabeth Kubler-Ross whose proper Swiss father expected her to dedicate her life to bookkeeping for him.

## Supportive

Supportive people often naturally give you accurate, positive feedback on your strengths, and comfort you when you are plagued by doubts. They keep your weaknesses in proportion. They are interested in learning more about each phase of the career search process and enjoy witnessing your progress. Supportive people know when and how to comfort you on a bad day, perhaps with tea and a walk rather than advice.

Another way family and friends can be supportive is by providing good role models. Shoshanna Krall felt okay about leaving a "good" job and facing financial uncertainty and the unknown when it became obvious that the job was "so boring that is was liable to turn me into a raving monster who would eat my own liver." She notes that her family members have always willingly faced challenges in reaching for true career satisfaction throughout their lives. "Most important was having family members who refused to be limited to the mainstream and parents who have gone back to school in their fifties."

You may want to focus on bringing new supportive people into your life, especially for this transition. One client didn't believe her mom could be taught to be supportive, so she arranged to give a call to a friend's mom to hear a motherly voice say, "You can do it. I know you are so great!"

**Teachable**
Teachable people are of genuine goodwill, but need coaching to understand how to be really helpful. You might want to share parts of this handbook with your eager, but misguided supporters, so that they better understand each stage of the process. For example, you might need a listening ear during self-assessment, a baby sitter for networking events and a cheerleader prior to interviews.

A useful coaching technique is to praise the person for their positive intent, followed by modeling what you're looking for. "Honey, I love it when you tell me that I am smart and can do anything I set my mind to. It would also be helpful if you would tell me about the specific skills that I use when I am being 'smart.' Is it my intuition on how to handle that cranky neighbor? My ability to figure out complex instructions for the DVR? See if you can 'catch me being smart' and describe what you see. I'm just too close to me to see myself accurately."

Of course basic psychology teaches us to increase desirable behaviors by being generous with compliments and recognition. This may only require taking a moment to exclaim: "Mom, I love it when you take the kids to the park so I can focus on the job search!" You can also offer something positive to replace annoying comments and behaviors. "You know, mom, it would help relieve my stress if you didn't ask 'Have you found anything yet?' when you return from the park. It would make it more fun to relax with you and chit-chat."

List people in your life who can help during your career transition and job search:

| Name | Help I can ask for |
| --- | --- |
|  |  |
|  |  |
|  |  |
|  |  |
|  |  |

# How Long Will It Take?

As you prepare for this career transition journey, remember that it is simultaneously a strategic, step-by-step process and a somewhat unpredictable journey. Examine preconceived notions about what it takes to make it, and expect a few surprises as you go through each phase. Be aware that when you come from your deepest interests and values, people tend to respond affirmatively and help you in totally unexpected ways. Stay open to see where light appears under a door that initially appeared unwelcoming and tightly shut.

Your expectations and emotions around what **success** will look like:

| What people think it looks like | What it looks like when you do it on your own | What it looks like working with a career professional |

Over the last fifteen years, Vicki has gone through this process with hundreds of clients and has seen clients meet their goal of a new job or career in as little as two months and as much as two years of committed attention. Statistics say that it takes an average professional six months to get a new job in the same field; statistics say that it can take up to two years to change careers entirely. Below are six factors that can either help your transition move quickly or be a barrier that you need to acknowledge and address to move more smoothly towards your career vision.

Two months to two years is quite a range. To get a closer estimate for your situation, examine these six factors that correlate with a faster or slower transition. The purpose of this section is to help you establish a realistic time-line and make intermediate steps or back up plans while working towards your goal of a new career path. Reflect on which of these factors can be improved, moving steadily towards the stronger option. If you have more challenging factors in your situation, be prepared to make a plan that will allow you to pinpoint solutions. If you have the advantage factor, think about how you can leverage it to save time. Be thankful for it. If the idea of a two-year career transition intimidates you, think about what support you need to help with the challenging factors.

**Financial Resources vs. Financial Crisis**
It is ideal to have the funds to support yourself while you gain new skills, carry out strategic volunteering and network in professional associations. If you are in financial crisis and don't have the option of staying in a current job, you may need to consider temporary employment, drawing on the comfort of knowing you are meeting your primary needs for food and shelter.

If you need to stay in your current position for longer than you hoped, consider it temporary, and draw comfort knowing that your basic needs are being met. You still have time to explore and connect. Explore options to work part time to allow more time for pursuing your true interests. As always, live simply and experiment with lifestyle choices to reduce expenses and help create and expand your options.

If you need a new job right away, go to **Phase Three** on Finding a Job. Then, when your basic needs are met, return to Self-Assessment to reset your compass towards a career that matters.

**Available Time vs. Time Crunch**
Most job searches proceed more quickly if you have more time to commit to learning new skills, networking, and crafting resumes. You've probably heard "It is a full time job to get a job." We disagree. While learning new skills, networking, and crafting resumes can become enjoyable, we think that strategically committing twenty hours a week is plenty.

If you are currently locked into working forty or more hours a week, you will be limited to an evening or two per week, which may slow progress.

When time is limited, we encourage you to think creatively about how to do double duty. For example, can your employer send you to a technical training relevant to both your current position, and (unbeknownst to them) in high demand for your future desired career? Perhaps you can become more strategic with your volunteer activities. For example, if you are looking towards the still-growing area of energy efficiency, you could duck out of the SOLV beach cleanup and volunteer on a committee for the Association of Energy Service Professional (AESP).

**Geographical Restrictions vs. Geographical Freedom**
Because Portland is full of wonderful professionals with deep backgrounds in creative fields, sustainability and social justice, competition is fierce for positions in organizations with strong reputations. If Portland is your first choice, then you might want to set a period of time in which to find a new position. If job openings are too sparse when the time is up, then consider a broader geographical range.

Vicki had a client with a bachelor degree in biology along with experience managing an outdoor school. Over six months Wanda only saw a few openings in Portland, and most of those stated that master degrees were required or preferred. She switched her attention to the SW United States and quickly landed her ideal job as Director of a Wyoming Audubon Center.

**Technical Competence vs. Technical Phobia**
During the economic downswing, aspects of many jobs have been automated and/or two positions may have been combined into one. The result is that positions often have a longer list of technical competencies, usually software programs. Professionals in most fields are expected to be equivalent to new graduates who are competent in PowerPoint, Excel, and basic databases along with programs specific to their field. If technology is a weakness for you, possibly a phobia, we have written a separate section to help you take this challenge on one little techno-step at a time.

**Expertise in robust industry where you have worked vs. Expertise in crowded new industry**
It is common sense that it will be faster to find a position in an industry where you have a depth of expertise, particularly in a growing industry. Assuming that you have decent references, if you have ten years of experience retrofitting residences for energy efficiency, you should be snapped up. At the other extreme, if you are a new graduate in Interior Design, you will need to plan on a longer transition since you will not be the first one chosen as long as the building recession continues.

**Emotional Resilience vs. Emotional Vulnerability**
Being able to bounce back from rejection is key to success. When you find a job that you really want and put considerable effort into tailoring a resume and cover letter, it is exciting when you push the "send" button or drop it in the mailbox. Your sense of hope, however, may sag when days creep by, and you haven't gotten a call for an interview. Currently, most employers do not send any notification that your resume has been received, and they actively discourage phone calls. It is even more discouraging when you feel that you gave an outstanding interview, really resonated with your interviewees, and then you are not selected for a job.

It is crucial you realize that a rejection from a future employer is not a rejection of you as a valuable human being. Instead, it is a statement that another individual had skills, expertise and characteristics that are a better fit as they see it. Naturally, you will be disappointed. If three days on the couch, in the woods or reading a mystery novel doesn't get you into action, you might consider therapy to bolster your resilience.

**Include Others in Your Plan**
The length of your career transition will impact others in your life. We encourage you to sit down and explore how you can move towards greater resilience, more financial security, greater technical competence, etc. You may need to experiment with lifestyle choices in order to support and continue your efforts. For more **Career Services** information, please see **Appendix F**.

Generally, it is more difficult for you and people in your life at first. As your vision becomes something you trust more and question less, consider what you still need in the way of resources, routines, and activities, so that you have what you need to go after what matters to you. There is more information about **Community Resources** in **Appendix D.**

*Life is indeed difficult, partly because of the real difficulties we must overcome in order to survive, and partly because of our own innate desire to always do better, to overcome new challenges, to self-actualize. Happiness is experienced largely in striving towards a goal, not having attained things, because our nature is always to want to go on to the next endeavor.*

-Albert Ellis, Michael Abrams, Lidia Dengelegi,
The Art & Science of Rational Eating, 1992

# Reducing Negative Self-Talk

If you're unhappily employed or unemployed, some ways of thinking and talking to yourself can be helpful, while others will not be. We call the latter "show stoppers" because they stop you from showing up to take action towards your career dream. Try the following techniques to help you reduce negative self-talk.

**The Mr. Spock**
First, identify the inner voices that masquerade as an adult, parent, or the voice of reason. They may be internalized from your parents, grandparents, or other sources. Your job is to expose their habit of exaggeration and their "know it all" tone of voice. They sometimes use exaggerations like "no one," "never," and "always." They sometimes sneer! Your goal is to invoke Star Trek's totally logical Mr. Spock to change the vocabulary to express a more accurate, objective reality.

*Show Stopper Self-Talk*: I'll never get into a key organization like the Bureau of Planning and Sustainability, Weiden + Kennedy or Laika Studios. *Everyone* else is more experienced; besides, no one is hiring in this economy.

*Rational Self-Talk*: There are not very many job openings at this time, so I need to find out what I will need in my portfolio to become competitive.

**The Bridge**
You may have a dream of working for a renowned creative firm. However, the gap between where you are and this dream may be so large that you are immobilized. Simply repeating a grand affirmation may not feel credible. Writer Sid Smith suggests breaking the gap down into a series of smaller "bridge beliefs" which he defines as "a belief or observation that feels just a little bit better than your current belief, feels completely true, and you have no resistance to this belief." (Go to www.sidsmith.com to read more about bridge beliefs.)

*Show Stopper Belief:* I'll make $60 thousand in my first year as a life coach.

*Bridge Belief:* For now, I can get and enjoy a job where I facilitate the growth of a team of co-workers while I start building my coaching practice.

**The Erin Brockovich**
Choose a real-life hero or heroine, from the public arena or from your life – someone like Erin Brockovich, who has overcome even more obstacles and fears than you face. Read about them. Put up their photographs and quotes. Celebrate how they did not "play themselves small."

**The Compassionate Mom**
Hush your negative thoughts as if you were comforting a child. When you started believing and internalizing toxic messages, you were in a young and vulnerable condition. Treat yourself as you would treat a tender infant who deserves unquestioning nurturance and comfort. Learn to recognize when you are in this state and what you can do for self-care and comfort. Get in touch with people who make you feel safe and smart and who believe in your success.

**The Zen Cloud**
Remind yourself that periods of fear are a natural part of being human and taking risks. Buddhists say that pain does not come from the actual situation but from how our minds get attached to what we desire. We believe that a temporary feeling is real and permanent because it often shows up in our body as a real feeling.

*Show Stopper Fear*: Your stomach is tight and you cannot eat as you imagine an upcoming interview. *Zen-Cloud Option:* Imagine your fear sitting on an ugly but natural rain cloud. Then picture a weather map on which the cloud system drifts off the chart. Enjoy a cup of tea as you watch it move on.

**The Woody Allen**
Use humor to disarm your show-stoppers. In *Everything You Always Wanted to Know About Sex*, Allen's character is making love to his girlfriend, but is having trouble getting aroused. The camera cuts to inside his head where we see a mission control room full of technicians trying to figure out what is holding up the mission. They discover that it is a half-crazed priest shouting, "Blasphemy! Blasphemy! Sex between unmarrieds!" It takes two burly bodyguards to drag the priest away.

*Show Stopper:* You keep resisting applying to law school, and instead replay your friends' snide comments about manipulating, money-mongering lawyers.

*Woody Allen Option*: You imagine an equally absurd but aggressive action, in the mode of the Woody Allen movie, that allows you to drag away your own deeply embedded and critical self-talk.


*Our deepest fear is not that we are inadequate. Our deepest fear is that we are powerful beyond measure. It is our light, not our darkness, that most frightens us. Your playing small does not serve the world. There's nothing enlightened about shrinking so that other people won't feel insecure around us.*

– Marianne Williamson

# Income for the Transition

**Temping**

Temping is the colloquial term for working through a staffing agency. Staffing agencies earn their money by helping employers who are temporarily short of help. Employers use staffing agencies for several reasons: seasonal flux in workload, to avoid paying benefits, and/or to try someone out before permanent hire. The last arrangement is called "temp for hire." You will be paid by the agency, not the employer.

Temping is particularly well suited to those who have strong clerical and computer skills. Most jobs these agencies fill are clerical positions for people with intermediate Microsoft Office Suite skills that include Word, Excel, Access and basic PowerPoint. Receptionist positions are plentiful, and fast typing skills are important. Temp agencies hire accountants, as well as production and warehouse workers. It takes persistence to get your foot in the door. Temp agencies are working for employers, and you are the product. You have to convince the agency that you are a good product that they can sell.

Here are tips for gaining access to temp jobs:

- There are a lot of agencies. They don't all offer the same type of positions or even use the same procedures to "hire" their workers and place them. Do research online (www.net-temps.com/staffing-agencies/Portland/1/) and pick two to three agencies that appear to have jobs, or categories of jobs, that fit your profile. Then carefully follow their procedures. After you apply on their website, ask for an interview and computer skills test. Be persistent. Call weekly, or even daily, early in the morning to show your interest. Some of them will ask you to update their website weekly with your availability.
- Temp agency staff recruits at career fairs, which take place at colleges, universities and other public venues. Go to these fairs during a slow time. We recommend mid-to-late afternoon, not early or at lunchtime. Make eye contact, offer a solid handshake, have your resume ready, and ask specific questions regarding their openings and preferred method of hiring. Get their business cards so you can follow up after the fair.
- Target your resume VERY specifically to the skill set needed for the type of job you are most qualified. List at the top of the resume a summary of qualifications and key words that are your most employable skills. Chances are the person reviewing your resume will spend less than a minute to find key words matches for open positions.
- After you are in their system, check in regularly. Be persistent! Take any jobs they offer to start off with. Once you show you are a reliable worker, you can become more selective.

Our clients bring back good reports about the following general/clerical staffing agencies:

- **NW Staffing Resources** has jobs with government and nonprofits. Two of our clients got jobs with the United Way through NW Staffing Resources. (www.nwstaffing.com/)
- **DePaul Staffing** has a reasonable number of placements in government and nonprofits. They give placement preference to people with disabilities, so if you have a documented disability, even a minor one, you may have a leg up. People without disabilities do get jobs as well. (http://www.depaulindustries.com/staffing.html)
- **Boly:Welch** has jobs that are typical business community positions, with a concentration of clerical positions. This company is a local, woman-owned business with a reputation for treating temps decently. (http://www.bolywelch.com/)

- Creative Staffing Agencies
- **Aquent** is a creative placement agency in a national company with a local presence that is the most active creative staffing agency. Aquent places experienced copywriters, marketing professionals, programmers, web designers/developers, and more. (http://aquent.us/)
- **52LTD (Limited)** calls itself a hybrid model, functioning both as a design firm and as a small

creative staffing agency. (http://www.52ltd.com/)
- **Jackie Mathys**, a long-time Portland recruiter for creative directors and other very experienced Creatives, has joined forces with Steve Potestio to form **Mathys+Portestio.** (http://www.mathys-potestio.com/)

## A Bridge Job

A bridge job provides a link between your old career and your new one. You had hoped to just pop the door open and be inside a career matched to your interest, values and skills. Your transferable skills were obvious to you, but, alas, not to prospective employers. So to become competitive, you may need to pry that door open with a bridge job. The job might last a year or so, and it is likely closer to your old field and/or is not at an optimal salary. For example, job club graduate, Sam wanted to work marketing certified lumber products (and now does). However, he was willing to work at Parr Lumber, if needed, to learn more about certified and non-certified wood products.

## Part-time Work

Part-time employment has the merits of giving you some income, structure to your week and a chance to be with familiar people. This can be a pleasant counterpoint to the stress of foraging in new career arenas. Job club graduate, Alison, reduced her workweek as a crisis counselor to fewer shifts while developing her expertise in transportation options, where she now works.

If staying in an existing job or field on a part-time basis is not a good option, other short-term part-time work may help, particularly seasonal jobs. Examples:
- **Norm Thompson** offers part-time sales jobs for the winter holidays.
- **Willowbrook** offers teaching positions at a summer arts camp.
- **Home Depot** and **Starbucks** sometimes have weekend work available. (Note: Both companies are unusual in giving benefits to some part-time employees.)
- **Sylvan Learning Centers, New Horizons Computer Learning Centers, and community colleges** are always hiring part-time instructors and/or tutors.

## Gigs

Gigs are short term and one-time projects for which you can be paid.
- **Craigslist** gigs connects you with people posting ads. (http://portland.craigslist.org/ggg/)
- **Taskrabbit** allows you to create a profile and chat online with people seeking help. (http://www.taskrabbit.com/)
- **Gigwalk** offers nationwide gigs, requires you have a smart phone, and has a competitive model where you "unlock" better paying gigs by doing great work. (http://gigwalk.com/)

## Community Resources For Your Transition

During your job or career transition, you may experience a high degree of economic and psychological stress. For example, you may be very short on funds, lack health insurance, or have difficulty paying bills. You may be racking up credit card debt in order to survive. Perhaps you have kids, and they too are doing without during your time of transition.

Excellent community resources are available during this phase of your life. Don't be afraid or embarrassed to use them! You don't have to be in a dire emergency to ask for help. The "safety net" the community provides is designed for everyone, including many middle class and educated folks who are now needing support. The economy is in bad shape. You are not alone! When you're back on your feet and earning good money, you can always give back by donating to or volunteering for agencies that helped you.

You may be surprised at how many resources are available, even in this time of limited public and private funding. The government still offers a variety of resources, and many more are available through nonprofit programs. Some may be free, others may be offered on a low fee or sliding scale basis. Please go to **Appendix F** for links to specific community resource information.

# Ten Strategies to Simplify for the Transition
## Contributed by Ursala Garbrecht

After analyzing your career transition situation, you'll know if it's long enough to merit lifestyle changes. Simplifying your life is both a spiritual and financial transformation. Each of the practical tips below can help you save money and nurture your physical, emotional, and spiritual wellbeing. This is a challenging and rewarding transition. Which tips are most relevant for you?

1. **Sell or donate things you no longer use.** Simplify your space by purging the things that no longer serve you. Let go of the old and make way for the new. This psychological transition is also practical. Take valuable items to one of Portland's many consignment shops to make extra money. You'll feel extra special in your new interview outfit if you got it at a second hand store using the in-store credit from purging old clothes or furniture.

2. **What skills can you barter to do what you love?** Select activities that are nurturing, active, and build community to help you stay resilient and positive. Learn skills and meet people who can be supportive or have connections in your field. For example, barter your computer skills for a haircut. I have gardened, done administrative work, been the doorperson, decorated, and recycled at events, done WordPress and written content for websites, and painted for trade.

3. **Downsize your living situation.** If you have the skill set you want, good connections, and a clear direction, wait out the transition in your current living situation. However, if you know it may take a while to gain skills, connections, or even decide on your field, consider downsizing. Move farther out, into a smaller space, or consider living in community so that you have support while you build skills, connections and career goals.

4. **Grow your own food.** With a little time, seeds, and soil, you get exercise and nutrition. Help the earth as you connect with nature. Food purchasing choices save more fossil fuels than bike commuting, even if it's 10 miles. That's something to feel good about. Pick up this popular Portland hobby, talk to neighbors working in their yard, and build your network naturally.

5. **Find free activities to entertain youself and meet new people.** Accept invitations or host gatherings where you can invite or meet new people. Potlucks keep expenses down, and networking is more natural when you already have things in common. Get some kitchen staples so you can get into the habit of cooking and eating at home. While you are cooking, you can meditate on your next strategic career step. Use the library instead of buying books.

6. **Shop in season at farmers' markets.** Eating healthy is cheaper if you buy local produce in season. You'll spend $5 for a box of Venezuelan blueberries in January or $8 on a quart of local ones in the summer. Learn to can and ferment to make foods last longer. You'll consume good nutrients to keep you sharp and ready to take on the challenges of an exciting new job.

7. **Join a class, group or club.** What types of people inspire you? What clubs are related to your career exploration? Pass up the $50 concert ticket and take guitar lessons instead. Classes give you the confidence boost not being met by a job. Toastmasters will help you build public speaking skills, while a running club might help you meet people from all walks of life.

8. **Travel using public transportation, biking and the local community.** Ditch the car and tune up your bike or learn the public transit system. Use Craigslist rideshare for longer distance traveling. Stay with hosts while you travel using www.couchsurfing.net. Maybe you find out you would actually move to a new city for the right job.

9. **Find gigs to earn some money.** Tell people you are looking for odd jobs. Check craigslist "gigs" (http://portland.craigslist.org/ggg/) or other community boards to find one time or short-term opportunities. Meet and help people, gain insights about what you want, learn new skills, and keep some money coming in. I have babysat, done administrative work, created WordPress sites, gardened, painted, edited, cleaned houses, and written web content for money.

10. **Re-organize your finances.** Mint (www.mint.com) is a free online finance organization tool. Analyze your costs and strategize how to reduce them. I found parking tickets and late fees pretty costly. I changed my travel methods and bill pay timing to reduce costs.

# Faith

The more spiritual version of the quote we introduced earlier is, "When God closes a door, s/he opens another." And the less spiritual punch line is: "What they don't tell you is that it is Hell waiting in the hallway!" It rattles the best of us to not have any indication of how long we should prepare to hang out in that sometimes dark and frightening place.

While you may not have been through this type of transition, remember the other difficult transitions that you have made and the roles played by religious and/or spiritual traditions, rituals and beliefs. If you are not employed at this time, you have the gift of time to add new tools or practices to those that are time-tested. However, if you are employed and engaged in a job search, finding time to brush your teeth may feel like all you can manage. During such a rushed and stressful period, you may need, more than ever, some of the simplest and most portable of practices, like conscious breathing and short prayers that can bring calm to your bus ride.

In the last decade, many people have drawn sustenance by combining a variety of faith traditions. For example, a million people from myriad religious and spiritual traditions logged on when Oprah partnered with author Eckhart Tolle for an online discourse on his book, *A New Earth: Awakening to Your Life's Purpose*. Vicki and Cynthia are both eclectic, drawing from Judaism, Christianity, Sufi (Muslim) and Buddhism, during challenging times.

Our experiences and those of our clients, has shown that faith can play an essential role in several ways: it can help you discern your calling, celebrate your gifts, accept the unknown, keep problems in perspective, and engender courage to take action.

**Discern Your Calling**

The phrase "discerning your calling" originally comes from the Christian faith, used when young men and women were "called to the ministry." The phrase has a broader interpretation, however, generally referring to a compelling feeling that you must use your mind and vigor to help heal some of the world's problems – from hunger to preserving salmon.

Your guidance could come in the form of a clear direct voice, "be a nurse," or a repetitive dream image of the salmon laboring to swim upstream. Or you may note that you feel a spiritual pull every time you are in the wild. Alternatively, you can use faith to let go of self-pity and trust that you will receive guidance when the time is right.

> *Sometimes I go about in pity for myself,*
> *and all the while a great wind is bearing me across the sky.*
> – Ojibwa saying

Whether you believe that a calling comes from an external deity, from inner spiritual direction or elsewhere, the voice that calls to you may not be as specific as you would like. Did you hear "salmon" or did you hear "poverty?" You may need more clarity. All faiths offer ways to quiet your "monkey mind." Perhaps you meditate, or pray, or go for a walk in the woods. I have particularly enjoyed the Sufi tool of "Remembrance," which helps quiet the mind to tap into our divine inner wisdom.

> *When you mediate, invite yourself to feel the self-esteem, the dignity*
> *and strong humility of the Buddha that you are.*
> – Sogyal Rinpoche

**Celebrate Your Gifts**

The self-assessment phase of career transition is about naming and claiming your gifts. You might stammer in stating your strengths in the world if you believe this comes from your ego and implies that "I am a better speaker/writer/programmer than you are." Alternatively, you can experience your strengths as gifts that have been given to you to use in the world. Your voice will carry this conviction and be received as such.

Vicki listens to Jimmy Carter's tapes because he exemplifies, for her, competence in the world coming from a place of humility. Strong in his Baptist faith, he sees his gifts as coming through him from God. Some women eschew the major religions because of the hierarchy that places men above women. As an alternative, they turn to the goddess earth religions to celebrate their strengths, attributes and power.

**Accept the Unknown**

You can, and should, use your rational mind to estimate the chances of reaching your career goal on a timeline. However, even if you promptly and diligently follow through on all tasks, you can't control when the market will provide more or fewer job opening, the qualifications of competing candidates, or when you will meet the ideal connector through networking. It is necessary to accept that you don't have complete control of when you will start your next job. The oft used Serenity Prayer may come in handy: "God, grant me the serenity to accept the things I cannot change, the courage to change the things I can, and the wisdom to know the difference." (Attributed to Reinhold Nieburhr.)

Both Western and Eastern religions provide tools to help us during times when our future is unknowable. "When God closes one door, s/he opens another," reflects a belief that there is a God or a Power with a very specific plan for your life, along with a timetable that you as a human being cannot know. Eastern religions remind us that, at any point, on any day, at any minute, you can bring your attention to the present, without judgment, thereby easing your focus on the future. It is a great way to re-shift your focus and remember who you are, which is much more than your unemployed status.

*If you let cloudy water settle, it will become clear.*
*If you let your upset mind settle, your course will also become clear.*
— The Buddha

**Get Out of Your Own Problems**

If you are not employed during your search, we suggest ignoring the career search pundits who recommend spending 40+ hours each week on your job search. Unless you are in training classes, we don't see much is gained by dedicating more than 30 hours per week. That leaves ten hours to balance between enjoyment and service. You can do something wonderful and refreshing, like dusting off your guitar, meditating or taking your kid to feed baby goats right in the middle of the week. See **Gifts to Give Yourself During Career Transition Stress** for more inexpensive, wonderful gifts that you can give yourself.

Ammachi (known as Amma or the "Hugging Saint") is a current popular Indian guru who asks her followers to do two things: pray and serve. Jesus repeatedly commanded his followers to take care of the poor and the sick. If you are unemployed, you may have a unique opportunity to serve.

Fortunately, all faiths offer tools to abate fear. Many religions offer the solace of picturing God, goddesses, Christ, spirits at your side or even carrying you through the parts of the process where you need spiritual companionship. Whatever your personal beliefs, use your faith to steady you as you wait in the hallway. And in keeping with our hallway metaphor...

*Faith is taking the first step even when you don't see the whole staircase.*
— Martin Luther King, Jr.

# Research and Networking
## for
## Career Exploration
### phase II

52

# Phase II. Career Exploration: What's Out There?

The first phase, **Self-Assessment**, helped you to articulate your strengths and needs systematically in relation to your career goals. It was an inside job. This second phase, **Career Exploration**, will create a structure for you to see how your skills, values and interests match the external world of decently paying work. We'll guide you to identify many job titles and then winnow them to a few that you can research in depth. You are beginning to drill down. Since you need to find a career that will "feed the belly" as well as the soul, exploration provides information about compensation and job outlook for each type of job on your preliminary list of meaningful jobs.

Many creative people and those who want to make a difference can generate a bountiful list of options, but they are more challenged when forced to focus, prioritize and get out to talk with the right people. The extrovert runs to a dizzying array of activities, thinking that networking with a lot of people is the key. The introvert stays home or talks to a cherished friend about their most recent dream or reads another career transition book.

We present you with a series of keys to unlock the many doors in the hallway. Your pace and the way you approach career exploration must be consistent with your own personal style. A planned exploration will help extroverts focus energy on meeting the right people and pacing themselves. Introverts can dispel notions that they need to mimic the extrovert's networking style.

**Transition from Self-Assessment to Career Exploration**
The phases of career transitions are rarely exact and linear for the creative career seeker. For example, you may have thought for a while about pursuing a career as a publicity agent. You're ready to begin the research, but you also want to simultaneously uncover other options. Begin this section by completing the pre-assessment **Career Exploration Checklist** to decide how to organize your research and exploration. A post-assessment checklist, found at the end of this section, will allow you to track your progress and determine when you are ready to leave this phase.

**Introduction to LinkedIn and Social Media**
Social media is key for quickly finding the people to help you network. We will help you explore how to notify and leverage your current network to let them know about your career process and help you get in touch with the people who are already working in your fields of interest. The ethics of LinkedIn specifically allow you to start contributing your perspectives by becoming active in groups. This can be a powerful way to both show your passion and talent as well as experiment with what it feels like to engage in your potential new field. Your web presence can help you streamline the process of selecting your top field of interest.

**Creating a Basic Message**
When you completed the self-assessment phase, you created a one-page profile of your interests, personality style, values and skills as well as what you want from employment. It is helpful to begin talking to people close to you about these findings. As you do so, you'll be converting your findings into a verbal form.

You will be trying out various word choices, and as you do so, essential features will become sharpened. For example, Sam could begin to say to himself, his career counselor, his wife and his brother something like: "I have found that I want to use my long-term passions for wood and the outdoors. However, I am not a 'tree hugger.' I am practical and want to use my understanding of small business and rural communities." After practicing with family, Susan overcame her natural modesty and learned to say, "I am a good designer with intuition for the creative use of materials in a built environment, in the home or outdoors. I want to use my CAD skills, but also crave getting out and interacting with people about their creative projects."

It's a mistake to wait to create a basic message to use in networking until you have a clear job title (For example, I want to be a project manager in a company that makes shoes using renewable materials.) This level of specificity may come at the end of your research or may never come. But, stating the parts that you are clear about in a new and concise way is extremely important. You know that you are moving along when you find yourself talking more about where you want to go, than where you have been. One result is that you feel better; a second is that people will take your cues and direct you towards people and organizations that can educate you about your top career interests.

**Job Titles**
Once you can summarize your findings from your self-assessment, you're ready to brainstorm an **exhaustive list of possible jobs or specific organizations** that might be a fit. It is important to give yourself several weeks to expand the list. After you have created a complete list, your task changes dramatically. This is akin to the pivot point in a Tango. Expanding options is over; it's time to winnow to the top four possibilities, so that you can research them in depth. We encourage you to keep at least one dream job and one pragmatic job on this short list.

**Research and Exploration**
With this short list, you are ready for research and exploration. Internet research gives you the basic understanding of a job and a working vocabulary. You may want to write down the questions that you have about job titles on your short list. What are the entry-level jobs? How important are certain computer skills? Is it fun? Some of these questions can be answered by exploring written resources. Websites often include information about the profession and a chance to peruse typical position openings, typical salaries and qualifications. Books and professional journals are available from the library or bookstores. The Bureau of Labor Statistics (www.BLS.gov) and Oregon's OLMIS (www.OLMIS.org) websites are excellent starting places to research typical job titles to learn about expectations, salary and educational requirements. Also check out the broader, 10-year projections for these industries.

Internet research is important, but talking to people is the heart of the research and exploration process. Informational interviews and finding groups for networking are the keys. Initially, your research may be broad and exploratory. Marcelle, for example, was new to Portland and wanted to learn about many groups related to natural resources, particularly as it involved water and/or GIS (Geographic Information Systems). Later, she focused her exploration by choosing three target organizations to attend regularly.

**Curious Minds Want to Know**
You can think of research and exploration as if a professor gave you an assignment to research a career field that you find exciting. Remember that the facts and perspectives you learn about will slowly form a picture that you can later evaluate. Many career seekers falsely think that they need to force a career decision. The mood plummets on a day when a disheartened librarian reports on the four years she has been a clerk to compete for a library position at the downtown library. The mood soars after the informational interview with the passionate librarian at OHSU.

Chill – and enjoy the conversations in your informational interviews.

# Career Exploration Checklist: What's Out There?

Date of Pre-assessment_____

- ☐ **Brainstorm at least 15 job titles/organizations/careers**
  Reduce to 2 - 4 job titles/careers to research.
  1._____  3._____
  2._____  4._____

- ☐ **Identify research questions.** What do you want to know about employment in each career choice? Be sure to ask about degrees or certifications required to be competitive. (Use another sheet if you are researching more than two job titles or careers.)

Questions for Career/Job Title #1_____
  1._____
  2._____
  3._____
  4._____
  5._____

Questions for Career/Job Title #2_____
  1._____
  2._____
  3._____
  4._____
  5._____

- ☐ Create a **LinkedIn Profile** and invite connections.

- ☐ **Develop a strategy for meeting or being introduced to 3-6 people who work in each arena** or have that job description. (e.g., connect using LinkedIn, ask 4 or 5 people you know each week if they know someone, join or attend professional group meetings, do targeted volunteering or an internship).

  _____
  _____
  _____
  _____

- ☐ **List several people in each arena whom you can ask for an informational interview.** Then call or email them.
  1._____  5._____
  2._____  6._____
  3._____  7._____
  4._____  8._____

- ☐ **Carry out informational interviews and follow-up activities** with people whom you interviewed (send articles of interest, thank you, etc.)

# Brainstorming Possible Job Titles, Organizations and Career Arenas

The goal of this brainstorming is to produce a comprehensive list of actual job titles/employers/entrepreneurial businesses that match your interests, psychological type and skills. Set aside your "critical editor" who eliminates ideas because they are not practical. Include fantasies that you have had since childhood (a professional photographer of railroads?) as well as jobs with a lot of openings (Nurse? Computer tech?). If a specific organization calls to you, add it, even if you do not have a specific job title ("Use my PR skills for Mercy Corps" or "Do Web design for Weiden + Kennedy").

Stop yourself from editing out options based on fears. Vicki talks to her own fears, in a firm, calm voice: "Step aside. I promise you will get your time later." The following activities may help you to shake loose some options hiding in forgotten compartments of your brain.

- Imagine that someone else asked you, "What would a good career choice be for someone who has _____, _____ and _____ passions and _____, _____ and _____ skills?"
- Take a few close friends out for a beer or tea. Summarize your findings or bring your summary with you. Ask them for suggestions, from the obvious to the wild.
- Review jobs lists that match your Myers-Briggs type, in books like *Do What You Are* by Paul D. Tieger and Barbara Barron. If you are working with a career counselor, he or she can administer the Strong Interest Inventory, which compares your interests to more than 200 job titles.
- Use resources such as the *Dictionary of Occupational Titles*, OLMIS, or the yellow pages in *Cool Careers for Dummies* (Marty Nemko, Paul Edwards and Sarah Edwards) to familiarize yourself with little-known emerging job titles.
- After you've completed your list, you need to assume an entirely different mind-set. Instead of creative expansion, you need to evaluate options and reduce the list to a manageable two to four priorities. These are the ones you will research in greater depth.
- You may also discover ideas just below your conscious awareness using journaling, dream interpretation, or meditation. Don't rush the process. Give yourself at least a week.

| | |
|---|---|
| 1. | 11. |
| 2. | 12. |
| 3. | 13. |
| 4. | 14. |
| 5. | 15. |
| 6. | 16. |
| 7. | 17. |
| 8. | 18. |
| 9. | 19. |
| 10. | 20. |

# Short List of Possible Jobs

The purpose of this exercise is to select two to four job titles, organizations, freelance ideas or arenas that you will systematically research. This selection will help you move from a broad exploratory mode into a more focused research mode.

Go back through your list of possibilities and put a "$" symbol next to each listing that appears to be financially practical. Now, go back over the list and put a heart symbol next to listings for which you have an interest or passion. There may be a few listings for which you need to do some quick research in order to rate them. (Will it really take five years to become an architect?)

It is now time to select two to four from the list. Most likely, any candidates with both a positive financial outlook and a lot of heart will rise to the top. Include in this final cut at least one with a lot of heart and at least one that appears financially practical.

1._____

2_____

3._____

4._____

**Reflection on the Short List**

The purpose of reducing your career candidates to a few is to go deeper into an internal and external assessment of each possible future. While this chapter emphasizes researching external factors, you may also want to use this list for a more focused internal exploration.

If you are inclined towards journaling, we encourage you to write about your imagined life if you were to live out each of these futures. Not surprisingly Anais Nin, the consummate model of reflective journaling, recommended this technique to young artists, including Judy Chicago, when they were struggling with questions of career direction. As a young artist, Chicago was torn between art, activism and teaching. "Anais suggested that I use writing to 'try out' the paths I could see myself taking and as a method of exploring the many directions to the arts. She said that writing allowed one to 'act out' what one could not actually live out."

If you find it hard to leave some of the options behind, start with six and do the preliminary research on the Internet to learn about job descriptions, pay and outlook. Then, within a week or two, select the final four. It is a bad idea to keep too many doors open – it can lead to aimlessly wandering in and out of each option.

# Researching Job Titles

Now that you have identified four possible job titles, it is time to use the following powerful web resources to learn more about these job titles:

- **US Bureau of Labor Statistics (BLS):** Between five and ten pages are dedicated to each job title. It comments on the nature of each job, working conditions, training, qualifications, earnings, related occupations and sources of additional information.

- **The Occupational Information Center** (at www.qualityinfo.org/olmisj/OIC) gives the viewer occupational descriptions, compensation, occupational requirements and projected need. The level of specificity is useful for an introductory exploration of common careers, but its database of 700 careers is less than a quarter of the estimated job titles. For example, we entered 'graphic artist' for career exploration and found that it was lumped into a section of Artists & Related Jobs.

- **Oregon Career Information Systems (CIS)** provides the best information on career outlook and compensation in Oregon as well as detailed descriptions of job responsibilities and needed training. This powerful database compares salaries and outlook in Oregon as well as national averages. One of the coolest features of Oregon CIS is that it links each career to available training programs in Oregon.

  *Online access to CIS is available through the Multnomah County Library website (at http://www.multcolib.org/). Search for "career information system." Also, Peer Advisors are available to help you navigate the CIS system at Portland Community College (PCC) career centers, including PCC Sylvania, open every day and Wednesday until 7 pm. They will also give you a password so that you can continue this research at home. (PCC phone number: 503-977-4891)*

- The **U.S. Department of Labor's O*NET OnLine** system (at http://online.onetcenter.org) offers reports on many job titles; enter one of your titles into the Occupation Quick Search window and see if an O*NET Report is available. If so, there is a wealth of information awaiting you. If not, there may still be some information available (such as employment statistics and education requirements). The O*NET report includes a list of tasks for the job, tools and technology needed, and skills. It also suggests job titles that may be similar to the title you selected.

# National Career Trends

The U.S. Bureau of Labor Statistics (BLS) publishes the exhaustive *Occupational Outlook Handbook* (OOH) that contains data, commentary and charts pertinent to hundreds of career fields. Its dominance in the field has led it to being dubbed "the bible of career trends." Current versions can be found in bookstores, college career centers, and public libraries.

We recommend that you rely primarily on Oregon trends for your final career decisions, unless you are leaving the area. Regional economies are more likely to influence your job prospects than national trends. It's wise, however, to use national data for job titles and job descriptions, and to be generally informed about national trends.

In the section in OOH on Job Outlook, job titles are described with key phrases that tell you how fast the occupation is growing, with estimates of future supply and demand. Should you rely on these indicators in making a career decision? Consider them as a factor, and in balance with what you learn from your informational interviews with people who have their ears to the ground in your field. While the predictions based on economic recovery projections may waver, other predictions related to demographics are more dependable. For example, good news for jobseekers is that more than 60% of hires will be to replace folks who will retire during this decade.

There are other predictable and stable trends that you can rely on for the future. These will occur in Oregon as well. Such trends include:

- **Jobs for the multicultural work force, particularly Spanish-speaking people.** An analysis of the impact of immigration policies and analysis of birth rates in immigrant families has led to accurate, early predictions and planning for a multicultural America. There will be increasing demand for professionals who speak Spanish, Russian, Chinese and other languages, and who have cultural competence in those areas as well.
- **Jobs with seniors.** America is "graying" and there are significant, growing opportunities to work with elders. This trend will predictably increase as the surge of baby boomers hits retirement age during the next decade. Some things we know about the boomer generation:
  - They are big consumers of personal services, from massage therapy to counseling.
  - An increasing number are single. Aging single homeowners need more resources to stay at home, often with their pets as trusted roommates.
  - They will increasingly live in assisted living centers and advocate loudly for yoga, healthier foods and more broadly based spiritual development.
  - They are not likely to fully retire and more likely to start small businesses or work part-time. Hence, services that support home-based and small businesses will be in demand.
  - The needs of this population lead us to ponder low-impact travel programs for elders, holistic assisted living facility management, therapeutic bodywork and grief counseling for pet loss.

The fastest growing industries between 2010-2020 will be health care, personal care and social assistance, and construction. You must look carefully at both the rate of growth and actual numbers to determine whether the number of anticipated openings over the next decade will provide the level of opportunity you are seeking.

**Health Care and Social Assistance**: This sector is projected to gain the most jobs. Health care is inextricably linked to both technology and the graying of America. The shortage of experienced nurses and nursing assistants will continue. New careers will marry health care and technology.

**Construction:** More than one fourth of new jobs will be in this field as the economy improves. Jobs in this field will not return, however, to their pre-recession levels.

**Jobs in sustainability:** Some of the gains made over the last few years, spurred by the green stimulus funding, will be maintained. For more information, see **Trends in Sustainability**.

# Oregon Career Trends

In this economic climate, job availability and projections are a huge factor in your career decisions. If you want to stay in Portland, you'll need to combine your passion with some solid facts about job availability. Data and reports generated for Oregon are more current and reliable than the parallel national data. The Oregon Employment Department carries out comprehensive studies of the current status of hundreds of job titles as well as predictions for change. Between 2010 and 2020, major trends in Oregon are predicted to grow in the following areas:

- **Healthcare occupations will grow 28**%, a 32% increase in healthcare support jobs and a 26% increase in healthcare practitioners and technicians.
- **The construction industry will rebound with a 25%** growth rate, but not reach pre-recession highs.
- **Business and financial occupations will grow eighteen percent,** with the biggest growth among financial specialists and advertising/marketing/public-relations professionals.
- **Professional and computer-related occupations will grow sixteen percent.** Computer-related occupations represent 21% of that increase.

**The Oregon Employment Department** (www.employment.oregon.gov/) creates a host of publications available in print or for download. This site tracks local **labor trends, Oregon careers, Oregon wage information and projections by industry and occupation,** and posts **current job postings**. It will also inform you on the minimum requirements for education or training for each career.

The Department's data is summarized in the **Oregon Labor Market Information System** (OLMIS) at www.olmis.org/olmisj/OlmisZine, a powerful interactive informational database that helps you **explore career options, locate training programs and find career trend information** on more than 700 occupations. Check out the "Occupations in Demand" link to find current jobs in demand. Look for reports that address local, regional and statewide employment trends, including occupations in demand in Portland (Region 2).

One of the most powerful data tools is "Occupations," with two particularly useful links:

- **The Occupational Information Center** contains extensive data on job outlook, wages, education requirements and other key occupational information, with sample current job openings in Oregon. For example, if you input "occupational therapist," a one-page summary will include the number of projected openings, average wage ranges, and similar job titles you might consider. A new and exciting feature is the listing of current job openings in the state. This answers your questions: What position openings are *really* out there? Which employers are hiring in my field?
- **The Skills Explorer** allows you to match your unique set of skills by industry. Hit "search" for a skills menu, select your skills, and then it will generate a report listing occupational titles that match your skills.

**The Oregon Employment Department/OLMIS** site is friendly to use and packed with helpful data, so we encourage you to take the time to get familiar with how many ways it can help you during your career research.

# Portland Career Trends

Major cities begin determining occupational outlook by analyzing national data and statewide trends for applicability to their region. Portland, for example, as the only metropolitan city in the state, has become a center for medical specialization and research. It is therefore logical that the national data on trends in health care occupations would be particularly relevant for Portland. Keeping abreast of local news and trends is important during the research phase, particularly for those who are intellectually stimulated by new developments and can tolerate the risk that goes with them. In addition to seeking an understanding of how national trends will impact the city, the city seeks to shape and proactively anticipate new job trends. The Portland Development Commission (PDC), Portland Business Alliance (formerly Chamber of Commerce), and the Mayor's office work to bring and develop industries that are consistent with the region's values of minimizing pollution and maximizing quality of life.

**Resources for Local Trends**

The **Oregon Employment Department** (www.employment.oregon.gov/), especially Portland's downtown office, is a good place to research career trends and target organizations. You can pick up several of the department's print publications. In addition, the Employment Office has computer programs that help career seekers identify job titles that match their skill sets. And, of course, the Employment Office carries out its primary activities in matching registered job seekers (whether or not they are receiving unemployment benefits) with job listings. Even if you are not ready to apply for a job, reviewing job titles that match your skills will give you ideas for possible job titles to research.

**College and university career centers** and their staff are generally versed on local trends in their fields. Community college career centers, in particular, include resources at no or minimal cost, such as computer programs that identify job titles to match your skills and values. Advisors in specific programs, such as Interior Design at the Art Institute or Horticulture at PCC, should be able to let you know where their graduates are working.

**National Trends Mirrored Locally**

To forecast the job scene in Portland, we first reflect on the 2010-2020 **National Career Trends** and **Oregon Career Trends**. Portland's future jobs are intertwined with most of the same unpredictable economic and political forces that will drive country and state. Since we're not economists (nor psychics), we rely on the best estimates of the Bureau of Labor and Statistics (BLS), which bases its calculations on an optimistic outlook for the decade between 2010 and 2021. BLS predicts modest, but steady, economic progress as well as a large number of job vacancies created by Baby Boomers continuing to retire. Generation X and Y had been told to expect Boomer retirements earlier, but they were delayed by the recession. The real impact will be felt over the next five to ten years, when for every four jobs created from economic growth, five jobs will be created from people leaving the workforce. This will create openings in nearly every profession with the exception of print-related occupations such as postal work.

Paralleling the industry growth trends outlined in **Oregon Career Trends**, Portland growth will be most active in these categories:

- **Services** will growth the most rapidly, but unfortunately will be comprised of low paid positions that require little training, such as retail, security guards, and janitors. If working as a server or cook is a stop-gap measure for you, it's heartening to know that the number of these positions will continue to grow across the food continuum - from swanky Blue Hour to the neighborhood McMennamen's to growing assisted living facilities.
- **Office and administrative support** is another huge growth category. Over half of the open positions are replacements for retirees. Medical secretaries and others requiring strong

computer skills will lead the growth spurt in the office and administrative category.

- **Professional and related** category will also gain momentum as the recession recedes and Boomer retirements continue. This category includes engineers, computer specialists, social workers and teachers. Many jobs as teachers, social workers, and staff for the city government are tied to available tax revenue, and considerable reductions were made at the county and city level in 2010-2012. If the recession continues and politicians are assertive about balancing the budget, new government jobs will be limited. It will be several years before the retirement of older government workforce opens more positions and by the end of the decade, even elementary and secondary teachers will see increasing numbers of openings.

These professional categories will see the most robust growth:

- **Professional healthcare** positions will lead the growth pack with 18 out of the 50 fastest growing occupations in the tri-county area: nurses, occupational therapists, massage therapists, and medical assistants will all be in demand by the ageing population.
- **Professional computer related** occupations, especially computer software engineers, computer support specialists, and computer systems analysts. Our software industry is particularly robust, continuing to attract and retain men, but very few women.
- **Office Construction** will rebound from the dramatic hit this job category took during the Great Recession, but it will not return to pre-recession levels. The recovery, along with replacements for retirement will create openings for carpenters, plumbers, electricians and building/retrofitting for energy efficiency.

**Uniquely Portland**

**Young and Educated**: Portland's workforce is distinctive from the rest of the state in its young, well-educated workforce. Even during the recession, Portland continued to be a magnet for 22-35 year old progressive, creative, outdoor-oriented college graduates. This trend magnifies the job problems of college graduate without the type of advanced "hard" skills that populate the requirements section of position announcements. Competition is particularly keen for progressive businesses and organizations with a positive work culture. A consequence for educated, non-technical job seekers is that you need to research less popular employers and create relationships through networking.

**Culturally Creative**: It's not hard to see that Portland is also culturally distinctive from most of the rural areas in Oregon—just view a few episodes of the satirical comedy, *Portlandia*, including cameos by Mayor Sam Adams. *Portlandia* captures Portland as fresh, idealistic, organic, and innovative. These light-hearted sketches are congruent with Portland's more serious designation (since 2008) as a hub for Cultural Creatives. According to author Richard Florida, Portland is one of the top fifty cities characterized as having a high density of writers, designers, psychotherapists, and traditional/holistic health care providers. Cultural Creatives value sustainability, education, and innovation. Florida identifies Cultural Creatives as often needing achievement and independence, as well as welcoming risk taking—a strong recipe for entrepreneurs. As a result, Florida predicted in 2008 that Portland, and cities like it, were poised to become innovative economic engines.

Given that Portland hit double-digit inflation, did the prediction have any meaning? Can it still come true? Perhaps. Being a culturally creative city has given us direction to counter the recession. In May 2012, *Where's The Bottom*, (http://wheresthebottom.wordpress.com) a city watchdog group, ranked Portland as the 13th fastest growing/recovering job market out of a field of 51 cities. This may be because two core values associated with cultural creativity—sustainability and entrepreneurialism—are at the forefront of Portland's planning.

# Portland for Creatives

**Portland's Wealth for Creatives**

The signs of Portland's love of the art, music, and writing are everywhere. We jam the banks of the Willamette for the Blues Festival, attend readings at Powells, and support BodyVox's edgy dance troupe. We frequent comedy clubs and listen to indie bands.

*The Wall Street Journal* broached the possibility that Portland may become the country's next art capital (May 2012). The author queried, "In what U.S. city might you find an 'alternative' art exhibition space on a 200-ton, 135-foot decommissioned crabbing ship?" The article noted that we crave national attention, while simultaneously thumbing our noses at the typical New York or LA gallery scene. We even poke fun of ourselves in zany sketch comedies on *Portlandia*. With this panoply of inexpensive creative options, Portland is heaven for those seeking a creative life.

**Portland's Dearth for Creatives**

Portland's creative scene is robust for people living modestly or with a secure second income. Unfortunately, only a small percentage of artists can charge enough to make a robust living, and we have only one Arlene Schnitzer (wealthy art patron). For those who need a salaried position with benefits, options for working in the arts are even more limited.

Your financial options also depend on how you define Creatives, a term whose meaning can vary widely, and overlaps with the use of the terms *artists, musicians and writers*. We would like to explore some of the definitions and the job-related implications of each.

**Definitions of Creatives**

**Fine Arts** focus on art forms developed primarily for aesthetics and/or concept, rather than practical application. Historically, the five great fine arts have included painting, sculpture, architecture, music, and poetry, with drama and dancing considered minor arts. While the focus of these art forms is not primarily practical, the artists themselves have to solve the practical problem of supporting themselves. Few full-time, paid employment opportunities, such as playing with the Portland symphony, exist. Most local fine artists grapple with compromises and select one, or several, of the following:

- **Teaching at a college** is attractive because the schedule offers generous vacation allotments and support for continuing to develop your art form. A Masters in Fine Arts (MFA) is the terminal degree required for a full-time teaching position in studio arts at a community college or four year university. Most courses, particularly at community colleges, are taught by part-time, temporary "adjunct faculty." Contracts to teach these individual courses are plentiful at the five community college campuses in or near Portland as well as at PSU, and private colleges. The downside of being an adjunct faculty is that the pay is poor, schedules are apt to change without warning, and benefits accumulate slowly.
- **Non-arts job in an arts organization is** inspiring to some artists because it allows them to be immersed in the fine arts, even if their job function is program management, education, fundraising or directing. Portland's arts organizations are financially supported through a mix of paying attendees, private patrons, and government funding. For example, with help from small National Arts Endowment (NEA) grants, the following organizations have paid staff positions: *Literary Arts, Inc.*, *Miracle Theatre Group, Portland Center Stage, Portland Youth Philharmonic Association,* and *White Bird (dance)*.
- **Find a subsistence job** that interferes minimally with time for your art. This usually works best when combined with a simple lifestyle and/or a partner with a steady income. Start up a conversation with many young baristas or bartenders and you will usually find a musician, writer, or other artist.

- **Seek outside funding** to support your art. Local writer and presentation coach, Gigi Rosenberg specializes in the business side of being an artist. We recommend her book. *The Artist's Guide to Grant Writing,* which Gigi designed to "transform readers from starving artists fumbling to get by into working artists who confidently tap into all the resources at their disposal." Written in an engaging, down-to-earth tone, this comprehensive guide includes time-tested strategies, anecdotes from successful grant writers, and tips from grant officers and fundraising specialists.

### Cultural Creatives

While fine artists are defined by the products that they create, *Cultural Creatives* are defined by their beliefs and values. In 2005, author and sociologist Richard Florida coined the term *"Creative Class"* and *ranked Portland as one of the cities with the highest densities of Cultural Creatives*. This group comprises about twelve percent of all U.S. jobs. It includes a wide range of occupations (e.g. science, engineering, education, computer programming, research) with arts, design, and media workers forming a small subset. Florida considers people in all of these professions to "fully engage in the creative process" (2002, p. 69). While the science/engineer subset of Cultural Creatives might disdain tattoos or Flash Mobs, they are very innovative, creating commercial products and consumer goods. The primary job function of its members is to be creative and innovative, and their advanced skills have recently attracted employers in desirable industries such as biotechnology. With this broader definition of Cultural Creatives that includes creative thinkers, there are well-compensated options in Portland.

The mayor and city council's disposition towards the arts make a difference. Ex-mayor Sam Adams was a strong proponent of the arts and also believed in the tie between the arts and the economy. In *The Oregonian* (June 2012), Adams touts, "An investment in arts education is an investment in our future economic success."

**Creative Industry or Creative Services** refers to a range of economic activities concerned with the generation development of knowledge, information, and ideas. These Creatives work in advertising, architecture, illustration, print and web design, fashion, film, performing arts, publishing, R&D, software, toys and games, TV and radio, and video games. In general, people thrive in these industries if they enjoy the interplay of business and technology with creativity.

In order to garner full-time employment in the creative industry as web/print designer, copywriter, music illustrator, illustrator, or videographer, it's usually necessary to have a well-developed, high quality online portfolio. While some pieces can be from student projects, others need to be from clients. To develop their portfolios, many Creatives begin as freelancers and then move to agencies or in-house positions.

Even after they have launched their careers, Creatives (in the Creative Services Industry) in Portland tend to move in and out of the following types of relationships to an employer:

- **Freelancing**, finding your own clients, often keeping a second part time job, while you build your business and portfolio. Freelancing has the upside of flexibility, well fitted for one member of a family, while the other person holds down a more steady income and generates the medical benefits. A proclivity for technology and/or an entrepreneurial spirit are correlated with significant economic success. Most Creatives need to develop a niche (or a few niches) to compete in Portland's robust freelance scene. For example, Christian Columbres, a photographer, specializes in architectural photography; Jill Kelly, an editor, has developed a steady stream of dissertations to edit.

- **Working for Agencies.** Portland has hundreds of small agencies, located in NW Portland and the Pearl. In addition, it has two large agencies: Weiden+Kennedy, with international dazzle, and Waggener Edstrom, an international public relations firm. Agencies generally have younger employees who respond to trends and periodic breakneck deadlines. The pay and benefits are generally good at these agencies, but they usually expand and shrink when they lose or gain major clients. The most common position titles are Creative Director, Project Manager, Account Manager Copywriter, Designer, Producer/Content Manager, Web Developer, and Copy Editor.
- **Creative Staffing Agencies** provide temporary projects for Creatives, usually placing people with at least three to five years of experience. Aquent, (www.aquentus.com) Portland's most active creative staffing agency, typically has half a dozen openings. Listings include Sr. Illustrator, Sr. Interactive Developer, and Content Manager.
- **Working In-House for Employers**. Large companies, educational organizations, medical facilities, and government agencies usually have in-house creative departments. Companies with local corporate headquarters, such as Norm Thompson and Nike have a team of graphic designers, copywriters, and photographers who design their catalogs, trade show booths, packaging, and promotional activities. These positions often list extensive technical requirements, and it's vital to build competence in these technical skills to compete for these popular positions. This is especially true if you don't have an inside connection.

Illustrious non-profits, such as Mercy Corps or the Humane Society are particularly competitive because they combine social contribution with creativity. Unless you are well networked, you may need to take a minimally paid or unpaid internship with such a desirable employer. We suggest that you initially build your credentials with a less prominent, but decent organization.

*"Sometimes the road less traveled is less traveled for a reason."*
- Jerry Seinfeld

# Careers in Fundraising and Development
## Contributed by Brenda Ray Scott, CFRE and Adept Diva Consulting

Securing rewarding work in the development and fundraising portion of today's nonprofit sector is more challenging than ever. This article is designed to introduce to you the work of fundraising and development professionals and to provide insight about where to look and what to look for in finding a position that suits you.

**What is Fundraising and Development?**
According to Lilya Wagner in her book, *Careers in Fundraising*, "Fundraising is part of philanthropy, defined by Robert L. Payton as 'voluntary action for the public good.'" (Ref. Robert L. Payton, Philanthropy, 1988. New York: Macmillan Publishing Co. and the American Council on Education.) The profession's largest internationally recognized professional organization, Association of Fundraising Professionals, defines development as: "The total process by which an organization increases public understanding of its mission and acquires financial support for its programs." A fundraising professional manages the process of creating the messaging and procedures that help match a donor's interest in investing in community needs with an organization that meets those needs. Fundraising professionals work in a variety of roles including the executive who leads the entire process i.e., Vice President of Development to the professionals who focus on a specific area i.e., grant writing to those who provide logistical and administrative support i.e., Development Assistant.

**Current Trends**
Despite economic uncertainty, a career in fundraising and development represents a solid choice for those currently working in the nonprofit sector, in fundraising and development, and those seeking to transition into the field. This optimism is being expressed amidst a backdrop of less than encouraging compensation news as reported in a story in the *Chronicle of Philanthropy*. (This is a "go to" resource for both the newer and the more seasoned fundraising professional.) According to this article, the median salary of fundraisers was $66,000. Also, pay increased by only 1.5 percent—not enough to keep pace with inflation. Fundraising professionals working at federations such as United Way earned a median salary of $52,000 and those working for international groups earned more. (*The Chronicle of Philanthropy*, "Fundraisers' Pay didn't Keep Up with Inflation Last Year," May 8, 2012, Flandez, Raymond.)

**Salaries – A Sampling of the Portland, Oregon Metro Market**
Salaries listed below are based on a sampling of job descriptions and survey information from nonprofits in the Portland, Oregon metropolitan area. Higher education and healthcare institutions typically offer greater compensation. Compensation increases also when a professional possesses certification such as a CFRE (Certified Fund Raising Executive):

| Position | Salary | Level | Experience |
|---|---|---|---|
| *Development Director | $50,000 - $63,000 | Management | 7 + years |
| Capital Campaign Manager | $45,000 - $65,000 | Management | 5 + years |
| Major Gifts Officer | $45,000 – 70,000 | Senior | 5 – 7 years |
| Planned Giving Officer | Varies | Senior | 5 – 7 years |

# Careers in Fundraising and Development
## Contributed by Brenda Ray Scott, CFRE and Adept Diva Consulting

| Annual Giving Manager | $40,000 - $50,000 | Professional | 3 – 5 years |
|---|---|---|---|
| Grant Writer | $40,000 - $45,000 | Professional | 5 + years |
| Events Manager | $41,000 - $59,000 | Professional | 3 + years |
| Development Assistant | $28,000 - $35,000 | Administrative | Entry level |

**\*Note:** Other titles for executive roles in fundraising and development include Vice President of Development, Vice President of Advancement, and Chief Development Officer. These titles are usually associated with larger organizations and larger fundraising operations.

### Qualities of a Successful Fundraising Professional
According to the Association of Fundraising Professionals, qualities of a good candidate for development professional are:
- A passion for achievement
- Great "people person" skills
- The ability to solve problems with creativity and flexibility
- A focus on results
- The ability to juggle and multi-task
- A strong personal code of ethics

### Skills of a Successful Fundraising Professional
The following list of skills is not intended to be exhaustive, but to provide an idea of what skills as typically sought in a fundraising professional early in their career:
- Self-starter, able to successfully coordinate multifaceted events, timelines, competing priorities, projects and duties both independently and in collaboration with other team members;
- Excellent interpersonal skills and pleasant manner dealing with the public, other employees and volunteers;
- Excellent oral and written communications skills; and
- Willingness and ability to work occasional weekends or evenings.

### Other typical qualifications for fundraising positions:
- Undergraduate degree, in any field of study, typically business, communication or non-profit management
- At least three years of experience in development, sales or equivalent; and
- Strong computer skills including MS Office, relational database software i.e., Raiser's Edge or similar donor management software.

### About Brenda Ray Scott and Adept Diva Consulting
Brenda Ray Scott, CFRE, is Principal of Adept Diva Consulting, a fundraising consulting practice based in Portland, Oregon. With nearly 20 years of experience, Brenda has raised millions of dollars as staff and consultant with a variety of organizations—large and small providing them with grant writing, corporate and foundation relations, and sponsorship management. When she's not working tweeting, posting, blogging, or speaking about fundraising, or enjoying time with her family, she's a passionate community activist serving in a number of hands on and volunteer leadership roles in her neighborhood, her daughter's school, and county government. Learn more about Brenda at http://www.linkedin.com/in/brendarayscott and @adeptdiva.

# Going to School

**The Decision to Return to School**

There are pros and cons in going back to school, so consider as many aspects as possible before making this life changing commitment. School is expensive and time consuming, so do your research to ensure this is the best decision for you right now! Going to school will change your life in several ways. You will have less time for family, friends and hobbies. You will likely take on debt, and your current income flow will likely be reduced as well.

Before you decide to go back to school, first find out whether the degree or certification is really required. You can research online and complete informational interviews to find out whether this educational standard is a) required b) preferred or c) entirely optional. For some careers, the credential may be absolutely required by state or corporate regulations. For others, the certification or degree may be only preferred or optional, and used as a rough indicator of maturity and skill. Sometimes these are also used to screen large applicant pools. Here are several ways to find out more before you leap into school:

- Take a look at 20 or more current posted jobs in your targeted field in Seattle or San Francisco and track the percentage of jobs that require, prefer or make no mention of the educational credential in question. You can certainly track local jobs on Portland Craigslist (http://portland.craigslist.org/) but the market may be too small to ascertain a trend.
- Ask in informational interviews how important the degree or certificate may be in your job search.
- Review LinkedIn profiles to find out what type of education folks in your desired field have obtained. Go to "Advanced Search" and put the desired job title under key words. It will show you people who hold the job title that you desire. Look at about ten to see if they all have the "required" educational backgrounds. If not, see what other route they took to get the position.
- Unless the education is absolutely required for the job, seriously consider an intensive networking effort and other activities that will build relevant work experience before you make a commitment to attend school.

**Benefits of Returning to School**

Even if you don't HAVE to go to school, you may decide to pursue this avenue for several reasons. You may want a degree for your own edification and sense of accomplishment, and to obtain it before educational costs rise even further. Also, having a credential or degree can meet the following needs:

a) Increase your competitiveness in a tight job market, and allow you to compete with folks who DO have the degree.

b) Help network and build your resume **while** you are in school through coursework and internships.

c) Build your confidence and competence, which tend to erode if you are unemployed.

**Building Contacts in School**

Going to school in your targeted field can help you build a lot of contacts and networks because of several convenient structures in the school setting. Your instructors or professors will know people in the field. Many programs require or offer internships, an ideal way to earn credit AND build experience, contacts and references. You can become visible in your field and in the community through both formal internships and informal volunteering, such as working on committees and boards or helping to plan events. Again, having the school and your instructors behind your efforts can build credibility and connections. You may get your dream job during or right after you complete your degree, certificate, or training program. It may be entry level and therefore not pay very much, but you'll be launched in the field and ready to work your way up and into higher wages and more satisfaction.

**Internships**

Colleges use a variety of terms to describe internships. They may be called practica, externships, cooperative education, or clinicals. They all mean pretty much the same thing. They all provide a structured, unpaid experience during which you explore a field, practice skills, undergo evaluation, and/or earn credit. If you already have significant skills, an internship might include wages or a stipend. Internships are available in both the nonprofit and for-profit sectors.

If you are not a student, you can still arrange a for-credit internship. In the Portland area, for example, you can meet with an advisor at one of Portland Community College's Cooperative Education offices, pay tuition for the credit(s), and set up an internship. You will need a site that has agreed to host you and provide weekly supervision, and you will have to set learning goals. Your credits and tuition will be based on the number of hours you want to volunteer.

Internships also may be arranged without any reference to colleges or credits; however, state law does limit unpaid internships in the private sector to arrangements that lead to college credit. For information on a non-credit, self-designed internship, look at the article titled **Internships: Posted or Self-Designed** for guidance on how to set up a useful experience that will help you build your skills, resume and contacts in the field.

**Selecting Schools**

**Undergraduates or those seeking technical certifications:** If you need to obtain a technical credential, complete specific technical classes, or accumulate freshman or sophomore level courses, seriously consider attending a community college. They are low-cost, accessible, have open admission for many courses and programs, and offer extensive support resources. In the Portland area, Portland, Clackamas, and Mt. Hood Community Colleges as well as Clark College in Vancouver, Washington, offer a wide range of technical courses and programs. In addition to lower-division liberal arts classes at PCC, for example, over 50% of the students currently have a bachelor's degree and attend for specific career-related training.

Academic Advisors and Faculty Advisors are available to help you discuss options, investigate programs, plan your schedule, and identify campus resources that will help you succeed. Campus staff can also provide expert help by analyzing transcripts and help you plan your transfer to a four-year university. They can also help you navigate the Byzantine maze of financial aid, scholarships and other tuition payment options.

Many people assume that community college education is inferior to that received at a university or private college. This is incorrect! Community colleges offer small classes with passionate instructors (who don't have to publish or perish, as university professors do), lots of diversity, and multiple extra-curricular activities to enhance lower division liberal arts education.
Community colleges have theater, newspapers, clubs, student government, debate teams and multicultural events. They provide a lot of student support for retention and high performance, Mt. Hood Community College, for example, includes Women's Transitions Programs (http://mhcc.edu/StudentServices.aspx?id=499), TRiO Student Success Programs (http://mhcc.edu/StudentServices.aspx?id=511), and other types of support. All this for a fraction of the cost of other colleges and universities!

**Bachelor's Degree Completion Programs**

Degree Completion programs are generally offered by local, private colleges and tailored for working adults with classes offered on evenings, weekends, and online. They are designed for people who have completed a few years of lower division work. Some include credits for learning acquired through life experience, which shortens the length of time it takes to complete a degree. While the tuition is generally higher than upper-division coursework at a state university, the adult-friendly policies and accelerated schedules often lead to earlier completion. George Fox University, Linfield

College, Marylhurst University, Concordia University, and Warner Pacific College are all fully accredited and offer degree completion options.

**Graduate Studies**
The Portland area offers a wide variety of public and private universities with graduate programs. Again, do your research. Talk to program advisors and faculty as well as current and former students. You will get a lot of important insider information, particularly about new programs. Apply to several programs that are appropriate to your goal and then make an informed decision after you have all the information, including financial aid and funding information. If your research has revealed that a program is very competitive, it is important to attend informational sessions and hold informational interviews to learn how to increase your ability to compete successfully. For many graduate-level programs in social service and health care, volunteer and work experience are as important as GPA. If you are willing to relocate, you may want to consider universities in other areas of Oregon or Washington as well.

**Getting The Skinny**
Schools recruit students. Schools and programs sometimes tout statistics that may be inflated. Watch out for hype and avoid for-profit schools, which often cater to working adults but may be overcharging and under delivering results. Trade schools have a poor reputation for high costs, fast pace, lack of student support, and poor employment outcomes. Advisors at private trade schools are usually paid to recruit students, so you need to dig deeper to truly evaluate the merits of the program. Often, you can find the same or better education for a lower cost and at a more reasonable pace elsewhere.

**Online Education**
Think carefully about online courses and programs. Although online education is highly convenient, especially for older adults with families and jobs, it may contain hidden downsides as well. Learning online can be stimulating and effective, especially with high quality instructors who know how to build community and dialogue in a virtual setting. You will need to be quite comfortable and skilled, however, with a) technology b) time management skills and c) written communication. Also, if you are an extrovert or a highly kinesthetic learner, the lack of physical and visual contact with your teacher and fellow learners may be difficult. You may want to look for "hybrid" programs that include both online and in-person activities.

The higher quality on-line programs are affiliated with a traditional reputable school, from Stanford to Oregon State University. Those that are purely for profit such as American InterContinental University and Phoenix University have a very low completion rate. Finding out a program's completion rate is an important indicator of the level of quality and support.

**New Programs**
Colleges and universities sometimes launch new programs, particularly in cutting edge fields such as sustainability, web design, and other areas. Always do your research to determine how well established a new program has become, talk to current students, and make sure you feel confident about the program's quality before entrance.

**Balancing School and Life**
Returning to school as an adult is challenging, especially if you are working, have a family or have high living costs associated with owning a home. Look at prospective programs and courses and investigate institutional resources and flexibility. Here are some important questions to consider if you have larger commitments:
- What percentage of this institution's students are adult learners or parents?
- Does this college or university offer onsite childcare?
- Can a full time program be modified to allow part-time attendance?

- Are there evenings, weekend or online classes available that would meet your needs?
- Does the institution offer a variety of support systems, such as a women's center, an intensive new student orientation program, counseling or health services, low-cost health insurance, writing tutors, and flexible part time jobs on campus?

Avoid going to school full time and working full time. There are too many students undertaking this enormous task. Too much stress can result in illness, poor performance, neglected children and failed relationships!

**Paying for School**
The rising cost of education is big news these days. Tuition has skyrocketed while financial aid programs have shrunk. Undergraduates and graduate students are leaving school with large loan debts. Here's where research pays off! See the Appendix section on **Funding for School** for more details.

# Crafting Your Initial Basic Message

After you have selected two to four areas for in-depth research and exploration, you will want to network to meet people who know about your area(s) of interest. Some of this networking will be fairly structured through informational interviews, and some of it will be more casual. Initially, this networking will be broad and exploratory. Later, when you have a clear career goal and are looking for job openings, you may return to many of the same individuals for additional, more focused help. When you meet people, they will be better able to help you if you provide them with a succinct statement of you skills and the area in which you want to work. We call this pre-planned statement your basic message.

We tend to think that people will easily recall our career focus after hearing it once, but this is not true. If you are a career changer, you will need to repeat your basic message repeatedly to people who knew you in your past career. It is natural for people in your life who first met you when you were a legal secretary, to think of you as a legal secretary. The key to a useful basic message is to select vocabulary that reflects your core strengths and the areas where you want to use them. Then, push yourself to use your basic message often.

When you meet friends and acquaintances, your natural tendency may be to repeat the story of the ending of your last job, reveal your utter confusion, or replay the discouraging news of the down economy. If you lead with these topics, the natural rejoinder may be: "Oh, yes. I heard that there were 542 applicants for two openings at Krispy Kreme." However, it is just not in your best interest to lead with downers. In contrast, your basic message should leave the messy past and the horror stories where they belong—shared only with a few intimate people.

Your basic message is strength-based and future-oriented. You can begin using it at any time that you have a few points of clarity; you do not have to know your specific job goal. A simple formula is to break it down into your core skills, passion and/or experience and the general type of environment in which you want to use these skills. Here are some examples from four successful jobseekers.

- **The core skills, passion, or experience you want to bring to the next job.**
  - **Norm**: Background in journalism that developed in radio
  - **Bev**: Organizational abilities, positive interpersonal skills, computer skills and passion for connecting people with resources
  - **Laura**: Offer strong organizational skills and attention to detail
  - **Alicia**: share leadership, PR and communication skill (phone and in-person)
- **Between one and three general arenas in which you want to work.**
  - **Norm:** Nonprofit/government agencies that provide low-income people with basic needs
  - **Bev:** Arts, spiritual, or higher educational organization
  - **Laura:** Green collar job creation, entrepreneurship, agriculture
  - **Alicia:** Organizations committed to housing, environment, or international issues
- **Put these together into a coherent basic message.** If the areas you are exploring are in different aspects of your skills and experience, you will need to develop other basic messages to use in these different contexts.
  - **Norm:** I want to use the writing and research skills that I developed as a radio journalist in a position in government or a nonprofit. I am committed to using these communication skills to advocate for people and/or help them be aware of services available to them.
  - **Bev:** I want to bring my organizational abilities, computer skills, positive interpersonal skills and passion for connecting people with resources to an arts, spiritual, or educational organization.
  - **Laura:** I want to use my unusual blend of left brain/analytical abilities with my right brain/creative people skills. I care about the creation of jobs with sustainable small businesses, unions, or agriculture.

- **Alicia**:
  *Basic message #1*: I would like a position with an environmental organization that makes use of my leadership, PR and communications skills.
  *Basic message #2*: I want a position where I can share my passion for travel and my background leading international Habitat for Humanity trips. I want to be able to apply my leadership, PR and communication skills (including intercultural communication).

**Use the space below to craft your own basic message.**

# Your Approach to Social Media

In order for you to decide how much to include social media into your job search, we would like to make clear our use of terminology for "web presence" and "social media," two terms that are playing a growing role in career transition.

"Web presence" is the term for what people will find when they enter your name into a search engine, such as Google. Many employers state that they view candidate web presences on-line. Web presence is the entirety of what a person will find on the Internet if they search for you by name. It might include some one-way communication, non-interactive profiles like a bio you have placed in a directory such as GoodTherpist.com. The sites provide the reader with posted information. If they want to go to the next step, follow up communication takes place off the site.

In contrast, "social media" is a cluster of web-based tools, which are used to turn communication into interactive dialogue among organizations and individuals. Social media sites are generated by the users themselves and are excellent tools for building relationships and showcasing expertise to potential employers. At this time, the biggest social media sites are Facebook, LinkedIn, and Twitter.

To get a sense of both "web presence" and the role played by "social media," google the phrase "Vicki Lind Portland." You will get a full page of links to descriptions of Vicki as a career counselor and/or marketing coach. This is Vicki's "web presence," which includes a web site and a few YouTube videos with client testimonials that allow you to learn more about Vicki. In addition, you will see that she is active on LinkedIn. You can see her recommendations and who is in her community. You can join her LinkedIn community by inviting her to be one of your contacts and stay abreast of her new activities. You can also see that she is active in a second social media site, a blog called *Career Transition: Finding a Job Worth Having,* and you can build a relationship with her by commenting on her blog articles.

Now google your own name and see if you like both the quality and volume of your presence. Does it say what you would want it to say to potential employers? In general, the more "presence" you have focused around how you want to present yourself to employers, the quicker people will find you and the more your expertise and strengths can be visible and known.

As you weigh how much time to commit to your web presence and/or social media, consider the following:
- 45% of employers view potential candidates online
- 24% of employers said they made a hire after reviewing a social media profile
- 33% of employers admitted that they decided NOT to offer a job after reviewing a social media profile (July 2011, *Social Times*)
- In a recent poll of 500 recruiters, 66% said they used LinkedIn, and eight percent use Facebook regularly to look for job seekers.

Now that we have made the case for attending to your web presence, it is time to evaluate the emotional side of your decision. Most of our clients fall at either one end or the other on the spectrum.

**Technophobes** dislike and distrust social media, and we suggest that you start with one thing: A LinkedIn Profile. If you need help, get it from a career professional, accountability buddy, and/or webinar. Read the other sections on LinkedIn and social media in this handbook, but avoid taking on anything else if it increases your anxiety. Then proceed with a guilt-free, robust job search using other strategies.

Keep an open mind to returning to one or two social media tools in the future. And, if you are networking with younger people, omit the telltale sigh and groan whenever social media comes up. Just nod and smile knowingly!

**Techno-lovers** are intrigued by the possibilities presented by new technology and you can quickly lose yourself down a rabbit hole on social networking sites. Limit your time in front of the computer and use your time strategically to build new relationships and find position openings. We recommend that you set a boundary for the amount of time you spend on social networking sites and blogging, and that you make sure to be focused in that allotted time. You know when you find yourself watching your friends goofy YouTube video clips you've crossed the line.

While you might not love all technology, if you already use Facebook, this is an excellent time to re-evaluate how you might want to change your relationship to it given that you are now in career transition. Here are two examples of people already enjoying Facebook who have adapted their relationship to it since searching for employment. Erin Butler was excited to deepen her knowledge of online job search and personal marketing options, so she started investing time in blogging, websites, and other social media. She moved her professional relationships over to Twitter and LinkedIn, leaving Facebook solely for friends and family. Ursala Garbrecht already had a developed community of friends and professionals on Facebook, many who are creative entrepreneurs and use it regularly for business purposes. Her approach was to adjust some of her photo and content choices. She shared more content related to potential career directions, like her blog posts, photos related to passions, and helpful articles she found online, and she lessened politically charged content. There is no right approach, so it's best to assess your personal situation and decide from there.

Both traditional, face-to-face networking and social networking have the same goals to develop contacts with specific people who may be able to help:

- Introduce you to people working with your targeted employer.
- Introduce you to leaders in your industry.
- Gain interest in getting to know your expertise to give you a recommendation.
- Expand your understanding of a new role or industry and be on top of current trends.
- Team up, learn, and partner with you.

# LinkedIn: Profiles and Inviting Connections

Did you know that networking connections play a role in getting a job an estimated 60 to 70 percent of the time? And that LinkedIn is a primary networking resource? Job seekers should take the LinkedIn community seriously because the potential benefits are extensive. With regular use of this site, you can renew past professional relationships and confirm current ones (primary or first degree), and create new relationships (secondary or second degree) by being "introduced" to others online. You can draw on these connections to set up informational interviews, volunteer opportunities, and gain insider information to prepare for interviews. You can promote your own skills and the unique talents you bring to the table and research targeted employers who need them. In addition, you can follow potential employers and build relationships by joining groups.

While everyone is not cut out to become a regular and proficient LinkedIn user, every job seeker should have the kind of basic LinkedIn Profile that we describe below and should at least "connect" with the people that he or she knows. Think of it as today's phone book, but with a focus on each person's professional background and skills presented in a consistent and easy to access format. Prospective employers and people in your network expect to be able to find you on LinkedIn to get a quick electronic introduction to you. And, like all first impressions, you want the reader to think well of you and want to build the relationship with you.

If you are ready to go beyond the basics, we encourage you to move forward to the article called **LinkedIn for Networking and Job Search**, where we will guide you through the more advanced functions of getting introduced to new people and finding jobs. We will also introduce you to using LinkedIn groups. LinkedIn has thousands of interest groups, some local and some national. The majority of the largest groups are employment-related, including topics ranging from career search to trends in smart technology. Groups support a limited form discussion area, moderated by the group owners and managers. By joining groups in your field of expertise, you can share ideas and learn about new trends.

## Creating a LinkedIn Profile

You can create a LinkedIn Profile immediately, even if you are not yet in active career transition. A few years ago, having a profile on LinkedIn was a tip that a person was looking for a new position, something you might not want your current employer to read. Now, just about half of all professionals have LinkedIn profiles with a person joining every second. It has become the networking hub for those in business as well as job searchers.

Your initial profile will recount your professional and educational history. As you proceed through the research and career exploration phase, you will be able to update and focus your profile to fit your new job target. For example, Vicki worked with a recent college graduate with a major in environmental science and quite a bit of relevant volunteer work. As he became clear that he wanted to compete for positions in SE Portland where he would be doing outreach to expand solar programs, he realized that his four years of Spanish language was very relevant. He then added it to his LinkedIn profile, which took 60 seconds.

## Ten Tips for Your First LinkedIn Profile

1. Use the free level rather than paying for whistles and bells that you won't use. Most job seekers find this free level meets all of their needs.
2. Select an attractive headshot photo with a nice smile. It is harder for people to remember you or form a relationship with you without a photo.
3. If you have an advanced degree or certification, include the Initials after your last name. For example, Vicki thinks that "Cynthia Dettman, JD, MSW" is pretty darn impressive because the JD quickly connotes a sharp analytical ability and the MSW a sympathetic ear.

4. The space right under your name is usually used for a current job title and employer. If you are not employed, it is best to list your profession or some skills you offer. For example; "Copywriter and Proofreader" or "Environmental Marketing Specialist." You have up to 22 spaces, and it will create the first impression for the reader.
5. For longer sections, such as the Summary, it's a good idea to initially do your copy in Word and then cut and paste it into LinkedIn when you feel good about it.
6. For your work experience, include less copy than on your resume with plenty of white space.
7. If you know key search words that are used in your field, use them. If not, you can research and add them at a later time after you have reviewed position announcements and gotten familiar with their vocabulary.
8. Turn on the check box under your contact settings that you are open to career opportunities.
9. When you are first working on your profile, you might not want others to see your editing process. What you can do is adjust your "privacy controls" by going into the "settings" menu. Click on your name in the upper right corner to see the "settings" drop down menu. You can "turn on/off your activity broadcasts" and "select who can see your activity feed" and select "only you" until you have a decent draft. Then change it to be visible to the public.
10. A complete LinkedIn profile includes recommendations. Ideally these are from past bosses, colleagues, or clients. LinkedIn recommendations have largely replaced written letters of reference.

**Inviting People You Know**
Do you ever wish that you had kept track of an old colleague, like Jennie, with whom you had fun and learned a lot? You heard that she moved to New Jersey and went to law school. Now, your sister-in-law is moving to New Jersey and doesn't know a soul. You could probably track her down through a mutual friend, but it would take too much time. This scenario is about as outdated as a phonograph record. By adding colleagues and professional acquaintances you care about to LinkedIn, you will always be able to contact them. Unlike a mailing list or old-fashioned Rolodex, the person will update his or her own whereabouts and professional activities.

Both your friends and people in their network become potential resources for you. For example, if you have 50 connections and your connections have an average of 50 connections, there would be 2,500 people your friends and colleagues could potentially call on to help you in your networking and job search.

LinkedIn has three functions that help you build a network of people you know.
- You can select the **high school and colleges** you attended, along with the year you graduated. You'll receive a list of people on LinkedIn from your graduating class. Then, you can decide if you want to invite any of them to be your contacts, either because you want to stay in touch and/or because they work in your field.
- You can **select past employers** by the year you worked for that employer.
- You can ask **LinkedIn to review your email address book** (Outlook, Gmail, etc) and indicate who is also on LinkedIn. In Vicki's case, about half of her email addresses were also on LinkedIn.

When you invite someone from your past, it is important to write a personalized message rather than the standard, cold default, "I would like to invite you to my LinkedIn Network." Instead, something that is both a reminder and engages the reader such as, "I see from your profile that we both went on to become social workers. I'm glad to be back in touch." Or, "Remember me—I'm the one that wrote the two-page memos that were so annoying when we worked at B&G?" Vicki calls this type of message "rewarming the relationship."

We recommend that you include friends as well as professional contacts. Even if the person is not in your profession, they may have someone in their network who can be of help. Vicki invites people to be in her network if she recognizes their name and face. On Facebook, your "friends" have the option of writing derogatory comments on your "wall." Such as "She is a knucklehead and stole my boyfriend." There is no counterpart on LinkedIn, so your contacts cannot post any negative information. However, those of you who are therapists cannot invite or accept invitations from recent or current clients.

In sum, you have met and had positive interactions with hundreds of people who would like to help you network and find a new job. They can't help if you lose touch or don't keep them updated on your professional needs. LinkedIn makes it easy for those who want to help you to do so. How can you resist this good-willed tool for letting your network be of service, often in surprising ways?!

**True Life Example of How a LinkedIn Profile and Connection Has Helped:**
Deb Merchant invited a colleague she had worked with in the past to be a contact. He saw from her profile that she had left her most recent employer. He told Deb about a position as Grants Manager at SOLV, a position Deb had not seen on the job board. As a result, she applied and now holds this position.

While LinkedIn offers training webinars and a help function, you may want additional guidance. We recommend attending a LinkedIn workshop (more information in **Appendix F)** and/or reading social networking handbooks, such as *How to Find a Job on LinkedIn, Facebook, Twitter, My Space and Other Social Networks,* by Brad and Deborah Schepp.

# Informational Interviews

Informational interviews are an integral part of your career exploration process. They allow you to access a new field and its key players. The answers you get can help you shape a resume that targets the transferable skills most appropriate to your desired field. In this phase, it's not essential that the person you're interviewing has direct knowledge of job openings. However, if this is a quality exchange with you, he or she may be able to lead you to position openings after your search becomes more focused. He or she could be one degree of separation from the person who ends up hiring you.

If you find yourself procrastinating, start by promising yourself that you will NOT make any cold calls. Cold calls (such a chilling name!) bring up the expectation, often realistic, that the reception from a stranger is bound to be off-putting. I believe that cold calls should be reserved for extroverts. If you are more introverted, start by practicing interviews with people you already know. Afterward, you will need to take the plunge and make "warm calls." These are calls you make when a person you know recommends you call someone they know.

Ideally, the person you know has contacted the new person and they are expecting your call. For example, when I work with clients, I give them the names of past clients who are now working in the desired field. I then call the past client and get the pleasure of catching up with them. I ask them if they can do an informational interview with my current client. Based on the warmth of their connection with me, and their memories of being in a job search mode, they are usually happy to oblige.

Many of my clients are surprised that they enjoy informational interviews after overcoming their initial hesitation about calling and asking for someone's time. If the tired word, "networking" is unpleasant to you, call it "having interesting conversations with people who share you interests."

Before your informational interview you should see if the person giving your informational interview has a profile on LinkedIn. This will allow you to see their career history. In addition, check out the groups that the person belongs to and review some of their primary contacts. You will then be able to ask them about the usefulness of specific LinkedIn groups and may feel comfortable asking for specific introductions.

The **following guidelines** will stimulate your thinking. Chose four or five that truly pique your interest; the whole list would take a few hours. Find a balance between thoughtful planning and allowing time for spontaneous exchanges.

- You're most likely to get an informational interview if a mutual friend, colleague, or friend of a friend has referred you. This is called a "warmed" lead.
- When you make contact, tell the person that you value his or her time and will bring some specific questions with you. Ask if it would be helpful to send the questions in advance. Preparing questions will help you shape the interview to meet your needs.
- Start by suggesting a 20-minute interview at this person's place of work. If someone says that they do not have time, ask if you can have 5 minutes now or later, when it is more convenient. Also, if that person can't be of help, ask him or her to suggest someone else whom you might contact.
- Generally, you'll want to bring a resume, or send it ahead if they prefer. Another option is to ask if you could send a resume as follow-up to the interview. This way you have a reason for a second contact and can adapt your resume to what you learned in the informational interview.

You may not get answers to all of your questions. The purpose of an informational interview is to gather information and build rapport. If the person would be a valuable addition to your network, the rapport may be the most important component of the interview.

**Possible Questions**

Tell me about your career and how you became a _____.

- What degrees or training did you have when you entered this field? Is that typical? What degrees and skills help someone advance in this field?
- Do you think that the organization is committed to sustainability? If so, in what ways?
- Tell me about your typical workday.
- What are your most favorite/least favorite parts of the day? How much time is on the computer? How much interacting with people? How much outside of the office?
- Where is the field going? Where is the most growth in jobs expected?
- Are there some specialties or job titles within this field or closely linked to it that I might explore? Are there any specialized skills or knowledge for which there is increasing demand?
- What are the entry, the mid-level and the high salaries in the field?
- Are there local professional organizations with open meetings that I might attend? Journals that you recommend?
- Could you give me the names of two or three people to whom I could talk further?
- May I contact you again if I have any additional questions or when I begin my job search?
- May I check back in with you in few weeks or months to see if any new positions have opened up?
- Do you use LinkedIn for networking? If so, are there some people in your network who you think will be helpful for me to meet?

**Follow up right away** with a thank you in a format that is consistent with the culture of the organization. For example, a thank you to someone in a small conservation-minded nonprofit might enjoy a hand-written note on a Sierra Club card; a person in a hip creative firm might prefer a witty e-mail. Hopefully, the thank you letter will be the first of many exchanges. Stay in touch and find ways to build on the connection. For example, if you see an article that might be of interest to the interviewer, you can send it along. You never know when someone will develop into a significant professional relationship.

**Potential Informational Interviews:**

Name_____ Phone_____ E-Mail_____

Name_____ Phone_____ E-Mail_____

Name_____ Phone_____ E-Mail_____

Name_____ Phone_____ E-Mail_____

Name_____ Phone_____ E-Mail_____

Name_____ Phone_____ E-Mail_____

# Requesting Informational Interviews

**Letter Based on Referral**

Dear Pat,

Barry Bestman, whom I met at the sustainability conference last month, suggested I contact you about my interest in environmentally sound building practices. I currently work as a sales representative designing and selling decks and backyard fences. Because I am bothered by the large amounts of beautiful cedar used for suburban fences and decks, I am exploring new career directions. My strengths as a salesperson include explaining complex choices to people in simple language and calculating use of materials; but honestly, I'm not comfortable with any type of "hard sell" if the customer is ambivalent about a purchase.

I would be grateful for any suggestions that you might have about how I can plan a career transition. I'd like to contact you in the near future to "pick your brain." I have a few purchases that I want to make at Environmental Building Supply, so I'd be glad to come by and take you out to coffee or tea.

Sincerely,

Ruth Chapman

**Letter Based on Previous Encounter**

Dear Ms. Rydell,

I really enjoyed meeting you after your presentation at the PRSA. Your talk was very inspiring, particularly the campaign that you organized to help people understand emergency preparedness. I followed up your suggestion to read Stanford's new book on the psychological impact of 9-11.

Throughout my career in insurance, I have volunteered for nearly every committee related to helping people think about preparation for the unexpected – from hostile colleagues, to war, to volcanoes. In preparation for a career change, I returned to college and have a freshly minted BA in communication.

I am now researching the field of public relations in the nonprofit sector. I would welcome the opportunity to hear more about your insights into the profession. Your position sounds very much like the type of work I'd like to do eventually.

Thank you for considering this request. I'll contact you next week to see if we can schedule a time to meet.

With appreciation,

Ronnie Brown

**Sample Telephone Script Based on Referral**

Hi, my name is _____. I was talking to Francis Talt who was in a job club with me, and she suggested that I contact you. Have I caught you at a good time? (If yes, continue). Francis tells me that you are a great person to talk to about a career in fundraising. I'm exploring this field and have done some Internet research. I wonder if we might be able to have a short meeting so I could ask you about your career and get your perspective on the direction this field is taking?

# LinkedIn: Expanding Your Networking

You've already read **Introduction to LinkedIn: Profiles & Inviting Connections** during phase II of Career Exploration. Now that you've investigated other aspects of your career, it's time to revisit LinkedIn and more clearly share what you offer and what you want.

**Update Your Summary**

At the time you posted your profile, you were probably not as clear about your job goals as you are now. Although your basic message may not yet be finalized, you are probably clearer on which skills you want to bring to which type of position and/or organization. Your basic message will help you review the Summary section on your Profile. The Summary section is particularly critical if your most recent job experience does not showcase the skills you want potential employers to note.

The Summary section is the next most important section of your profile, after the Header, and it is vital to include your primary keywords. While the Summary can be up to 2000 words, it will usually be three or four very short paragraphs. Because it is not possible to use color or bold in the copy, your only option for maximum online readability is plenty of white space and/or bullets.

**Example #1**

Here is a strong example that summarizes experience, what he brings to the company, and a "call to action." In this case, "the call" is to review the writer's strong recommendations on LinkedIn.

**Summary**

Actively seeking opportunities.

I have 11 years experience and a proven record of researching, designing and implementing innovative marketing and program strategies for energy efficiency, renewable energy, and greenhouse gas mitigation. These strategies are strengthened by customer insights and result in measurable energy and emissions reductions as well as non-energy benefits valued by customers. I have produced results for government, non-profits, Fortune 500 companies, energy utilities, and a large state university.

Please see my recommendations from supervisors, colleagues and partner organizations for more insight into my **accomplishments** and work style.

**Example #2**

This teacher has selected the highlights from her career and uses bullets for the Professional Summary section from her resume.

**Summary**

- Highly qualified English and humanities classroom teacher since 2000. Skilled in working with both high achieving and low performing students
- Developed model high school literacy coaching program. Created school-wide reading strategies resulting in raised reading state test scores
- Researched and presented K-12 cross-content literacy strategies at several professional development venues
- Led yearlong professional learning teams that stimulated teacher collaboration
- Excel at mentoring and supervising new teachers

**Researching Target Employers**

Vicki recently had a newly unemployed architect in his fifties come into her office, perplexed and frustrated that the Human Resource Department at a growing sustainability company would not review his resume and answer what he perceived as a reasonable question: Where do you see my skills fitting in your company? He did not understand that, in the fifteen years since he last looked for a job, the curtain has fallen between job searchers and HR departments. In today's environment the onus is on the job seeker to network with people working in the desired organization and LinkedIn is the key tool.

We encourage you to identify and "follow" ten to twenty target companies for many reasons:
- Receive notices when new positions are posted to see if they match your skills set and to determine if the company is expanding.
- Learn who in your network is connected to employees of the targeted company and to ask for introductions, possible networking meetings, and/or informational interviews.
- See which groups and professional associations employees belong to so you can engage with them, either in LinkedIn groups or at face-to-face events they attend.
- Target the cover letter to the person who has posted the position.
- Prepare for an interview, showing off your research into the company and its employees.

**Expanding Your Network**
Now that you are proud of your Profile, you will want to maximize the number of people who see it. The more people who are in your network, the larger the chances are that they can introduce you to someone in your new career field and/or a targeted business. Aim for 100 or more contacts by examining your current network. You can see how many "Connections" you currently have under the "Contacts" tab. Make sure you used each of LinkedIn's four tools for finding people who you already know under the "Add Connections" tab.
- **Import email addresses** from your computer by clicking "See Who You Already Know on LinkedIn." Once you upload your addresses, you can see a symbol next to the people who are on LinkedIn. Remember to send a personalized message when you invite people from your past.
- **Locate "Colleagues"** who have worked with you in the past by selecting the tab that will review your experience section and show you names of people who also worked at that organization. Using this function Vicki located Jeff Barnes, who she had worked with twenty-five years ago at Linfield College. They met for lunch and found they both had an interest in LinkedIn. They had fun reuniting and ended up planning and offering a workshop together!
- **"Alumni"** is a similar function to "Colleagues," scanning profiles to show you people who graduated from the same colleges as you have listed under Education on your profile.
- **"People You May Know"** provides names on your home page of people it "guesses" you may know based on location, key words, and people you know in common.

Unfortunately, we all get LinkedIn invitations and scratch our heads. "Who the heck is Leo Johnson?" and toggle between thinking that we have had a senior moment or that Leo's invitation is spam. Since you don't want to accept anyone who you don't know, you have three choices.
- Select "View Invitation" and choose "ignore."
- Read the person's profile and, if they are in your industry, send them a note that says, "I may not recall meeting you, but because of our common interest in Reproductive Rights, I am glad to accept you into my network."
- Respond with a message, "I may be forgetting that we have met. I would appreciate it if you could refresh my memory and let me know how we could be of help to each other on LinkedIn."

We suggest that you treat your LinkedIn Network like a closet. Every few months, go in and discard contacts who you no longer remember or trust. (Use "Remove Connection"). The person will not get a notice that they have been moved to the Goodwill bin.

You may also want to organize your list so that it is easier to find who you want. Use the Advanced Option link in the upper right hand corner to select one of three filters to show:

- Only people with new connections
- Only connections by location
- Only connections in your professional area (such as biotech or marketing)

**Getting Introductions**

Once you have a network of at least one hundred contacts, you can begin to search to be introduced to Second Degree Contacts, people who your contacts can introduce you to. Here are three approaches.

- **Reviewing Your Contact's Contacts (Second Degree).** You can choose a few of your contacts who are most likely to have contacts in your chosen new field. Whenever someone has accepted an invitation to be in your network, you can see the profiles of the people in his or her network. When you find someone you would like to connect with, use the "Get introduced through a common connection" function, and explain your interest in the introduction.
- **Searching by Job Title Key Words.** Go to the drop-down menu on the upper right portion of the screen and click "Advanced." Click on the "Find People" tab and input a job title, such as "Massage Therapist" or "Energy Analyst" and the city where you live. LinkedIn will show you the profiles of local individuals with these job titles. Look for the number 2, which will indicate second-degree contacts. Then you can ask your contact to assist you with an introduction. Even if this person does not know any of your contacts, it may be useful to examine the education and work experience that prepared him or her for their current position.
- **Searching by Employer.** Most mid-sized and larger employers have a LinkedIn page. Go to the drop-down menu next to the search box in the upper right and select "Companies." LinkedIn will show you people who work for that organization, once again indicating with a "2nd" if they are known to your contacts. Even if there are no people in this organization to whom you can be introduced, you can review employee profiles to see if you have a similar background to target the organization. In addition, you can see which LinkedIn Groups a person belongs to and join those groups to build the relationship.

**Making and Getting Recommendations**

**Give First**

If your nature is to be generous and help people, being a job seeker can be difficult because you feel like you are always asking people for assistance. Do you have twenty minutes for an informational interview? Do you know anyone at Mercy Corps Northwest? Could you proofread this cover letter? Making a practice of making recommendations to colleagues and professionals who have provided you services is a great way to balance the scale. It doesn't matter if the person for whom you initiate writing a recommendation is in a position to help you or not. Or, if you believe in karma. Our feelings confirm what science now tells us, that Oxytocin is released in our bodies when we do a good deed.

Under "Profile" select "Recommendations" where you can scroll down and either search for someone by name or select from your list of contacts. LinkedIn gives you an example to get started by suggesting three characteristics about the person/professional. According to Eric Butow and Kathleen Taylor in *How to Succeed in Business Using LinkedIn,* these recommendations are shorter than recommendation letters. "They should be brief, but certainly write things that are complimentary to the person's personality, capabilities, and talent…"And remember to make your recommendations actual and truthful. "If you don't, you not only harm your own integrity and that of the person you recommend, but you also diminish the integrity of the entire LinkedIn community" (29).

A recommendation should include:

- Your working relationship with the person: "employer," "colleague," "received services"
- What the person did "edited a manual," "delivered a workshop you attended," "supervised you"
- The results you received, both tangible and the feeling that you had: "I felt proud to have one of the highest ranking websites after J. helped me understand SEO."

**Ask Second**

Once you experience the pleasure of writing a well-deserved recommendation, you will have more energy to make a request yourself. Since recommendations show up under each of the positions you list in the Experience section, begin by reviewing bosses, co-workers, and clients you helped in different positions.

If your working relationship is fairly recent, you may not need to offer suggestions to the person making the recommendation. However, if you haven't worked together for a while, you will be helping the recommendation writer and yourself, by giving a few suggestions. It is often effective to tickle their memory about a compliment that they have offered in the past. "Dave, I remember how you commented on the tight meetings that I ran while we were at Metro and how my quick follow-up kept us on track. Since I'm using these skills in the jobs that I'm applying to, I would appreciate any references to skills like this about managing people and tasks." If you feel uncomfortable making this request on LinkedIn because you have been out of touch, you might want to give a phone call to assess the current warmth of this relationship from the past.

**Becoming Active in LinkedIn Groups**

LinkedIn Groups can play a vital role in career research, networking, and job search. During career research and exploration, they are an unparalleled resource for learning the inside scoop about possible career directions. During networking and job search, you can build to your professional community to achieve visibility and develop helpful new connections. When you are in active job search, you can get leads and assistance with interview preparation.

There are two easy ways to locate groups you may be interested in. First, go to the drop down menu titled "Groups" and choose "Groups You May Like." LinkedIn will show you a list based on key words in your Profile. You can also go to the search box in the top, right corner and change the gray box titled "People" to "Groups." Then search for phrases such as "Portland" plus "energy" or "medical writing." Initially choose six to ten groups to review and then pick a small number with content you enjoy that also appear relevant to your field. Notice that some groups have monitors and require you to apply. These are often correlated with higher quality content. Smaller groups have the advantage of letting your voice be heard and having more visibility and influence. Larger groups give you a wider range of perspectives and greater exposure.

**Using Groups for Career Research and Exploration**

- **Ask career research questions:** When researching a possible job title, select a large national group, that can help you filter and evaluate your research. You can also filter groups to ones your connections belong to, categories such as 'open' or 'members only' groups, and by language. For example, Teresa S. wanted to explore becoming a medical writer and how to best learn the needed skills. As she planned to become a mother, she valued a career that could be done from home, but she needed assurance that she could earn at least $45K after a training period. When she typed, "certificates medical writing" into Google, she found dozens of certificates related to medical writing, with an enormous range of costs and lengths of times. She joined two national LinkedIn groups "Medical Writers' Forum" and "Professional Medical/Science Writers" and asked the 4,6000 members which certificate were the most valid and why. She also asked if she was more likely to reach her financial goal if she chose a sub-specialty such as cancer writer or medical research writer.

- **Research typical career paths in target companies:** In addition to individual profiles, LinkedIn allows companies to have LinkedIn pages where information about most mid-sized to large employers can be found. These provide a goldmine of information on company size, recent hires and the backgrounds of employees holding different positions. A review of larger popular Portland employers such as New Seasons, adidas, and Mercy Corps indicated that about 60% of all employees are members of LinkedIn.

As little as five years ago, if you wanted to know how to prepare for a specific type of job in a company, you called human resources. You may have had a question, such as, "what background and degree would be helpful to plan a career in marketing athletic apparel?" In the current market, calling a human resources department yields recorded messages and/or unreturned phone calls. The contemporary alternative is to find the answer yourself by reviewing the "Experience" sections on the profiles of the company's employees who hold job titles that interest you. Rob Hall wanted to meet people and understand hiring preferences for marketing positions in Portland's energy efficiency companies. He joined the Association of Energy Services Professions NW and became active by reading and responding to posts. Rob noted that many of the members were employed by some of his target employers, and began participating in the live, local chapter of the association.

## Use Groups for Networking and Job Search

- **Comment and Post in Groups**: People, including hiring managers, are more likely to want to build a relationship if you share things that will be of value to the group. Find interesting discussions by seeing who liked a discussion and how many people commented. Share thoughtful comments you've reviewed for spelling and grammatical errors. *The ethics of LinkedIn avoid comments that promote the self in a way that presents as self-serving and focus instead on offering value to others.*
- **Ask thoughtful, informed questions:** This is another way to engage people, demonstrating simultaneously your expertise and your openness to learn.
- **Follow the most influential people:** Check the Top Influencers board and click their profile image to see all their group activity.
- **Review the Profiles of members:** Start working to get introduced to people who would further your goals in the group. Eventually these conversations can help to produce your own relationships with these individuals for informational interviews or for referrals to job leads. Start a dialogue before asking to connect because people can give an "I don't know this person" reply, and if you get 5 of them, your contact will be restricted to only those people you can connect with by email.
- **Invite people in local groups to meet**: An advantage of local groups (those that usually have Portland or PDX in their title or description) is that you can follow up and meet people. You have the ability to message members of your group. When career coach Liz du Toit moved to Portland, she wanted to build a network of like-minded individuals. She joined LinkedIn groups and scanned profiles of group members who shared her interests and passions. She then sent them a message saying, "We are both members of 'Portland Connect,' and I enjoyed reading your profile. Since we have a lot in common professionally, would you be interested in getting together?"

*"To me, if life boils down to one thing, it's movement. To live is to keep moving."*
-Jerry Seinfeld

# Networking SOBIN Style

One week Vicki had the pleasant synchronicity of attending three green events that were also attended by Sobin Hiraoka. Sobin was beginning an exploration of a career change from marketing electronic systems to working in the green field, possibly organic foods.

The three events were Green Drinks, Natural Step Network breakfast meeting, and a party given by Alison Wiley and Thor Hinkley, a couple working and living with sustainability as a center. Green Drinks and events by the Natural Step Network are two of the most prominent gathering places for a broad cross-section of Portland's sustainability community, so it was not a surprise that Sobin selected them for early exploration. The social invitation grew out of a bond from an informational interview.

But how did he garner an invitation to a holiday party attended by many green community leaders? It began when he attended a "Careers in Sustainability" workshop sponsored annually by Oregon Natural Step Network. As a panelist, Alison Wiley spoke about her expanded green Rolodex and database, and how she loved meeting and helping green career changers. Sobin was the only participant out of 26 who followed up by asking her for an informational interview. Alison saw his openness and enthusiasm for learning as much as he could about and from people on this journey. Invitations followed.

At the holiday party, I watched how Sobin combined contemporary networking techniques with what I assume is the gentle graciousness of his Japanese heritage. I invented this acronym based on Sobin's first name and his excellent networking skills:

**S-O-B-I-N:**

S: **Stay** late, ask for cards, and continue interesting conversations in greater depth, thus building deeper connections.

O: Be **open** and responsive to new ideas learned in these conversations. Spend more time listening than talking or trying to impress.

B: **Believe** with full heart in the importance of your new career and the contribution that you can make. In Sobin's case, he is enthusiastic and committed to the importance of affordable, local, organic foods.

I: **Initiate** contact. Sobin met Alison at the Careers in Sustainability workshop where she was a panelist. She stated she was happy to meet with those planning a career in sustainability. He asked for her card, and with a little nudge, he contacted Alison for an informational interview. She suggested that he also meet some of her green friends at her party that weekend. And, of course, he came early and stayed late at that party!

N: Have a **nice** thoughtful approach. Some of the advice about networking has an assertive type of style to it. Recommendations such as "play golf with people higher up in the organization" are a turn-off to many Portland-style egalitarians. Sobin exemplifies the nice, thoughtful approach that may be a better model for you. For instance, he is strong on greetings, follow-through, and congratulations for co-searchers who succeed, and expressing appreciation to those who help him.

# Staying in Touch with Your Network

The following emails are from job seekers who wanted to stay in touch with people they met through informational interviews.

**Question:**
When conducting an informational interview, how do you politely switch the interview back into "information-gathering" mode if your interviewee begins asking you a lot of "high pressure job interview" type questions, and you haven't had a chance to ask all of your questions yet?
– Marcelle

**Response:**
I've done a number of info interviews and they have never turned into a job interview type of scenario. Most people like to talk about their work and are expecting you to ask the questions—not the other way around. I see no reason why you would not be able to remain true to yourself. You are seeking them out for information as it relates to your career path. There is no place in this process for you to be asked high-pressure questions. My experience has been that this is a very informal process that is often filled with surprises. Have fun with it!
– Cyd

**Question:**
Hi all,

Before I got my current job at Regence, I had interviewed for a similar position at OHSU; I hit it off with the director and project manager of the department where I interviewed, but they were looking for somebody with more extensive certifications for the immediate opening and did not extend an offer to me. They said that they wanted to keep in touch and would contact me if they had other "generalist" positions that opened up—as far as I could tell, it seemed a sincere offer; it wasn't just a way to let me down easily. I since attended a workshop that they put on, and I think I made a good impression on them at the workshop. I told them that I had accepted an offer at Regence, and they both told me to still keep in touch—the project manager specifically told me that if I'm ever in a position where I was pursuing another degree part-time (a possibility), that I should definitely let them know because they would be having more part-time openings available.

So what I'm wondering at this point is, how exactly do I "keep in touch" at this point? I'm enjoying my current position, but OHSU is a place where I would eventually like to see myself, or would at least like to keep the possibility alive. The workshop that I attended is offered twice per year, but it's not the type of workshop that I would attend more than once. Any suggestions would be more than welcome. Thank you!
– Carrie

**Response:**
Hi Carrie,
Whew! This sounds like a very hot long-term lead to me. They really, truly do want you to keep in touch! Your note to us has lots of wonderful information in it. What better candidate than one who loves her job, is a steady employee, really likes the other one that interviewed her, and would like to eventually to work there!!??

One way to keep in touch would be to make sure you read whatever department newsletter comes out, then drop an email to the several people who interviewed you, with a little comment about some news item. You could include an upbeat note about what is going on with you. You could close by saying you are still very interested in joining their team if an opportunity comes up and hoping they are having a wonderful summer.
– Marty

**Response:**
Carrie,

I had a similar situation as you with someone who told me to keep in touch, but there was nothing to "bounce" that contact off of. So every 3-4 months I just sent an email saying that he had suggested we stay in touch and just thought I'd check-in. Then would briefly remind him who I was and why we were staying in touch. I also included some more thoughts on the topic we had discussed (we were both interested in adding a new service that I would provide to his program). I also, like you, checked for lectures that his organization sponsored and attended when I could. If he wasn't there I made sure I told him that I had been :-) He always thanked me for keeping in touch and always seemed to remember me and the goal.

Good luck!

– Carol

# Social Media: Twitter, Facebook, Virtual CVs, Websites, Blogging

The purpose of this section is to help you decide if or how you want to incorporate social media beyond LinkedIn into your networking and job search strategy. After you get the hang of LinkedIn, we suggest you explore at least one additional site as part of your regular job search and networking strategy.

These questions will help you decide which one you want to tackle next:
- Are these skills required or a competitive advantage for jobs you are seeking?
- Will you enjoy learning this technology?
- Do you need to combat possible ageism by showing that you are current on this technology?
- Do you have a family member or friend who enjoys this technology and can help you?

## Twitter

We turn to Joshua Waldman, a local social media expert and author of *Job Searching with Social Media for Dummies,* to help us understand the quickly evolving role of Twitter in the job search. Twitter has been called microblogging because you can only post brief blurbs of no more than 140 characters. Twitter is called "real time web," which allows you to follow leaders in your field or targeted employers without a time delay.

If you have a targeted company, leaders in your industry, and/or recruiters active on Twitter, you will want to start "following them." Tweet (post) information related to your accomplishments and ideas that are career or business related. To start with, post a brief and strategic profile, as well as a link to another Internet site such as your website and a picture. Then, tweet with a purpose to build a positive professional reputation.

And remember, tweeting, just like any other post on the web, will help you build your overall web presence. Having an active Twitter account will boost your rating when someone googles your name.

## Facebook

When the last version of this handbook was published three years ago, the recommendation was to use LinkedIn for job search and to keep Facebook for fun, social relationships. Because Facebook is so enormous (there are more members internationally than people in the United States), it has recently evolved into becoming a significant tool for job seekers. You may have heard some bad press about Facebook, thinking that it is for younger folks, largely for social purposes. Set aside your prejudices, and you will see that this site has matured and can also be effectively used for professional networking.

We strongly encourage you to consider it as a job search tool if you meet one or more of the following criteria:
- If you've already built up a network of friends and family members. With this existing network, you can publicize your job search and your talents, and ask for help in networking and getting introduced.
- If the employers that you are targeting have a Facebook Page, then you should indicate that you "Like" the employer and engage with them on Facebook. Organizations and businesses create these pages to interact with customers who like them. You can also conduct your research about the company from this page because it links to the company blogs as websites. In addition, it may contain information about benefits, culture, and hiring practices.
- If you are seeking positions that desire expertise in Social Media and you have not used it before.

New users can create a Facebook presence to show your more "human" side so that future employers and contacts can get a good sense of your qualities outside of your professional resume. You don't have to become a regular user to create a well-written profile that emphasizes your credentials, education and experience. Perhaps you can link to a presentation you made, articles you've written, awards you have received, or relevant photos or videos you have prepared.

If you are of the Millennial generation, you grew up learning about the Internet and the benefits and possible pitfalls of Facebook. Unfortunately, studies have shown that Gen Xers and Baby Boomers are more careless with their online privacy settings. So, if you are new to Facebook, we recommend *Job Searching with Social Media for Dummies* for a review of the best privacy practices for the job hunter.

If you decide to go further with Facebook, a next step is to look for folks in your Facebook network who might work at a company where you want to work. Facebook groups can also be helpful. We suggest checking out groups in the area of Business and Organizations. Join groups carefully, as some are very small and others much more robust and useful. Group discussion boards may include relevant topics of discussion and job postings as well.

You can look for job postings on Facebook using CareerBuilder, Simply Hired, and other job applications. You can also purchase an advertisement to show your skills and expertise on Facebook.

**What to Post on Facebook**
If Facebook has been part of your life since you were in college, you may have to go back and rethink your profile with the eyes of a potential employer. If you are new to Facebook, you may also wonder how much personal information to post. The best thing about the Facebook culture is that it focuses on playfulness and pictures while discouraging the stiff and boring. Consider that potential employers may be checking out your social as well as professional profiles. The following suggestions can guide you:
- Don't post references to drinking or sexual activities. Imagine yourself a potential employer in your field of interest: how would you respond to the information if you found it on an applicant's social media site?
- Reflect carefully on how much political material to print. Election years pull for a lot of emotions and hot rhetoric that go viral.
- Check your privacy settings on Facebook and other sites to ensure that only selected readers may view your personal information or selected portions of your Facebook page.
- Feel comfortable posting information and pictures about your hobbies, your travels, your family, and your volunteer work.
- Include any information that may be pleasing and interesting to a potential employer. These details can help present a fuller and more positive picture of your personality, talents, attitudes and values, which could not be captured in a resume.

**Virtual CVs (Curriculum Vitae or Resume)**
You may also want to create a "social" or "visual" resume, an electronic portfolio of your background, skills, services, products and accomplishments you can use to attract employers and business contacts. See for example the free template available at http://www.visualcv.com/. With this visual and audio display, you now have a site where you can direct all your readers, and which you can update just once to reach all the sites where you have a presence. You can include photos, references, examples of work, and other multi-media materials relevant to your credentials. Look at the examples on the template sites to see how folks have tailored their page to fit their background and industry.

Many online resumes are actually portfolios, particularly for careers in the creative industry. For example, look at Vicki's daughter Jessica Hurley's at http://www.visualcv.com/jessicahurley. Jessica's virtual CV includes video clips and covers of books she has written, features beyond the capability of LinkedIn. Also check out Cynthia's CV. Cynthia was amazed at how easy it was to set up (http://www.visualcv.com/cynthiadettmancom).

Once you have created this portfolio or resume, place a link to it on your LinkedIn profile, website, and all other sites where you have a presence.

**Websites**
If you are seeking employment, why would you consider making a website? During this economy, you may need to work on a freelance or project basis either until you find your ideal employment or until you decide to commit fully to running your own business. In a sense, you are in business for yourself for the interim, and all businesses are expected to have a web presence. For example, Meredith's ideal was to be employed as a massage therapist in a chiropractor's office. After a month with no results, she created a simple website, sublet an office one day a week and offered her services. This brought in some immediately needed cash during the transition, as well as impressing employers when she applied for positions. Potential employers were able to more fully see her specific strengths and professionalism; in addition, she was able to fill in the gap in her resume with web evidence that she was professionally active.

There are two avenues to creating a website. If you are in the creative services industry, your website will be seen as a work sample, and you will want to hire a designer/developer to create a customized site. For many people, using a template site like WordPress or GoDaddy is a viable option because they are low-cost or free. You can choose a format, colors and pictures that suit your tastes, upload your own pictures, audio, and video materials, and create an interesting, eye-catching presence. The templates are easy to use, and several companies offer excellent telephone support 24 hours a day if you run into trouble.

**Blogs**
Blogs are online sites where individuals and organizations post articles, comments, ideas, pictures, and videos on a wide variety of topics. Blogging is highly interactive. People read others' blogs, comment on them, and thereby build relationships, learn new things, and draw attention to their own blogs. Some blogs are highly personal and others are highly professional. Your purpose is to build and express your professional expertise in a few specialties relevant to future employment goals.

It will reflect poorly on your web presence if you start a blog and then post rarely or abandon it. Therefore, we suggest that you begin by becoming a blog consumer in your areas of professional interest.

Google a topic such as "Blog Social Justice" or "Blog Emergency Preparedness," and you will find a list of twenty or more blogs on each topic. After subscribing to several, you will be able to select two or three. Look for blogs that add to your knowledge and expertise, raise stimulating questions upon which you want to comment, and on which you would like to be seen. Begin by posting short, thoughtful, well-researched, and professionally worded comments on these blogs. After a blogging community knows you, you may want to ask if you can post an article as a guest. To determine if a blog is popular and/or seeking guest writers, you can use a directory of top-ranking blogs such as www.alltop.com or www.bloggerlinkup.com.

If you want to start a blog, your first task is to find a topic of expertise related to your industry or job function. It's only worthwhile to create your own blog if you have a plan and are committed to writing regularly. It is recommended that a serious blogger post several blogs (short essays/pieces/items) per week and regularly comment on other blogs in the same or similar fields. Less than a third of the blogs created remain active after a few months, so you must have a topic that is broad enough that you will be able to write a series of posts without losing interest.

Your review of other blogs will help you determine what is already being well covered. Questions to ask yourself in seeking a unique niche include:

- What do I have to offer that is different?
- Do I have "insider tips" or a novel interpretation of doing something that may benefit employers?
- Which areas in my industry do other people come to me for advice?
- What can I talk about for hours without becoming boring and repetitive?

If you do identify a niche topic with which you feel comfortable, your next step before making a commitment to start a blog is to reflect on your skills and aptitude as a writer.

- Do I enjoy writing, or do I often suffer from writer's block?
- Is my verbal expression and use of grammar good, or will I need an editor?
- Is my writing style engaging and professional to match my target employers?
- Will demonstrating strong writing skills be a competitive strength for my career goals?

Writing blog articles on your own or other sites builds your web presence and visibility. Social Media expert, Joshua Waldman, makes a strong case for developing your own blog in *Job Searching with Social Media for Dummies*. "Having your own blog, where you control the look, feel, and tone of the site is a great feeling. It's also one of the most powerful credibility builders in anyone's career." Blogging brands you as an expert in your field. Once you get going, you may be able to get a well known blogger to comment on your blog or refer other readers to your blog. You also want to offer information and assistance to others on the web, so it's clear that you are contributing as well as taking.

GoDaddy, WordPress, and Googlesites are free blog sites for those of you who are confident in your ability to commit to and manage your own blog. Vicki didn't want to commit a lot of time to blogging, so she banded together with six other career counselors who take turns posting longer articles every two weeks on WordPress (http://ccppblog.wordpress.com/).

**Summary**

We encourage you to reflect on your overall job search strategy before deciding if you want to invest time in these social media technologies. We always invite you to balance your comfort and enjoyment with selective areas in which to stretch yourself by learning new skills. If you are an introvert and enjoy spending time on the web, be careful to balance time online with getting out for old-fashioned face-to-face networking events.

# Strategic Volunteering

Why do we volunteer? Normally, we are driven by our passion to help our ailing communities and environment. We volunteer to support a political candidate who supports issues of which we are most passionate. We volunteer to teach art to children because we know how it feeds the soul. We volunteer for Growing Gardens because permaculture has captured our intellectual curiosity and will help the planet. We often want to do more than our schedules allow.

These are excellent motivations to volunteer when you are employed, but inadequate when you are seeking a career change. I urge career changers and job seekers to think more selfishly and strategically about their volunteer activities. Well-chosen volunteer activities can play a key role in helping you find and win a desired new job. Your volunteer choices will lead to employment to the extent that they provide opportunities to expand your network in a chosen employment arena, practice a needed skill, produce a work sample and/or become an inside candidate in the organization. Before jumping into a new volunteer activity, reflect on what you learned earlier in the exploration process.

By analyzing job openings that interest you and by conducting informational interviews, you can identify skills and experience that you lack that are desirable to employers. A volunteer experience or internship can strategically fill in the missing experience. Your research may have helped you identify the key players and employers in your desired field. Your chances of being hired are dramatically increased when employers have been able to observe you and your voluntary contributions to the organization. Susan, a member of the job club, moved into a position that opened up where she was volunteering. They did not advertise the position and even reconfigured it to better match Susan's skill set. When asked for advice for other job seekers, what she said was to the point: "Figure out where you want to work. Impress them with how much you can do for them. Keep hanging around until they hire you."

Strategic volunteering was key in landing a job for Teresa, now a research assistant for CARES Northwest (an assessment center for abused children), and Alicia, a program coordinator who does outreach for Portland's Bureau of Planning and Sustainability. Marguerite began her career search with a volunteer internship position at the Oregon Environmental Council to gain experience in the field of sustainability

**Case Studies**
- **Teresa:** Teresa had volunteered at the Oregon Food Bank for a few years but was not meeting new people who might be helpful in her network and was not expanding her skills. During her career transition, she reduced her hours at the Food Bank and strategically selected a new arena to try out as a volunteer. She found these volunteer positions through Volunteerworks, now managed by Hands-on-Portland.

  One of Teresa's strategic choices was to volunteer at CARES Northwest, a collaborative program housed at Legacy Emanuel Hospital that coordinates services for abused children. She wanted an inside view to see if she would like being in a clinical environment and to explore a large hospital as an employer at closer range. An introvert, Teresa had hated doing informational interviews and distrusted the limited peek hole they gave her into a work environment.

  As a CARES volunteer, Teresa initially was content with entering research data into a database. She enjoyed being around intelligent, committed professionals who began to trust her accuracy and attention to detail. Impressed with her abilities, they created a part-time paid position and within a few months, upgraded and expanded it to Teresa's goal of four days per week, so that she could spend her fifth day playing the pennywhistle.

Five years later, Teresa happened to wander into my garage sale and said, "I wish that other people got to know what it's like to go do something you love every day. I didn't even know that there was something like this out there!"

- **Alicia**. At the outset a of her career transition, Alicia's interest was divided among three core passions: international travel, housing issues and the environment. These interests kept her plate full of worthwhile, diverse volunteer activities, but she lacked a focus for a next career move. A breakthrough occurred when Alicia realized that the term "outreach" captured the role where she excelled, irrespective of the purpose of the organization. It became clear that her love of people and extroverted personality were assets for both the networking process and a potential position.

  The Master Recycler program in which she was enrolled required volunteering and she selected an outreach activity, assisting at an information booth at the Portland Home and Garden Show. At this event, she met and had lively conversations with several people from the Bureau of Planning and Sustainability. Soon after, she saw an ad for a position in the Bureau of Planning and Sustainability doing outreach for the multi-family housing sector. She contacted the people she had met at the Home and Garden Show for additional background information. While her resume could have been lost in a sizable stack of applicants, she was already a familiar name who had made an impression with her vivacious smile and friendly manner. The contacts that she made during her strategic volunteering helped her plan the interview, which, in turn, gave her the opportunity to win the job.

- **Marguerite** left the work force after the birth of her son. When he started kindergarten, she was ready to expand her circle of influence once again. Though she had previous work experience in the fields of education and conflict resolution, she was now drawn to work in the field of sustainability on behalf of children. As a new parent, she felt an increased sense of responsibility for caring for the earth. While raising her son, she became passionate about limiting exposure to everyday household chemicals for the welfare of all family members and the earth too. When the Oregon Environmental Council posted a job announcement for an Environmental Health Education Intern to support the Eco-Healthy Child Care Program, she knew she had found a good fit. She interviewed for the position and got it on the spot. The interviewers told her that they loved her cover letter. Marguerite's strategic volunteering gave her the on-the-job experience that she was lacking in the competitive field of sustainability.

**Locating Places to Volunteer**

Once you have decided on the type of volunteer position (or positions) that could help you better compete for your desired position, you need to locate an organization that will respect your contribution and offer you a true opportunity for professional development. Opportunities are plentiful and may be obvious to you at this juncture. If not, I recommend the following:

- **Post your specific need on a listserv** or Website in your arena of interest. The richest local resource in the nonprofit arena is CNRG (http://www.CNRG@yahoogroups.com) and the richest local resource for Creatives is Craigslist (http://www.craigslist.org). Be specific about what you want and what you have to offer.
    - "I seek to volunteer 15 hours per week in an organization that promotes justice for underrepresented populations. I wish to use my legal skills (new law degree) and/or my accounting background."
    - "I want to volunteer evenings and Saturdays to use my background in graphic design and newsletters. I can design brochures, ads and possibly Websites (would need some assistance here). Prefer SW Portland location."

- Approach one of your targeted organizations. Once you have a selected career arena, it is helpful to make a list of the organizations where you might like to work. For example, if your target is helping low-income or immigrant populations with job skills, you might have identified community colleges, Stand for Children and Head Start as possible employers. Searching their Websites and/or conducting informational interviews will reveal optimal volunteer activities.
- **Volunteer for a professional association.** One of the easiest ways to access friendly people willing to give you informational interviews is through professional organizations. For example, Rick, who is interested in an entry position in development at a nonprofit, is volunteering on a planning committee for the NW Association of Development Officers. Other members of the committee are senior development officers who are well steeped in the traditions of the profession. People who experience your skills first hand by serving on a committee with you also can be potential references.
- **Search options through "Volunteer Here" and "Oregon Volunteers."** Hands on Portland (formerly Volunteerworks) manages the most thorough volunteer matching service in the metro area. At http://www.handsonportland.org you will be asked to indicate the location, social issue and population that you would like to serve. Oregon Volunteers is sponsored by the Oregon Commission for Voluntary Action and Services (www.Oregonvolunteers.com). We reviewed a few hundred of the four thousand opportunities listed at this site. The vast majority of the positions are in social service, health and educational organizations. Duties within these organizations included clerical, fundraising, teaching/mentoring, counseling, computer, event planning and public relations.

**Conclusion**

In addition to helping you find a job, strategic volunteering can offer you a place to contribute where you can forget that you are unemployed; to locate people for informational interviews; to go when your days have no structure; to meet kindred spirits; or to make a difference.

# Sample Request for Strategic Volunteering

May 13, 2008

Sara Leverette
Oregon Environmental Council
222 NW Davis Street, Suite 309
Portland, OR 97209

RE: Environmental Health Education Intern Position

Dear Ms. Leverette:

When my five-year-old comes to me in a decade and asks me what I did when I heard about global warming, I'm determined to have an answer for him. We biked and walked more and drove less. We reduced our carbon footprint. We shopped at farmer's markets and were thoughtful about our consumption. The birth of my son took my passion for the environment to a new level. We used cloth diapers and purchased organic clothing, toys and body products. We converted to gentle earth-friendly cleaning products for our laundry and our home. At some point I stumbled upon Tiny Footprints and have been an OEC Website devotee ever since.

I have spent the last number of years nurturing my family (who knew I was getting on-the-job training all the while; over these years I learned about and became passionate about the very issues that OEC addresses.) I cared for my mother through years of declining health, and I became a mother myself. Last fall I began to prioritize expanding my influence beyond my family. I believe that my life experiences over the last several years have trained me to be a better employee and a more human being than my formal education ever did.

I have worked as an educator – formally and informally – in school classrooms, in homes, in community centers, in mediation centers and more. My focus has always been helping people live better lives through conscious choices. With more than five years experience assisting in the administration of busy nonprofit mediation programs and conducting mediations myself, I know how to build rapport with people from all walks of life, how to communicate well with people, and how to resolve problems. I have demonstrated success in resource development and have excellent research and writing skills. Mostly, I am eager to make a difference in the issue of the day—the environment. I have a strong work ethic, and I am always eager to take on new challenges. I am confident that I would be a valuable addition to the OEC and would love doing the work. I look forward to hearing from you so that we may set up an interview.

Sincerely,

Marguerite Aichele-Smith

# Deciding on a Career Objective

Your self-assessment and research may have produced a clear career objective in an arena with a reasonable number of professional positions. Ideally, your objective is neither too narrow (I want to be an advertising executive for Weiden+Kennedy) nor too broad (I want to use my excellent communication skills in sustainability). Optimally, your objective will be within the range of the examples below. A good objective naturally points you towards a strategy.

- **Sam:** I am looking for a position in which I can use my love of wood and my small business marketing background in an organization committed to sustainability. My research has revealed that there are two leaders in this area in Portland, The Collins Foundation and the Certified Forest Products Council. My strategy is to send them my resume and offer to volunteer or do an entry level job in order for them to observe my abilities at close range.
- **Susan:** I seek a position to use my strong writing, analysis and policy development skills in addition to expertise gained through my master's degree in international environmental policy. I will volunteer for one of Portland's two organizations in the field. Since these are small organizations with limited opportunities, I will also target the large humanitarian aid organizations such as Mercy Corps.
- **Judy:** I am looking for an entry job in development as a step towards my goal of becoming a development director. I seek to use my strong writing and team-building skills in an organization that shares my commitment to equity for marginalized populations.
- **Marguerite:** I am looking for a job where I can use my strong teaching and writing skills to educate adults and families about that which I am most passionate—creating homes and learning environments that are toxin-free and earth-friendly.

You may have reached this juncture with one or two career options that beckon strongly, only to find that they are extremely competitive. It is not surprising that many of the most rewarding jobs in the arts, environment and community have more qualified people than projected openings. Should you really make a commitment to your burning passion to become an art therapist, for example, if you read that there is a very poor prognosis for openings? If you truly have a burning passion, it may drive you to outdistance the odds. You may want to offset discouraging news by reading autobiographies and seeing movies of your career heroes/heroines, who "followed their bliss."

Some of the following strategies may help you integrate the discouraging information into your unique situation. You may decide to make some realistic compromises, and feel very peaceful and "adult like." Or, you may make more aggressive plans to compete well in a crowded field. You could, for example, adapt your career plan to include two unpaid internships so you can develop an adequate network. Looking at a negative prediction for job outlook, some folks face squarely the need to relocate to a region with greater opportunity.

Others make a financial plan that takes into account a longer transitional period. Your own tolerance for risk and your financial situation will be considerable factors. Is there someone in your life who can pick up more of the financial burden during your transition? If you are partnered with a supportive spouse who earns a solid income, you can plan a longer transition and training period than a single parent with no savings who holds the same coveted goal.

One of the purposes of identifying three or four areas to research is that you will have a fallback position if one turns out to be unrealistic for you at this time. If the odds are too discouraging, you may need to give yourself a day or even a week to grieve the lost dream (for the time being) before you begin to gather information about another option.

As an outcome of this phase, it is optimal to have one clear career objective and a possible back-up plan. For example, Sam's objective was to work for an organization that supports certified forest products. His back-up objective was to work for any lumber company that sells certified forest products to learn more about the lumber business.

Some enthusiastic folks complete their research and find that they are still interested in three or four career directions. For example, one client continued to be interested in housing, international travel, recycling and public relations. It may be difficult, but necessary, to approach your creative-divergent spirit with a strong, authoritative tone and say: You must decide on no more than two focal points, lest your networking and search become too fragmented.

While we strongly advocate for developing a clear focus, we also believe in keeping your eyes and your heart open to the unexpected. One of our clients whose focus was on business writing said an opportunity in PR "just splashed down on me. Hallelujah!"

Even if your career decision is based on sound research, making a final commitment to a clear career objective can be frightening. Creative people often yearn to keep all options open. At this juncture, religious people pray for discernment of God's will; spiritual people meditate so that they can hear the clear, calm voice from within. Others just close their eyes, and with a metaphorical hand at their backs, they jump. Once you have a clear career objective, you'll be energized to move into the next phase, **Finding the Job**.

# Post-Assessment Career Exploration Checklist: What's Out There?

Date of Post-assessment_____

☐ **Brainstorm at least 15 job titles/organizations/career arenas.**

Reduce to 2 - 4 job titles/arenas to research.

1._____  3._____
2._____  4._____

☐ **Identify research questions.** What do you want to know about employment in each arena? Be sure to include questions about degrees and certifications. (Use back of sheet if you have 3 or 4.)

Arena #1_____
1._____
2._____
3._____
4._____
5._____

Arena #2_____
1._____
2._____
3._____
4._____
5._____

☐ Create a **LinkedIn Profile** and invite connections.

☐ **Develop a strategy for meeting or being introduced to three to six people** who work in each arena or have that job description. (e.g., connect using LinkedIn, ask 4 or 5 people you know each week if they know someone, join or attend professional group meetings, do targeted volunteering or an internship).

_____
_____
_____
_____

☐ **List several people in each arena who you can ask for an informational interview.** Then call or email them.

1_____  5._____
2._____  6._____
3._____  7._____
4._____  8._____

☐ **Carry out informational interviews and follow-up activities** with people whom you interviewed (send articles of interest, thank you, etc.)

# Finding the Job
## phase III

# Phase III: Finding the Job

You have now reached the practical core of this handbook, the section that lays out the techniques to get a job. You have arrived here in one of three ways:

- You read and did the exercises in **Self-Assessment** and **Career Exploration,** which led to a heart-felt career objective. Happily, your research indicates that it is a reasonably practical choice. You are enjoying your increased clarity and are eager to land the job to match.

- You skipped ahead to this section because you already know your career goal and feel stuck on the implementation of your vision. You may be one of the lucky ones, blessed with a clear calling without a lot of meandering to get there. To ensure that we are, indeed, on the same page go back and read **Deciding on a Career Objective**.

- You skipped ahead to this section because you need a paycheck soon and cannot afford the time to research and discover your true calling. We are completely sympathetic. Your priorities are consistent with Maslow's Hierarchy of Needs. Maslow verifies that people cannot attend to their highest needs for self-actualization if more basic physiological and safety needs are not met. You can always keep your pledge to return to the earlier phases at a more propitious time.

If you are starting with this chapter, it is vital for you to get up to date on the role that social media now plays in both career exploration and job search. Start with **Your Approach to Social Med**ia followed by **LinkedIn: Profiles and Inviting Connections**. Proceed to **LinkedIn: Groups and Networking** followed by **Social Media: Twitter, Facebook, Virtual CV's, Websites, and Blogging**. While we encourage you to have this overview of social media, the most important task is to create your LinkedIn profile and invite your contacts to join. The rest is optional.

At this juncture it is also helpful to foresee and plan to address challenges. Turn to **Resources and Barrier Grid** where you initially summarized your key resources and barriers. Review the activities that comprise a robust job search and think of how you can include your sources of support in this final stage. Conversely, think of your identified barriers and how to inoculate against them during the job search. For example, if a resource is attending a weekly job search group, maximize your attendance. If a barrier is your dislike of writing resumes and cover letters, find a friend or professional to make sure you get the good ones out of the door. In addition, it may be helpful to review and decide if your current spiritual and emotional practices are sufficient to counteract the stresses and implicit periodic rejections that are part of finding a job worth having.

A robust job search includes targeting your resume, finding jobs through postings on the Internet, networking, strategic volunteering, applying for jobs and interview preparation. Once again, the **Job Search Plan Checklist** found at the beginning and end of this section provide a road map.

## Targeting Your Resume

You probably have a resume that you dusted off when you began this career transition. Good. Now that you have a more focused direction and know what employers are looking for, you are ready to improve your resume. This will allow you to move quickly when an opportunity is presented. We recommend that you expand your resume into a three or four-page master that includes a comprehensive list of the keywords, skills, accomplishments, and experiences that might be relevant to your next position. When you apply for a position, you will cut and paste from the master resume the two pages of copy that are most relevant.

We have had clients set goals to send as many as ten or more resumes out per week. Setting such a quantitative goal usually means aiming for some long shots. For most people, we recommend applying for fewer positions and spending more time targeting each resume. You probably need to schedule at least a half day to do a credible job of customizing a resume and cover letter. This time includes introductory research on the organization to use language and examples consistent with their culture. Resume wordsmithing can be painstaking, but we believe it is constitutionally good for you to continually revisit how your skills and experience match those requested by employers.

**Finding Job Openings**
There are two broad types of activities to find job postings: **Finding Job Openings on the Internet** and **Networking.**

Using the **Internet** is not just a matter of checking out Indeed.com and other job sites. It includes building relationships on LinkedIn, subscribing to a few lists, such as CNRG and Mac's List (both send pertinent announcements to you on a regular basis), and checking desired employer websites.

There will be a continual interaction between networking on the Internet and meeting people in person. For example, in **LinkedIn: Groups and Networking** you learned how to build an initial online relationship with someone who is an expert in your field. If the quality of your online interactions is positive, you may suggest getting together for tea. Conversely, you may meet someone face-to-face at Green Drinks, get their card, and invite them to be a connection on LinkedIn. To strengthen this relationship, continue to interact both online and off. You never know when a key person can tell you about a job or introduce you to someone who can hire you. We have included an article on **Social Media: Finding the Position Openings and Getting Insider Help** that works hand-in-hand with the social media articles in **Career Exploration (Phase II).** The huge majority of people who find jobs through social media are able to do so because of the relationships they built prior to seeing the job posting.

**Networking** begins by revisiting people you already know to update them on your more focused objective. Begin by refining your basic message and challenging yourself to use it regularly. Your first audience may be yourself in the mirror followed by family members. Eventually, even an introvert can progress to a room full of strangers at a professional event in his or her field. It is a time for you to breathe optimism and belief into your words. To quote Bob Dylan, "You either got faith or you got unbelief. There is no middle ground."

**Applying for Positions**
Generally, it's a good idea to review your favorite Internet job sites a few times a week. Don't be surprised if you only find one position where your skills match those in the posted qualifications. Next you will need to note if a closing date has been posted and organize your schedule to respond as quickly as possible. For popular jobs, some employers begin interviewing before they posted closing dates. So aim for applying within a week after posting.

A second step is to see if any of your contacts can put in a good word for you. Do learn how to do so using social media, check out **Social Media: Finding Position Openings and Getting Insider Help.**

**Cover Letters**
A **cover letter** is written to match each position for which you apply. In one page, you summarize how your strengths are a match to the position and organization. If someone noteworthy in the organization referred you to the position, you begin by referring to this person by name. As opposed to the resume, the cover letter can include some personal style in your prose. For example, some playfulness might be a good match for a young ad agency, whereas a very direct style might be more in sync with an engineering firm. Because people in nonprofits and sustainable businesses are driven by passion for their mission, it is important to include your familiarity with their work and share your feelings about their mission.

**Interviewing**

In today's market, where good employers usually have many well-qualified candidates for each position, the interview is often the basis for the final decision. You may be surprised to learn how much you can do to improve your interview by reviewing **Common Interview Questions, Telling Stories in a PAR Format** (Problem, Action, Result) and finding out **What Should I Wear?** Because Vicki did her last job search when she was 55-years-old, she is particularly aware of the challenges faced by older applicants. She wrote **Interviewing for the Older Candidate** so that older candidates may avoid increasing the risks of ageism.

**References**

Selecting and giving employers names and contact information for your references happens either at the time that you apply (if they make this request) or when you bring the contact information to the interview. In our practice, we see many, many competent professionals who have had a negative or "iffy" interaction with a previous employer. The **References** section offers suggestions on preparing your references in advance of a phone call from a perspective employer and guides you on the use of an "iffy" reference.

# Pre-Assessment Job Search Plan Checklist:
## Finding the Job

**Pre-Assessment Date_____**

❏ **Target your resume(s) to your career objective(s).**

❏ **Identify and review Internet job sites most likely to post appropriate job openings.**

❏ **Bookmark and periodically review Websites for desirable employers.**

| | |
|---|---|
| 1._____ | 6._____ |
| 2._____ | 7._____ |
| 3._____ | 8._____ |
| 4._____ | 9._____ |
| 5._____ | 10._____ |

❏ **Analyze job postings for required/desired technical skills; build one or two of these.**

_____     _____

❏ **Re-contact (phone/email/mail) people in your network who are most likely to hear about job openings.**

_____     _____

_____     _____

_____     _____

❏ **Carry out strategic volunteering or an internship to build the skills and/or contacts that fit your career objective(s).**

❏ **Become active in professional organizations/groups that can provide job leads that match your career objective(s).**

_____

_____

❏ **Develop an interview strategy and practice PAR (problem, action, results) stories.**

❏ **Customize your cover letter and resume for each position to which you apply.**

❏ **Research the organization prior to each interview.**

❏ **Interview with vigor.**

# Finding Job Openings on the Internet

**How has the Internet Changed Searching for Job Openings?**
The old style of job search was to curl up with the Sunday *Oregonian* and go through all of the sections and circle ads. Today, this method plays a negligible role in most job searches for two reasons. First, there are fewer and fewer jobs in newspapers. Second, the most effective way to find postings is searching by keywords, as well as job titles.

**How Much Time Should I Spend on Job Posting Sites?**
"Some people should devote no time at all to scanning postings; others should devote more than half of their job search time," says Marti Nemko, in *Cool Careers for Dummies*. If you often find postings that match your qualifications, go for it. If you rarely see postings for which you meet the requirements, networking will need to be your primary strategy.

Use the following questions as guidelines on how much time to spend on Internet job sites. The more "yes" answers you have, the more that these ads should be a part of your search.
- Do you write and customize resumes and cover letters with ease?
- Do you enjoy time on the Internet?
- Are you more likely to apply to postings than to network?
- Do very few people have your combination of technical skills in your field?
- Is your target job in demand?
- Do you work in technology?
- Are you currently employed in or near your target field?

**Should I Apply?**
The first consideration is to determine if you have at least a moderate level of interest. You can learn more about whether the job meets your true needs if you are offered an interview. If you are adequately interested, ask yourself if you are competitive for the position: What are your chances of getting an interview? To determine if you have a reasonable chance, scrutinize the qualifications listed in the ad. If you have at least 75 percent of the qualifications required, it is worth it to take the time to tailor your resume. The ad's wording can give you clues as to the relative importance of the listed qualifications:

**Note if the qualification is identified as "required."** A hiring manager told me recently that she makes the first cut in the stack of resumes by quickly seeing if the top two or three requirements are met. If not, she tosses it without reading the cover letter or the remainder of the resume.

**Note if the qualification is identified as "preferred" or "desirable."** It may not be a problem if you are missing a skill/experience labeled "preferred" or "desirable" rather than "required."

**Note if the qualifications are listed in a short want ad or at the bottom of a longer position announcement.** If an employer is paying for an ad by the word, they have usually chosen the most important elements for the ad. An employer who lists "experience with Raiser's Edge" in a three-line ad is very serious about this requirement. In contrast, an employer who places the same software in a laundry list of desirable skills at the end of a one-page position announcement is likely to be flexible about this "requirement."

**When Should I Ignore these Rules?**

There are four reasons to override our good advice and apply when you don't meet nearly all of the high-priority requirements:

- If you know someone of possible influence inside the organization who will put in a good word for you, consider applying. Vicki's daughter, Jessica, combed her network relentlessly until she found someone at Michael Hoff Productions who gave the person sorting resumes a call and said, "Don't overlook that Jessica. She is really great." And she got the interview.

- If you can take less than an hour to tailor a resume and cover letter, you may want to apply to some long shots. It's sinking too much time and pinning your hopes on positions that require qualifications that you don't have that leaves you feeling unwanted and unloved. And most employers no longer send out rejection letters.

- If you are applying in one of the rare fields that has more openings than applicants or requires a rare skill you possess, consider applying. For example, social service jobs that indicate "bi-lingual in Spanish or Russian reading and writing preferred" are going to have a limited number of applicants. These organizations will look more seriously at candidates missing some other qualification.

- If your heart's desire is to work for an organization and you have been praying or doing numerous affirmations, go for it.

- If you are still not sure how much job postings are worth your time, give them a test. Actively search for a month and send out resumes. It can't hurt and there is something satisfying about sending in a resume rather than networking, because you know, without a doubt, that there is an opening. Vicki had a client who recently came to her after sending out a few hundred unrequited resumes. Not surprisingly, he was in despair. It is better to reconsider a high-volume tactic after 20 submissions without any nibbles, usually because you lack some qualifications. Abandon the high-volume long-shot approach in favor of applying for fewer, better-matched jobs and working on other tactics outlined in this handbook.

**Organizing Your Internet Search**

Create a list of sites to check on a regular basis and determine the best time to do so. For example, Monday evenings might be your designated time to review your sites. Bookmark them for easy access. For most people, we recommend a mix of two or three general local jobs sites, 15 to 20 employer sites, and two or three career-specific listservs or job sites. Limit your time searching online to no more than 90 minutes, twice a week.

When you first start, it is worth your time to explore different key words to see which tend to be the best matches. Does the word "green" tend to pull up jobs about golf courses or sustainability? Does the phrase "communication coordinator" tend to pull up jobs that require numerous software programs?

**What Are Some "Good" Sites?**

- **General Local Sites**

  The following four general sites boast good volume across fields:

  - Oregonlive (same ads as in the *Oregonian* at www.oregonlive.com).
  - Oregon Employment Department site at www.oregon.gov/EMPLOY/index.shtml.
  - Craigslist at www.portland.craigslist.org and Indeed at www.indeed.com. Until recently Craigslist was free for local employers and thus, became very popular. However, an annoying aspect of Craigslist is that the site often does not disclose the name of the employer. If you select just one site to search, try Indeed because it searches numerous sites for local job listings including Monster (www.Monster.com).
  - Jobdango (www.jobdango.com) and Yahoo (www.yahoo.com). Search by job titles and key words in the job description and they will send you announcements that match your criteria.

- **Employer Sites**

  Most employers post jobs first on their own Websites, then (if at all) on other sites. Regularly checking the sites of your top 15+ desirable employers keeps you abreast of changes in target businesses or organizations and allows you to scan current job postings. This is particularly useful if you are looking at larger employers with more positions, such as the Red Cross or Outside In.

- **Sites Specific to Your Career Target**

  For a more complete list of job sites for your specific career target, review **Phase II: Career Exploration**. The most popular local sites for Creatives and people who want to make a difference are the following:

  - **Craig's List** (at www.craigslist.com or www.craigslist.org) is the undisputed queen of job sites for Creatives and includes a growing list of local jobs at nonprofits.

  - **CNRG** (pronounced synergy), at www.cnrg-portland.org. This listserv is the undisputed hub for job openings in the nonprofit arena in Portland. About 30 positions are posted each month in addition to hundreds of announcements about internships and volunteer opportunities. In order to avoid being inundated by non-job announcements, request the digest version and pick the most pertinent announcements.

  - **Professional Associations** are also useful sites to find job postings in your field. The main method of finding job openings through professional associations is to attend their meetings and get leads from other members. However, a few sites, such as those of the Public Relations Society of America (www.prsa.org), Willamette Valley Development Officers (www.wvdo-or.org), Women on Water (lists.onenw.org/lists) and Pacific Northwest Jobseekers (groups.yahoo.com/group/pnwJobSeekers) regularly post employment opportunities.

  - **RACC (Regional Arts and Culture Council)** lists Portland-area jobs in the arts at www.racc.org/resources/jobs

  - Mac's List lists Portland and Oregon jobs at prichardcommunications.com/macs-list.html

# Social Media: Finding Position Openings and Getting Insider Help

Job searching and networking are inextricable. The relationships you build during career exploration, both through social media and in face-to-face meetings, can be used strategically when you are actively job searching. The sites on which you have built relationships often include job postings. Individuals who have gotten to know you and your expertise will forward job postings to you. The opportunities to hear about position openings are strongest if your network includes leaders, managers, and/or recruiters.

The emphasis in this article is how to use social media to identify or create job positions as well as how to use social media during or after the application process. Now is the time to call on the people with whom you've developed a relationship. This is sometimes referred to as your "social capital."

## Relationships with Recruiters and Hiring Managers

If you have not yet developed active engagement in social media, you may want to skip reading the rest of this article for now. If you have built a community on any social media site, this is an excellent time to increase your engagement with managers or recruiters in targeted organizations. Recruiters, sometimes called "Talent Acquisition," can work internally as part of the Human Relations department for larger companies such as Nike or Portland Energy Conservation Incorporated. Recruiters can also work independently, receiving contracts to satisfy hard-to-fill positions for employers. Recruiters are sometimes called "Executive Recruiters," because they are most commonly engaged to find leadership talent or those with unusually advanced technical skills. Nearly every recruiter uses social media, particularly LinkedIn and Twitter to find employees for specific positions.

Once you have identified a hiring manager or recruiter engaged with your target companies or industry, you will want to start following them on Twitter. Whereas it might take weeks for a job post to show up on Craigslist or Indeed, you can find out about new jobs instantly as they are posted on Twitter. This gives you a head start to research the company, search your network for contacts, tailor a resume, and still submit your application within a week to give you a clear, competitive advantage.

According to social media expert Joshua Waldman, "local recruiters often post their job openings on Twitter first to test the level of interest to determine whether to post them to a job board later. Joshua recommends typing in "recruiter" at Twellow (www.twellow.com) or Listorious (www.listorious.com) to look up sample Twitter bios based on keyword searches.

One reason to follow hiring managers is to build relationships with them so that you will be known when they have an opening. Another approach is to learn about the hiring manager's problems and then suggest a meeting where you can pitch how you could solve the organization's problems. As a result, you could create an unpaid volunteer internship, be hired for a project, or become employed without the company ever posting a position.

## Shaking Your Networking Tree

You'll be following your targeted companies on LinkedIn. As a result they will send you position announcements as they become available. When you see one you would like to apply for, your next step is to find out who works in the company. You can review your network on LinkedIn to see if anyone is working there by going to the upper right corner of LinkedIn, changing the drop down menu to "companies," and searching for their name. The screen that will pop up will show anyone in your network who is currently working there. You might want to contact them for insider tips and see if it would be useful to refer to them in your cover letter. Ideally, if they are well positioned, they will pass your name onto the hiring manager or HR to keep an eye out for your resume. If you don't know anyone currently working there, you may find out if anyone you know worked there before by doing a "people" search for the company. Any of your connections who used to work there may be able to help you as well.

# Internships: Posted or Self-Designed

You don't need to be a student to benefit from interning with a desirable employer. You may be running into the most frustrating Catch-22 for career changers. How can you meet the requirement for industry-specific experience if no one will give you the chance to gain experience in the industry?

It is true that historically nearly all internships were planned and executed under the umbrella of a college or university. The school established a win-win relationship with employers. Students could work 10 to 20 hours per week to gain "real world" learning for 12 to 15 weeks. These free or minimally paid internships also gave students a way to use professional-level skills and generate references in a specific field. Often, they led to job offers after graduation.

Many nonprofit organizations are following this model and post announcements for paid and unpaid internships along with their paid positions on their Web sites and sites such as CNRG. Organizations understand that a volunteer has a weak obligation to the employer—they can stay for an hour or a year. In contrast, an internship includes a written agreement stating the length of the commitment, duties expected, and supervision that will be extended. In sum, it more closely mimics a paid position.

Private businesses are not allowed by law to benefit from unpaid labor unless the intern is a student earning academic credit. If you're not a student and would like to create an internship in a private business, there are two options. First, you can contact your local community college and ask to do the internship for community college practicum credit, which is not very expensive. Or second, you can call your proposed work for the business a "pro bono" project.

**Examples of Self-Designed Internships/Pro-Bono Projects**

**Alison Wiley**, a counselor, wanted to change careers and use her writing skills in a green company or organization. A recommendation from Richard Bolles in *What Color is Your Parachute* caught her eye. Bolles stated that you can create employment by making a proposal to a decision maker. You want to first meet and interview the employer, saying that you think you can solve some of his or her problems. In the first meeting, interview the employer about his or her challenges and ask permission to submit a win-win proposal at a subsequent meeting. Through networking, Alison met the president of a well-established engineering consulting firm committed to sustainability. She was able to obtain a meeting in which she offered to do a pro-bono project on the condition that a position would probably be created for her if her performance was satisfactory. He agreed, and after a few months, she moved from the pro-bono project to becoming an employee.

**Aron** is a Portland actor whose paid work as a customer service representative was too far from his passion for the arts, particularly theater. His career goal was to work in development and garnering funds for the performing arts. He submitted several applications, but fell short in matching the requirement for experience in development and/or knowledge of Raiser's Edge, the fund-raising software most often used in development. He wrote a letter that he submitted to the theatre groups that he most admired, offering his weekly day off to help in development with a large variety of tasks, from writing fund-raising letters to stuffing envelopes.

**Laura** is passionate about a range of social justice and sustainability fields, and her resume showed a series of short periods of employment and volunteer activities. She was able to review her values and commit to the following broad professional mission: "My mission is to help foster job creation through green collar jobs, sustainable business, or sustainable agriculture." With this strong focus, she identified a dozen nonprofit organizations with similar missions. She selected two for potential internships and sent them the letter on the following page.

# Sample Request for Internship

Mr. Tom Rinehart
Metropolitan Alliance for Common Good
1244 NE 39th Avenue
Portland, OR 97232

Dear Mr. Rinehart:

I am writing to offer my skills to Metropolitan Alliance for Common Good (MACG) with the purpose of completing a self-designed internship. I call this an internship rather than volunteer work because I can offer a steady commitment of 20 hours per week for several months without pay, with the goal of furthering my professional development. I am available to work either from my home office or at a workplace of your choice.

As you can see on my resume, I have 3 years of progressively responsible experience in small business administration, have coordinated a coalition, planned and implemented a successful press event, created curriculum and taught classes for various settings, topics, and audiences, performed street outreach, and founded a craft cooperative in a developing country.

I am ideally interested in using and further developing several of the following skills:
- **Imparting information**
  Education
  Outreach
  Public Speaking
- **Facilitating and Connecting Groups**
  Meeting Facilitation
  Creating mutually beneficial connections between organizations
  Planning, implementing, and following up on programs or projects
- **Organizing and Analyzing Data**
  Creating and analyzing databases and spreadsheets
  Researching and writing business plans or project proposals.

I have selected MACG to offer my assistance because the mission and goals of the Sustainable Works Portland Campaign resonate with my mission of promoting a sustainable economy through job creation. I would love to do everything I can to help this project take flight.

In return for my unpaid labor, I would ask for a commitment of at least one hour of supervision or guidance per week. At the same time, I am a highly self directed individual, able to recognize an unmet need in an organization and create appropriate solutions on my own. I would also appreciate the opportunity to participate in or observe select staff meetings or trainings.

My greatest strength as an employee is the ability to be both a left-brain and right-brain thinker. For example, I enjoy talking to people in educational and public speaking situations, but also excel at organizational tasks such as creating spreadsheets and reports. My references will attest to my strengths: I am committed, organized, honest, have integrity, friendly and fun to be around.

Please let me know if there are any unmet needs with which I can assist you. I will follow up on this letter within one week. If you have no need at this time, but are aware of any other associates or friends who might be looking for an intern with my skills and interests, please forward the enclosed resume to them. I appreciate your time in reflecting on this win/win proposal.

Sincerely, Laura

# Job Search for the Older Candidate

Vicki was in her fifties when she began searching for a half-time job with benefits to complement her true passion to build her practice as a career counselor. In spite of her expertise in the career search process, she often felt frozen. As an older job seeker, she had no doubt that she had more to offer than her younger counterparts. It was hard to stomach that she had to mute some of her strengths, particularly her independent nature, to successfully play the game and land a job.

Ageism is insidious and is difficult to confront for two reasons. First, hiring managers know that it is illegal to bring the subject out in the open. Second, in their young hearts, they do not believe that they are prejudiced. They believe that it is logical to be concerned because they believe older people will do the following:

- Miss more work and/or poop out just when the company is facing a dragon deadline
- Become a company mommy or daddy and tell others what to do with a wagging finger
- Want to do it the way it has always been done
- Not be able to keep up with new trends
- Get bored and leave too soon or retire soon

So to prevent employees from leaving too soon, the "clairvoyant" manager thinks that it is best not to hire them. Apparently, they have not read that research shows no correlation between age and job performance.

Fortunately, age bias in hiring is continually diminishing due to demographic trends. Because of the challenging economic times, aging baby boomers are staying with their employers into their 60s. And employers are delighted because of the labor shortage that is projected to begin in 2010. According to www.Go60.com "societal and cultural attitudes will have to undergo drastic and rapid change to accommodate throngs of active, healthier baby boomers as an economic powerhouse eager and willing to continue productivity."

To offset possible ageism remember these tips:

- Only go back 15 years on the chronological part of your resume (which is also standard practice).
- Leave the dates off your education on the resume.
- Get current on relevant technology, and take off outdated technical terms (Lotus 1-2-3, Mainframe, C++).
- Research employers who are typically friendly to older workers. Consider a casual visit to the place of business, reviewing photos on the Website, and asking people in your network. AARP (www.aarp.org) lists national employers who welcome older workers.
- Select careers (design, writing, accounting) that are driven by work-samples.
- Look at services geared toward older people where your ability to relate will be an asset (like hospice nurse, care manager or sales associate at assisted living facility).
- Carry out a robust networking strategy since the focus on age fades into the background once people get to know you as a person, your enthusiasms, and your skills.
- Review the section on **Interviewing for the Older Candidate** and practice.

# Telecommuting and Working at Home

Many new parents, particularly moms, want to stay home full-time or part-time with their children. Two full-time professional jobs in one household with two parents can be very stressful for many new families, especially if the household budget can't be stretched to afford a nanny. There just doesn't seem to be enough hours in a day or week to keep everyone nurtured, connected and clean.

First, the bad news. When Vicki was a young feminist she hoped that job-shares and telecommuting would be commonplace by now—a win-win solution for both families and employers. Many businesses avoid creating shared positions because of concern about paying benefits for both employees as well as logistical barriers that arguably could be overcome with a little good will. Similarly, very few jobs are posted for telecommuting other than telemarketing. These situations exist, but most arrangements for telecommuting are made after an employee has worked on site for a considerable period. The other bad news is that many sites on the Internet prey on this need and offer scams for how to make money at home.

If you don't want to work full-time and need medical benefits (but not a lot of income), your job search might be focused on the rare employer who pays full or partial benefits for half-time work. Examples include Starbucks, Home Depot, and Mercy Corps. Start by asking everyone you know about employers in this rare category. You may also consider getting a private policy with a high deductible.

Options for generating income at home dramatically improve if you don't have to worry about medical coverage and are blessed with a little entrepreneurial spirit. In tight economic times, employers work with a lot of contractors (i.e. the self-employed). Although the focus of this handbook is not primarily on self-employment, Vicki's private practice also focuses on self-employed people. She helps people develop marketing plans for providing creative services (writers, designers, videographers) and health/wellness services (acupuncture, counseling, massage, yoga and personal training). If you have the temperament to sell your services, with a little guidance, these are all very flexible options.

Working as a contractor or starting a home-based business is particularly attractive if you don't need to generate a full livable wage. We know several people who have earned up to $15,000 (a partial income) in their first few years of self-employment without being out of their home for more than 15 hours per week. Their job titles included the following:

- Bookkeeper
- Caregiver for other children at home
- Personal Chef delivering foods to client homes
- Personal or Business Coach (primarily with telephone contact)
- Senior Caregiver/ Nursing Assistant in private homes for 48 hour shifts, leaving time at home
- Programmers and other IT professionals
- Fiction Editor
- Artist making crafts for fairs and Etsy (www.Etsy.com)
- Virtual Personal Assistant
- Organizer
- Natural Resources Writer and Film Writer
- Graphic Designer
- Editor
- eBay Seller (but, we know many more who have tried and not made a viable income stream)
- eBooks Retailer (but, we know many more who have tried and not made a viable income stream)
- Nutritional Supplements Salesperson
- Small Farmer growing and selling food or herbs

We know people who have grossed more than $30,000 per year within the first few years while remaining largely at home in the following job categories:

- Translator (need second language at highly proficient level)
- Web Designer and Developer
- Graphic Designer (print and Web)
- Bookkeeper
- In-home Caregiver for seniors who are ill or at end of life (three 24-hour shifts per week)
- Editor
- IT Professional
- Medical Transcriber
- Technical Consultant
- Trainer/Facilitator

The following Websites may help you expand this list of options. In addition, you may want to search for one of the active blogs on which mothers share their experiences and resources about making money at home.

- **Home-Based Working Moms** (www.hbwm.com). This site "provides its members with support, networking, free advertising options, information, a monthly (print) newsletter, email discussion list, searchable member directory, member spotlights and corporate discounts on various products and services." Not everything here requires you to be a member. They list home business and work-at-home opportunities, some of which require you to pay fees but many do not.

- *Nice Work If You Can Get It: Websites for At-Home Jobs,* Sue Shellenbarger at online.wsj.com/article. This is a very good article from the Work & Family columnist for *CareerJournal.* She took the time and enlisted some help in finding "a few honest Websites that actually help people find real, paying home-based work." She agrees that most of these options are a better match for people who only need an income stream rather than a livable wage. Many of the jobs have minimum requirements for phone, office and computer setups. The links that she lists are a good place to start your search.

- **FlexJobs.com** was started by Sarah Sutton Fell. This site lists telecommuting and work-at-home opportunities, but not just any old listing from anyone who wants to post an ad. The FlexJobs team actually reviews and researches each posting to be sure it is a legitimate opportunity (temporary, part-time, or full-time). There is a $15 fee to try it out for a month, but this fee buys you a way to circumvent hours of chasing false ads. You can look at the list of posted jobs, but you cannot see the full posting until you register.

# The Spirit of Networking

Networking is probably the most overworked word in the career transition vocabulary. Magazines and Internet sites abound with articles with titles like "Five Easy Steps to Networking" or "Schmooze or Lose."

"Schmooze or Lose" captures the reason that most of our clients recoil from networking: The advice and examples in most business models seem inconsistent with their values and/or personal style. The word "schmooze" connotes getting to know someone expressly to advance your agenda—whether you like them or not. The article and scores like it assume a business/cultural context that is not relevant to many Creatives and idealists (e.g., "golfing and country clubs are still excellent locations for networking"). Deferential references to people "higher up" the organizational ladder may irk you if you are community-minded. In addition, introverts feel excluded in this conventional approach, which applies better to natural extroverts. It may be particularly helpful for you to glean truly useful information in this section if you are introverted, prefer a forest hike to a golf course, and don't like how "schmoozing" rhymes with "using" or "oozing."

We prefer to redefine networking into a more attractive model for the idealist and the creative career seeker. We offer the image of a net or web, particularly *Charlotte's Web*, to replace the image of the hierarchical, runged-ladder. When we see ourselves as part of a web, we are all interconnected in multiple directions around a common center. In Charlotte's case, the spider spun the words "some pig" in the center of her web. Imagine that Charlotte has woven a phrase in the middle of your career web that captures your career mission. A technical writer in health care might select "life-saving words" or a person in recycling might imagine "garbage reduction." The spokes radiating out from this core represent the people and organizations that connect with this central concern. The purpose of your networking is to meet as many people as possible with whom you share your passion in order to exchange ideas and leads. Generally, people are eager to talk to others who share their outrage about society's unhealthy direction and want to commit to healthy redirection.

### Networking for Introverts

Too many articles on networking are written by extroverts who assume that introverts can or would want to mimic them. They may believe they can show you that small talk is fun, whereas you probably would prefer to snuggle up with a book—even a dull book.

The following techniques were used by introverted clients who applied only what was consistent with their natural style. It surprises many introverts that networking can be done without gut-wrenching trauma.

### Examples:

- Several years ago, **Vicki** decided that she needed a half-time job with benefits to complement her beloved private practice as a career counselor. Although she can be outgoing in familiar settings, she has a strong preference to spend free time at home or with a few close friends. She kept avoiding, what she thought at that time, was required for effective networking—going out to varied activities to meet many new people. Finally, she decided to honor her own style and invite eight of her close colleagues to lunch to form an ad-hoc "advisory board." In advance, she reminded them of her top skills and challenged them to provide her with the names of organizations and specific people to contact. This brainstorming session generated about 15 leads including the name of a dean at PCC Rock Creek who hired her as a Career Specialist for that summer, followed by a contact at ProtoCall Services where she was hired for a half-time position on a mental health crisis line.

- **Marcy,** an introvert, came to Portland because of her husband's job; therefore, she didn't have a network of local friends or colleagues. Her gift and the motivating force behind her successful networking was her natural curiosity and her passion about map-making (GIS) and protecting natural resources, especially water. She used self-talk and the support of members in her job support group to get her to show up for a local GIS group, Green Drinks, and a gathering of Women on Water. In advance, she promised her support group that she would talk to at least two people she didn't know at Green Drinks as well as add some people to her LinkedIn virtual community. When she got to Green Drinks, she took a deep breath and said to herself, "If I'm only going to meet one or two people, I might as well meet someone who is well connected in Portland's green community. So she walked up and introduced herself to Will Vilotta who co-facilitates Green Drinks and has several hundred contacts on his LinkedIn site. Once she was into a one-on-one conversation with the ever-friendly Will, she no longer needed deep breathing or self-talk. Meaningful one-on-one conversations are safe and comfortable experiences for introverts. She also enjoyed reporting back to her support group that she had followed through on her intentions.

Once again, driven by her passion, Marcy attended a conference in California for GIS professionals specifically committed to natural resource issues. This conference was also attended by staff from Metro; Marcy planned to follow-up with these contacts upon returning to Portland. However, shortly after her return, Metro posted a GIS job and Marcy applied. She didn't have great hopes for an interview because she had not worked in the public sector and knew that Metro draws huge numbers of applicants. However, the hiring manager she had met at the conference knew her name, and she was invited for one of the coveted interview slots. She has now happily accepted the position as GIS Technician for the Portland Metro Natural Areas Program.

- **Patricia**, also schmooze-averse, wanted a position using her strengths in analyzing and organizing data and writing complex reports in service of sustainability. She wanted to stimulate people to keep their eyes open for position announcements that matched this skill set. However, as an introvert, she did not have a large network. And she was reluctant to both contact the people she had met and to initiate the requisite small talk. Instead, she signed up to organize the poster display booths for a large environmental conference. Her role was to contact each environmental organization to coordinate the details of their display. She left this targeted volunteer activity on a first-name basis with key players in her desired field. A strong writer, she periodically sent updates to this group via email and reminded them of her job search goal. When an appropriate project opened up at Metro, three people saw the match and forwarded the notice to Patricia, who successfully landed the position.

### Networking for Extroverts
One of the defining characteristics of an extrovert is that they enjoy meeting new people. Therefore, networking is easier for extroverts. Picture Bill Clinton's face and how it seems to genuinely light up when he meets strangers. It's been written that he started a Rolodex (for those of you who are new to this word, it was a circular holder for business cards that physically sat on your desk) of contacts his first year of college. He never stopped, and his database is now one of his most enviable tools. And, of course, he has zero compunction about asking everyone on the list for exactly what he wants.

### Examples:
- Another extrovert, **Macy Guppy**, began a career search by adopting the following advice offered by Marty Nemko, author of Cool Careers for Dummies. "Call 100, yes 100 people who like you—everyone from your parents' best friend to your ex-lover, from your old professor to your new haircutter."

- **Jessica Hurley**, Vicki's eldest daughter, is naturally social and stays in touch with an enormous network of friends and former colleagues. She eagerly goes out of her way to help people in her networking circles and seldom loses contact with old boyfriends, bosses, neighbors, and college mates. She keeps up her Facebook page and has hundreds of contacts on LinkedIn and Facebook.

People in her 30-something clan (as well as younger people) know they are always on call for one another and social media is the central connecting hub.

Jessica has obtained her two major jobs through this network. First, she decided that she wanted to use her creative and writing skills for an organization devoted to women's issues. She targeted a few ideal organizations and emailed her network to see who knew whom. A friend of a friend, whom she had met at a party, worked for Oxygen (Oprah's now-defunct women's Website). Jessica's contact put in a good word for her so that she won an interview. Once again, she drew on her network to research the people who would interview her to help her connect well at the interview. As a result, she was hired as the producer for Thrive, Oxygen's online health site for women.

In 2004, Jessica began a career transition seeking work in TV/video production. She had stayed in periodic contact with an old supervisor to express concern about his son's chronic illness and to say "hi." When a position came open at the TV station where he now worked, he sung her praises to the hiring manager. She is now a producer/writer for TV specials that focus on teen issues. Without the connection, her resume would never have been selected from among her more experienced competitors.

- **Alicia**, another extrovert, volunteered to staff a recycling program booth at Portland's Home and Garden Show. She struck up a lively conversation with some people who worked for the City of Portland's Bureau of Planning and Sustainability, introduced herself, and talked about opportunities at the office. The next month when a position opened up in this office, she was not just a name in the huge stack of applicants, and they recalled her energetic personal style. She won the interview and the job and was hired as a Multifamily Specialist.

**Is Networking Over-Rated?**
Experts state that between 50 percent and 80 percent of all positions are obtained by networking. Vicki did an informal study and reviewed the records of successful clients who have worked with her over the past two years. Networking played a role in 60 to 70 percent of the success stories. However, she found that the role of networking was quite diverse, with contacts helping in many different ways:
- Forwarded job announcements that otherwise would have been missed.
- Created a new position based on valuable contributions made during volunteering.
- Put in a good word to the hiring manager or search committee.
- Provided inside information and what to emphasize in the resume and interview.
- Made introductions to key decision-makers.
- Making introductions to contacts through LinkedIn

So we continue to urge the shy and the reluctant among you, as well as the vivacious and outgoing, to hone networking techniques that fit your style.

# Networking by Email

It is a good idea at this juncture to update your email addresses. Email can provide an excellent way to explain to friends and colleagues what you are seeking and how they can be of help. If you've been sticking all of the business cards you have collected into a drawer, now is the time to input them into your address book.

Facebook and LinkedIn also have options where you can select a subset of your connections or friends to send out a call for assistance to people who may want to help you.

Judy Brodkey wrote this letter and sent it through email to professional colleagues and more casual friends. She adapted it with a little more personal information for closer friends.

Hello…

I am writing to let you know that I've just resumed my job search. I am exploring opportunities to use some of my skills in program coordination, coaching, facilitation, and teaching/training. I am especially interested in health promotion and education but will consider other areas of interest as well.

Please let me know if you hear of any openings in Portland that might be a good match for me or if you think of other people or organizations I should contact as I develop my professional network. Also, feel free to pass along my resume to others who may be interested in someone with my experience and skills. (If you don't have my resume, I'm happy to resend it.)

Also, I continue to enjoy providing life coaching for individual clients. It's very rewarding for my clients and has been a joy for me. I offer a free exploratory coaching session for people interested in using coaching to live more fully and achieve their goals and dreams.

I'm happy to provide you with additional information and please feel free to send potential clients my way or suggest people I might contact about my services.

Thanks again for your help and being part of my extended network.

Sincerely,

Judy

# Your Networking Contact List

List 20 people whom you could call, email and/or meet for tea to network. Select people whom you can ask about job leads and/or contacts they may know inside of your targeted organizations.

The ideal candidate is someone in your desired job category or field. However, networking is based on the idea that your friend or colleague may have a spouse, sibling, or neighbor in your field. Remember Roy D. Chapin, Jr.'s aphorism: "luck is the time when preparation and opportunity meet."

If you are hesitant to contact people whom you do not know very well or have not seen for a while, begin with people you enjoy and with whom you feel comfortable. Even if they do not have a lead, you will enjoy the conversation. Consider your relatives, neighbors, past co-workers, people you have met at seminars, people you do business with, old classmates, etc. Err on the side of inclusiveness.

LinkedIn is designed to help you meet new people for professional purposes. Select one of your contacts who is well connected and may want to be of help. Review their connections and open the profiles of people who interest you. If you want your connection to introduce you, select the link in the upper right quadrant that says, "Get introduced through a connection."

In addition to LinkedIn, you may want to use one or more of the following techniques:
- Ask your two best friends to give you more leads.
- Go to an event or professional meeting in your field.
- Ask your career services professional, if you are working with one, for additional names.
- Check with your alumni association for names of local people in your desired profession.

| Date | Name | Phone | Email | Notes |
|------|------|-------|-------|-------|
| 1 | | | | |
| 2 | | | | |
| 3 | | | | |
| 4 | | | | |
| 5 | | | | |
| 6 | | | | |
| 7 | | | | |
| 8 | | | | |
| 9 | | | | |
| 10 | | | | |
| 11 | | | | |
| 12 | | | | |
| 13 | | | | |
| 14 | | | | |
| 15 | | | | |
| 16 | | | | |
| 17 | | | | |
| 18 | | | | |
| 19 | | | | |
| 20 | | | | |

# Resumes

Resumes and cover letters have one goal: to get you a coveted interview. Like everything else, resumes and cover letters have styles that are in favor and those that are out of favor. Beware of using ineffective, outmoded advice such as "resumes are one page; resumes are either functional <u>or</u> chronological; resumes should include hobbies and state, 'References available upon request.'"

Take a look through the samples in this book to see which ones you find easy to read and understand. We've left the samples in the font type, font size, and layout used by the author so that you can see an array. You will notice that these are all two pages, the most useful length for people with five or more years of experience. One page resumes are for people with very limited work experience and going over two pages is strictly for the academic world (curriculum vitae).

The first time you tailor a resume to a position, it will be particularly time consuming. It is most efficient if you add any new material you write to a master resume that you save. Eventually you will be able to quickly pull from the master the two pages of copy that are the best fit for any one position.

For most job seekers, the best resume format is a blend of a functional resume (organized by functional strengths) and a chronological resume (organized strictly by date). Your resume format will be predominately **chronological** if your most recent position is the most relevant to the prospective position (see Dan Triman). Dan's certifications and degree are his most competitive points, so he begins with them. For the engineering world, the perceived "softer" volunteer activities remain on the second page. Chronological resumes often include a brief "summary of strengths" or "profile" section at the top (See Jennifer Bloeser). When describing your accomplishments, use vocabulary that lines up closely with the wording listed as qualifications in the announcement. Larger employers are likely to screen resumes with software set to select those that use key words or key phrases listed in the requirements. Since a computer is reading the resume, be very exacting in using the exact terms or phrases in the announcement.

If your most recent job does not show your pertinent strengths, start with a strong **functional section** (see Owen Wozniak) Even if you have a strong functional start, you'll still need a chronological work history with short descriptions of your accomplishments and responsibilities at each place of employment. Hiring managers express frustration with resumes that focus exclusively on broad transferable skills without reference to where and when the skills were used.

**Resume Tips**
- Begin sentences with action verbs such as initiated, trained, organized, and motivated. End with quantitative or qualitative results.
- Tailor each resume for each position that you apply. One strategy is to develop a master resume with about three pages of material. When you apply for a job, refer to the position announcement and edit your resume down to two pages, using the most pertinent material.
- Include hobbies and community activities only if these are relevant to the position.
- If pertinent, professional organizations, community activities, or languages you speak make great additions.

# Accomplishments for Resumes

It may be helpful to forget about the resume format for a moment and start building a bank of your accomplishments, beginning each with a strong verb in the past tense. Notice that pronouns are not used in resume-speak. You can get ideas from old job descriptions, past performance evaluations as well as from position announcements. Or adapt those on the following pages to your own expertise and experience.

We suggest that you start by brainstorming accomplishments to get comfortable with the format and to practice articulating your strengths. At this point, you don't need to worry about exactly how they will fit into your resume.

1. _____

2. _____

3. _____

4. _____

5. _____

6. _____

7. _____

# Accomplishments for Creatives

**Acted** in TV and radio commercials, using up beat, friendly voice to engage audiences.

**Assisted** the Creative Department in the development of children's music videos and film/television-based toys.

**Analyzed** needs, wrote specifications, procured materials, and trained four technicians.

**Built**[*] successful relationships with local radio and print media representatives *that led to ongoing communication and media responsiveness.*

**Carried out** research and development in microphone design, stereo sound, and audio systems architecture.

**Created** high-impact graphics integrating typography, illustrations, and other design features.

**Collaborated\*** with team to respond to customers, *leading to a 25 percent annual increase in sales.*

**Coordinated\*** the convergence of company's content with Oxygen's television programming and health advocacy issues. *Won Webbie Award for best Health Site in 2001 and 2002.*

**Designed** and implemented a wide range of promotional pieces: advertisements, catalogs, Web page, invitations, business cards, and packaging designs for upscale wine wholesaler.

**Exhibited** paintings, collages, and sculptures in small galleries and restaurants.

**Estimated\*** time needs, *creating smooth flow from concept to manufacture of ceramic tiles.*

**Produced** articulate and illuminating press releases, keeping public abreast of Symphony events.

**Invented\*** video-assist device customized for stop-motion animation; *this became a commercial product manufactured by Animal Tool Works, Inc.*

**Managed** small team of graphic artists to meet graphic needs of five company branches.

**Planned\*** the 2009 Brooklyn Arts and Music Festival, generating creative ideas for community involvement and *increasing attendance by 20 percent to 30 percent.*

**Presented** videos and taught adults in role as cultural ambassador to nine Asian countries.

**Produced** stress-management and self-discovery related content for women's health Website.

**Resolved** technical print problems using expertise with papers, inks, and printing techniques.

\*These accomplishments include an effective result or outcome that is indicated in italics.

# Accomplishments for People Who Want to Make a Difference

**Nonprofit Director and Coordinator Positions**

**Convened and facilitated*** community forums and task-force meetings addressing complex issues to produce outcomes including strategic plans for Mid-Willamette Senior Services Agency and City of Salem Senior Center; *recognized with City of Salem Community Partnership Award.*

**Employed project management skills** to develop and implement unique social service and lifelong learning programs for senior adults including a senior peer-learning program with more than 80 members in less than 9 months.

**Evaluated** the effectiveness of the career development office and suggested improvements.

**Increased*** *membership renewal 7 percent in 2 years* by tripling annual contact with members.

**Represented*** agency as spokesperson with local, regional, and national media. Developed successful relationships with media *that resulted in effective coverage for agency.*

**Managed** project finances and cost accounting for $2 million annual budget, including making financial projections and monitoring costs.

**Negotiated** fair and clear contracts, from $500 to $200,000 with consultants and vendors.

**Supervised and trained*** eight employees using ability to clearly explain expectations while respectfully listening to perspectives of others. *Recognized on performance review for creating positive team morale.*


**Sustainability**

**Advocated** for sustainable building practices, promotion of eco-friendly products, and preservation of Oregon's natural beauty.

**Researched and evaluated** natural history recovery plan.

**Monitored** the effects of acid rain on aquatic insect development with team-members.

**Reduced** the number of commuter miles of State of Oregon employees by 19 percent in one year.


**Teaching and Social Service**

**Counseled** drug-addicted teens and family members in treatment center.

**Taught** applied math and project management to low-income participants in the Steps Program, serving predominantly women of ethnically diverse backgrounds.

**Engaged GED students** in preparation for testing by working from their existing knowledge bases and learning styles.

**Mediated** between runaway teens and their parents, working towards family reconciliation.

**Facilitated** parenting classes, encouraging use of natural consequences and reward as a disciplinary method.

*Indicates a result, either qualitative or quantitative.

# Sample Resumes

## Erin A. Butler

503.501.xxxx          http://www.linkedin.com/in/erinabutler          xxxxxx.xxxx@gmail.com

I have four years professional experience with technical writing and editing, with an M.A. in English education and a B.A. in English and studio art. My abilities to prioritize, organize, and collaborate closely with cross-functional team members enable me to efficiently implement projects simultaneously and facilitate desired outcomes.

### Core Skills

- Strong writing and editing skills
- Developing and delivering PowerPoint presentations
- Strong research skills
- Social and digital media
- Articulating core, underlying principles
- Collaborator
- Education and training
- Organizational and time-management
- Adapt to technology

### Writing and Editing Skills

I demonstrate attention to detail and commitment to quality in all areas of the written and spoken word. I excel at articulating clearly to varying audiences in order to clarify complicated or technical concepts. I have an accomplished track record for developing communications, presentations, and messaging processes through traditional and social media platforms.

- Eight years experience teaching writing, editing and evaluating student work
- Published poetry, literary criticism, and editorials in college publications. Art editor of student literary magazine
- Assisted Vicki Lind edit and format her book, *Finding a Job Worth Having,* using MS Word track changes
- Assisted Alison Wiley, a Portland author and blogger, proofread her novel, *Revelle,* using MS Word

### Technology and Social Media Skills

I adapt easily and quickly to technology and mutable software and am able to successfully articulate them to users of varying abilities. Currently expanding my basic WordPress skills. I trained new teachers as well as hundreds of people on computer software and programs.

- Microsoft Office Suite, Adobe, PDF, WordPress, Blogger, Open Office, Skype, Photoshop, iPhoto, Moodle (an online classroom), various online grading systems
- Social Networking platforms such as Facebook, Yelp, Foursquare, Twitter, Pinterest, blogs
- Created the unofficial Facebook page for Garden and Gun Magazine
- Proficient in style guidelines such as MLA, APA, and AP

### Professional Experience

*Friends of the Library Communications Committee and Libraries Yes! Campaign
        2012*

- Write content for the Friends of the Library newsletters and websites
- Wrote copy for email blasts, Facebook, Yelp, and Foursquare updates
- Target four social media networks to promote Portland library facilities and amenities

*ACE Academy for Architecture, Construction and Engineering*          *Portland, OR*
*2008 – 2012*
English Instructor and founding teacher of a project based, hands on school for 11th and 12th graders

### Written Communications and Technology

- Rapidly learned, mastered, and taught varied computer programs, online content, and style guidelines
- Articulated and edited the school's unique vision and English curriculum in documents such as the handbook, grade standards, newsletters, journal articles, and Facebook page

- Published feature articles in *Building Futures* magazine that explain ACE's educational mission to the design-build community and advantages of the school for prospective students
- Solicited and edited student articles for *Building Futures* magazine

**Teaching/Training**
- Collaborated with cross-functional teams, excelling at simultaneously keeping the end goals and necessary incremental steps in focus
- Researched and designed the school's senior project curriculum, articulating it from several models used across the country to one suited for the school's context.
- Researched, prepared and delivered exciting and informative PowerPoint lectures on a variety of topics, including sustainable building, construction site communication and Request for Proposal process

*Alexander Graham Middle School*                                          *Charlotte, NC*
*2004 – 2008*
6th Grade Language Arts Teacher
- Instructed and evaluated classes of diverse students in reading and writing
- Worked closely with five team teachers to make learning cohesive and interrelated
- Maintained professional and confidential communication with administrators, faculty, and parents to build rapport and foster a respectful working environment

*GrassRoots Recycling Network*                                          *Athens, GA*
*2002 – 2003*
Project Assistant for a non-profit, national recycling group
- Assisted in layout of printed materials, donor correspondence and general office duties

*Wake Forest University, Casa Artom*                                          *Venice, Italy*
*2001*
- Assisted twenty students and professors adapt to September 11 tragedy while living in a foreign country

*Custom Marketing Group*                                          *Atlanta, GA*
*2000*
- Researched and wrote short blurbs for a West Virginia advertising campaign
- Fact-checked and edited various tourism marketing brochures

*Travel and Leisure Magazine*                                          *New York, NY*
*1999*
Intern for Editorial and Art Department where I participated in the intense facets of a prestigious magazine
- Researched, wrote and fact-checked text for the "World's Best Awards" and short blurbs for on-line content

## Education and Licensure
*Master of English Education, University of Georgia*          *Athens, Georgia*          *2004*
*Bachelor of Arts, English and Studio Art, Wake Forest University  Winston-Salem, NC*          *2001*
*Oregon Initial II Teaching, High School Language Arts, Highly Qualified*          *2013*

# Lyn Bonyhadi

**(xxx) xxx-xxxx linkedin.com/in/lynbonyhadi**

xxxxxxxxxxxxx@gmail.com

*Program/Project Management • Business/ Partnership Development*

Creative, energetic and highly organized project manager/marketing professional with expertise in launching projects and programs, hiring and managing teams, forging partnerships, guiding branding efforts and managing accounts relationships. A knowledgeable and established member of the sustainable practices industry with a track record of delivering results for public, non-profit and business entities.

**Core competencies:**

- entrepreneurial aptitude for launching and managing new programs
- develop business plans, manage budgets, hire staff, improve efficiencies and craft strategies that exceed goals and grow programs
- expertise in crafting and executing marketing programs that generate award-winning results
- manage results-focused teams and promote collaboration
- solid project management, contract negotiation, budget management and resource allocation skills
- strength in account management, client relations and cultivation of community partners
- known for building bridges between the public and private sectors, then leveraging these relationships for various issues-based initiatives

## PROFESSIONAL EXPERIENCE

**Metro**, Portland, OR **2006 to August 2011**
*An elected regional government, Metro strives to make the region an extraordinary place to live, work and play. Metro serves more than 1.5 million residents in Clackamas, Multnomah and Washington counties and the 25 cities in the Portland region*
**Senior Development Partnership Coordinator**

- Entered the sustainability industry with no prior experience within sector; emerged as key convener on issues within the sustainable community.
- Recognized for aptitude in cultivating and sustaining collaborative relationships among private companies, government and non-profit agencies.
- Forged strategic partnership with Home Builders Association of Metropolitan Portland that earned national recognition for successfully moving sustainable practices forward.
- Reputation as dynamic educator and business strategist, frequently called upon by home builders and developers for education and marketing support.
- Launched break-though web-based resource that enables home builders to obtain immediate information and support related to sustainable practices.
- Developed and executed a "Green from the Ground Up" program for residential builders to educate them on sustainable site practices that drive market demand; program adopted by another sustainability organization that is taking the campaign statewide.

**ESP Commercial and Industrial Realtors, Inc.**, Portland, OR **2001 to 2006**
*Portland-based commercial and industrial real estate sales/leasing and property management firm*
**Commercial Real Estate Broker**

- In response to reputation for outstanding business development, was recruited by the company's principal to grow business centered on retail, non-traditional properties and owner-user buildings.
- Procured properties for sale/lease and developed compelling marketing materials.
- Leveraged outstanding verbal and written communication skills to develop offers, negotiate counter offers and craft closing documentation.
- Became one of the top producing brokers within the organization, increasing sales by more than 50% each consecutive year.

**MindFinders, Inc.**, Portland, OR **2000 to 2001**
*Provider of specialized consulting and professional search solution services for corporate clients in need of high-tech professional resources*
**Director of eCruiting**

- Built new recruitment division from concept to delivery with six key account managers.
- Demonstrated outstanding team leadership and development skills to empower team members to make informed business decisions that lead to increased client contracts.
- Team successfully filled more than 300 high-tech positions for 25 corporate clients.
- Responsible for key national accounts, including Dell Computers and National Semiconductor.
- Outstanding account management resulting in increased division sales of 50% over projected placements.

**Bonyhadi & Associates, Inc.**, Portland, OR **1995 to 2003**
*Entrepreneurial endeavor providing graphic and photographic services to advertising firms*
**Owner/Principal**

- As a result of successes with Will Vinton Studios (WVS,) launched an entrepreneurial endeavor that supported client pre-production print needs, including those of WVS and its clients.
- Provided computer style guides, graphics and photographic services for print applications, including packaging and point of purchases, for international advertising firms.
- Managed all business development, account management and day-to-day operational functions.
- Demonstrated outstanding negotiation skills with both vendor and client contracts.
- Key clients: MARS/M&Ms, ThermaCare products, Dr. Pepper 7-Up/ Hawaiian Punch, BBDO Worldwide, DraftWorldwide, Mead Office & School Supplies, Hollywood Video, Clorox, Albertsons, Jell-O and Kikkoman Soy Sauce.
- By consistently delivering outstanding product increased revenues by 25% each consecutive year.

## COMMUNITY INVOLVEMENT

**Community Cycling Center, Volunteer 2011 to present**
**Schoolhouse Supplies Board of Directors (2003-2005 President) 1999 to 2005**
**Portland Schools Foundation Board, Board member 1994 to 2003**
**Northwest Academy Advisory Board, Board member 1996 to1998**

## EDUCATION

**Pitzer College, Claremont Colleges, Claremont, CA.**

# JENNIFER A. BLOESER

xxxx SE xxTH AVENUE • PORTLAND, OR 97202
xxx.xxx.xxxx • xxxxxxx@jenniferbloeser.com
PAGE 1 OF 2

## PROFESSIONAL PROFILE

Natural resource management professional with a commitment to advancing ecological sustainability and stewardship.

- 10 years of experience in natural resource management, conservation, and restoration.
- 10+ years developing and implementing terrestrial and aquatic research projects focused on restoration, protection, and enhancement.
- Extensive knowledge of program development and project management.
- Proven experience in grant writing and management.
- Highly organized and able to effectively manage a complex workload.
- Experience managing staff, budgets, contractors, and volunteers.
- Extremely successful working with groups of diverse stakeholders on challenging issues in a collaborative manner.

## PROFESSIONAL EXPERIENCE

*Acting Executive Director*                                June 2008 - Present
Pacific Marine Conservation Council                        Portland, Oregon
Manage and administer all functions of the organization, including campaign strategy and oversight, staff oversight, financial management, public outreach, and board communication.

- Manage and integrate Science, Policy, Community, and Development/Grant programs, four staff and five consultants with an organizational budget of $650,000.
- Monitor program results and adapt programs to meet grant deliverables, increase effectiveness, efficiency and impact.
- Manage executive transition, organizational assessment, and strategic planning processes.
- Manage and assure timelines are met for deliverables of grants between $5,000 and $250,000.
- Lead the organization's development activities, including prospect identification, funder communication, grant writing, grant management, report development, membership and donor appeals.

*Science Director*                                November 1997 - June 2008
Pacific Marine Conservation Council                        Portland, Oregon

- Established objectives, funding requirements, and implementation plans for the Science, Policy and Community Programs and projects within the programs to promote natural resource stewardship and sustainability,
- Developed and managed research projects focused on fisheries sustainability and restoration.
- Composed reports and presented publically on a variety of community sustainability and marine fisheries conservation and management issues to conferences, private groups, and state and federal agencies.
- Planned, hosted and facilitated events and workshops from 5-200 people.

JENNIFER BLOESER RESUME
PAGE 2 OF 2

*Founder/Director*  
Bay to Dunes Environmental Education Program

January 1997 – December 1997  
Arcata, California

- Developed and managed bay, coastal forest and dune ecology and restoration programs and curriculum and instructed courses.
- Identified and cultivated funders, composed grant applications and managed budget.
- Recruited and trained approximately twelve volunteers in educational instruction.

*Course Lecturer: Fisheries Sciences*  
Humboldt State University

January 1995 - June 2005  
Arcata, California

- Lectured graduate-level fisheries management course.
- Lectured and provided lab instruction: graduate-level marine fish ecology course.

*Biological Science Technician*  
Redwood Science Laboratorv / US Forest Service

May 1996 - December 1997  
Arcata, California

- Developed terrestrial and stream restoration survey and data analysis protocols.
- Surveyed and assessed forest, river and stream sites for the development of area management plans.

## TRAINING / EDUCATION

| | |
|---|---|
| *Advanced Grant Strategies* <br> TACS | 2007 <br> Portland, OR |
| *Art of Leadership* <br> Rockwood Leadership Program | 2003 <br> Ben Lomond, CA |
| *Master of Science : Natural Resources/Fisheries* <br> Humboldt State University | 1998 <br> Arcata, CA |
| *Bachelor of Science: Marine Science and Environmental Science* <br> East Stroudsburg University | 1992 <br> East Stroudsburg, PA |

## COMPUTER SKILLS

Microsoft Office Word, Excel, Publisher, Access, and Power Point; Macs and PCs; internet research; QuickBooks

# CYNTHIA L. DETTMAN. JD, MSW

xxxx NE xxxxxxxx St.　　　　　　　　　　　　　xxx xxx-xxxx
Portland, Or. 97218　　　　　　　　　　　　　xxxxxx@msn.com

*An innovative leader in community college instruction and student services*

## Summary of Experience and Skills

* 12 years experience developing and managing collaborative, team-based college programs serving multicultural populations
* 9 years experience as a community college instructor and counselor
* Initiated and developed more than 10 innovative service and advocacy programs
* 12 years experience as a social worker and counselor in social service and education settings
* Excellent negotiation, conflict resolution, communication and training skills developed as an attorney and journalist

## Leadership and Administrative Experience

**Coordinator, Transitions/Transiciones Program,** Mt. Hood Community College, 1997-present.
Taught career development and college success classes; provided counseling; supervised staff and managed budget; developed and expanded award-winning career program for low-income women; doubled college enrollment and persistence rates; increased minority and immigrant participation by 30%

Created Oregon's only Spanish-language career program for low-income Latina women; provided leadership for advocacy and fundraising plan for 14 Transitions programs statewide; expanded volunteer program and training; wrote grants and raised funds for student aid; currently implementing new initiative to prepare minority and non-native women for health careers with multiple employer, agency and school partners;

**Program Developer/Grant Writer,** The Boys and Girls Aid Society, Portland Or. 1995-1997.
Lead successful, grassroots SE Portland effort to plan and initiate teen pregnancy program; partners included public schools, non-profits, and county; wrote successful grant applications to initiate project. Participated in team planning with agency staff, Portland Parks and Recreation, and national consultant to implement comprehensive youth empowerment project in North Portland. Developed and initiated volunteer program for agency's adoption services by involving parents and adoptees; trained and supervised volunteers.

**Cooperative Education Specialist & International Programs Coordinator,** PCC/Sylvania. 1994-95. Coordinated exchange program with sister college in Japan; helped students locate and successfully complete community-based internships; Co-lead grassroots effort among students and staff to develop and fund a new **Women's Resource Center**; trained students to be leaders and advocates; facilitated planning meetings; advocated for funding. Center still exists today and has expanded.

**Advisor, Multicultural Student Organizations,** Portland State University, 1993-94.
Advised all multicultural student organizations at PSU, including African American, Latino, Native American, International, and Gay/Lesbian clubs. Facilitated conflicts, advocated with administration, provided leadership training; participated in Dean of Students leadership team.

**Staff Attorney and Domestic Violence Advocate,** Oregon Legal Services (Albany, Or.) and APPALRED (Charleston, West Virginia) 1997-88.
Provided legal advocacy services to low-income families to combat poverty, including welfare, housing, consumer, disability and civil rights cases. Worked with state agencies to expand and improve services to low-income families; argued federal and state appellate cases involving civil rights; provided leadership training to low-income family advocates; developed volunteer lawyer program.

### Direct Service, Teaching and Communications Experience

**Founder and Director,** Support Network for Abused Persons, Fayetteville, West Virginia. 1980-82.
Lead rural, community-based initiative to start the first battered women's hotline in Southeast West Virginia; Worked with community volunteers, courthouse personnel, police and service agencies.

**Community Resource Specialist,** Steps to Success, Portland Community College. 1990-92.
Provided case management services to low-income women seeking training and job search support, serving predominantly African American women.

**Teacher/Trainer, Portland Community College and Mt. Hood Community College.** Taught numerous classes and provided numerous trainings to students on career development, college success, leadership development, and cultural competency. (1990-present)

**Newspaper Journalist, 1989, 1990-92,** The Gazette-Times (Corvallis) and the Oregonian; researched and wrote articles and wide variety of social, economic and civil rights issues.

### Sample List of New Projects Developed

Health Careers Access Project (2004-present)
Oregon Women Work! Statewide Leadership Development Initiative (2003-2005)
Graduate Intern, Americorps and Mentor projects, Transitions Program (1999-2003)
Transiciones (2000-2003)
GLAD (Girls Leadership and Development Program) 1995-97
Women's Resource Center, PCC/Sylvania (1994-95)
SNAP (Support Network for Abused Persons) 1980-82

### Volunteer Work

**Board Member, Hambleton Project:** 1999-2001 Provided leadership, planning support and strategic planning facilitation for non-profit providing services to lesbians with cancer.

**Volunteer Advocate and Board Member,** Center Against Rape and Domestic Violence, Corvallis. 1982-88 Provided crisis intervention services for battered women; trained volunteers, served on board of directors.

**Volunteer Legal Advocate,** provided volunteer legal services to farmworkers organizing in South Texas (1975); disabled miners in Kentucky (1976); low-income families in Boston (1977).

### Awards

**Exemplary Practices Award,** National Council on Student Development, 2000.
**Local Hero Award,** Bank of America, November, 2005 ($5,000 award for charitable donation)

### Education

**Master of Social Work.** Portland State University.
**Journalism Studies,** University of Oregon.
**Juris Doctor.** Northeastern School of Law, Boston, Massachusetts.
**B.A.,** Sociology. Summa cum laude, Oberlin College, Ohio.

# Resume Checklist

Many people are challenged by writing their own resume and tailoring it for each position. It will help you to use this checklist to address each section of your resume. Keep in mind that there will be some parts where you will want to consult with a career professional or trusted colleague to ensure that you've represented yourself optimally.

- Your name is in larger font for easy recall, contact information is smaller

- Short, clear objective or career title at the top

- Summary of qualifications or profile at top mirrors top qualifications and keywords from position announcement

- Experience from past jobs start with verbs in the past tense

- Improve or delete overused soft skills (for example: works well independently and in team)

- Format blends chronological and functional

- Work experience only goes back fifteen years

- Vocabulary and tone matches industry culture

- Relevant volunteer work/internships on first page

- Use numbers if they are impressive (for example: supervised 60 people, managed ten facilities)

- Dates of education eliminated if they show you to be younger or older than people who are usually hired in the company or industry

- Eliminated hobbies and personal interest section

- Proof-read twice before sending it out

# Cover Letter Formats: Letter Style

In addition to individualizing each resume to match the position requirements, you need to customize each cover letter. Generally cover letters are one page and up to 500 words in length. A common format follows:

---

**Cover Letter Format**

Dear _____ (get name if possible):

**OPENING PARAGRAPH:** State the reason for your letter, including the job title of the position you are seeking. State how you became aware of the position: referral, on-line site, Worksource Oregon, trade magazine, etc. The strongest referral source is a person who is known and respected by the person screening or hiring.

**SECOND PARAGRAPH:** This paragraph summarizes your knowledge and/or prior experience with this organization.

**THIRD/ FOURTH PARAGRAPH:** In one or two paragraphs, reiterate and possibly expand on one or two skills, accomplishments, or characteristics from your resume.

**CLOSING PARAGRAPH:** State how you can be reached. You may want to restate in one sentence what you can do for the organization.

Sincerely

---

Some companies prefer an online application and do not request cover letters. A few concise, targeted comments can be sent in the copy of an e-mail. In order to decide if you need a full cover letter, read the company's directions very carefully and follow them.

**Cover Letter Examples**

Your cover letters to non-profits and mission-driven businesses can include some personal style, beliefs or anecdotes that express your commitment to their mission. Below are two excerpts from cover letters where the applicant uses passion to connect to the purpose of the organization, as well as naming someone from inside:

- Example 1: Russ Parnell alerted me to the position you have open for an Administrative Assistant, and I am very interested in the job. As a longtime conservationist with a passion for rivers, rafting and a knack for organization, I am an excellent match for this position. A significant part of my work history includes exactly the kind of administrative support and experience with environmental issues you're seeking.
- Example 2: I care deeply about protecting open spaces and admire *Trust for Public Land's* tight focus on a practical mission — to put high-quality land in public ownership — and its entrepreneurial style. I'm especially drawn to *TPL's* vision of conserving land for people, from natural ecosystems to urban brownfields.

Show that you meet each job requirement in your resume, and expand on your most competitive points in the cover letter. Unless you have someone on the inside, working to get you an interview with the right person.

We have invited Susan Rich, to share her model and what she calls "kick butt" cover letters that go the extra mile and convey specifically how you will be a benefit to the employer. This approach is particularly well matched to a marketing position and/or a competitive business that will appreciate your drive.

# Cover Letter Formats: Memo Style

In an excerpt from the book, *Write it Rich,* Susan Rich, shares her model of what she calls "kick butt" cover letters that go the extra mile and convey specifically how you will be a benefit to the employer. This approach is particularly well matched to a marketing position and/or a competitive business that will appreciate your drive.

**Why do you need a kick-butt resume cover letter?**
Because today's job search is harder than ever, there are hundreds of applicants for every one job. We all know people who have been unemployed a year or more.

**What's my secret to a kick-butt resume cover letter?**
It's easy – but it takes a new way of thinking – about you, and how your skills and experience benefit a company. It's about showing – using facts, figures, and anecdotes – how you help solve a problem. It's a subtle mind-shift that yields a compelling resume cover letter.

**Here are 3 points I want to make:**
1. A cover letter is a sales letter. It presents the benefits of hiring you. Every sales letter is based on cause and effect: Do this, get that. Your cover letter should take this same approach: Hire me, solve this problem.
2. If a resume is a listing of job facts, your cover letter is the story of how your career is relevant to the position. There are 5 Must-Haves every cover letter should have, as described below. These should express the benefit of hiring you.
3. Excellent written and verbal skills are a common job requirement. Write a standout resume cover letter – and you'll prove you have the written. (You'll demonstrate the oral in the interview.)

**5 Must-Haves for every cover letter**
1. Headline – 8 out of 10 people read a headline…and not one word more. Your headline could be the first (and only) line that gets read. Write a good one and you'll get noticed. Write a great one, and the recruiter will keep on reading.
2. Opening hook – The first two sentences should include your name, and why you kick butt at what you do. Taken together, the headline and opening hook should express the primary benefits of hiring you.
3. Proof – After the first two sentences, the rest of the letter should build the case for talking to you. Include statistics and proof points that show why you are the best candidate for the job.
4. Ask – What do you want the reader to do? Interview you. Hire you. Ask for what you want. Remember, this kind of cover letter is a sales letter. You cannot make the sale unless you ask for what you want. You want a job, a chance to prove yourself. It's why you wrote the letter in the first place.
5. Closing – Summarize your skills and say thank you. End with one final benefit the employer gets from hiring you. Be sure to end the letter on a strong, upbeat note.

Read on for an example of my model of a memo-format. But first, let me explain.

**Memo Style: Speed the Reader Along**
Instead of writing a traditional business letter, I suggest using the memo format. The memo format drives the reader right into the heart of your letter.
Let's begin with the memo-style introduction: To, From, Regarding. This is where your letter shifts from a traditional business letter to a streamlined, sales approach.

**For the TO line:** If you know the name of the hiring manager, by all means, use it. And use it again on the "Dear" line. If you don't know the name of the hiring manager, simply type,

To: Hiring Manager on this line, and don't include a "Dear" line in the letter. Why? If you don't know who you are writing to, there's no point in stating the obvious. Instead, use your headline and first sentence to pull the reader into your letter.

**For the FROM line:** Your name. And here's why: Your name is your brand, therefore you need to state it as often as possible, that's what helps people remember you. In a 500-word letter you have 5 opportunities to use your name, and I suggest you try for all of them: Put your name in the

1. Contact information at the top of the page
2. From line
3. Headline
4. Introduction (my name is)
5. Signature

**For the REGARDING (or RE) line:** Put the job title and number here. This makes it easy for the reader to know which job you're applying for. That's important, because she might be reviewing several job openings. It also means you don't have to mention this detail in the first sentence of the letter, giving you more space to talk about your kick-butt skills.

Rich's fusion cover letter style supports the hiring manager by making it easy for them to see who you are and what you want. They can quickly see the heart of your skills and know what to do next.

# Sample Cover Letters
## Contributed by Susan Rich

To:    James Koenig, Special Projects & Operations Specialist, BEF
From:  Vicki Shane
Re:    Brand Manager Position

**Do you want to increase brand awareness, better serve your existing clients and foster client loyalty through entrepreneurial marketing initiatives?**

Dear James:

My name is Vicki Shane, and from the beginning of my career I have successfully managed client relationships both on a local and national level, all with the goal of enhancing business for stakeholders. My most recent win was with Meritpay (now Hopeful Giving). I created and implemented a collaborative marketing program that yielded a 50% growth in participation.
As your Brand Manager, BEF and its key clients will benefit from my proven experience in:

* **Client management**: 15 years experience with client relationship building, (both current and prospective), account services, and client support and retention within diverse industries.

* **Marketing**: More than 11 years experience with developing, implementing, launching and tracking marketing initiatives. including program creation, brand awareness and stewardship, process improvement, establishment of best practices, print production and comprehensive marketing outreach. Marketing outreach includes print, email, online, tradeshows and events management.

* **Content Creation**: Eight years experience in creating marketing and educational collateral, sales support materials, presentations and copy writing and editing. This also included creation of the greatest lead generating educational piece produced in company history for Meritpay. This is still in use today. I have attached it as one of my writing samples.

I am committed to working with an organization that makes a difference in the world, and I will thrive in a position where collaboration, creativity and out of the box perspectives are highly prized.

James, my diverse background, along with an entrepreneurial spirit and innate problem solving nature, make me an ideal candidate. I look forward to meeting with you in person to share the passion, detail-oriented approach and knowledge that I will bring to Bonneville Environmental Foundation.

*(signed)*

**Attachments:**
* Writing samples

    o *Auction Planner* – an educational piece created for a consultative sales process and lead generation tool

    o *2010 Prospectus* – a sales piece used to outline product offerings for 3 brands, including levels of participation available

* Resume

* References and Salary History/Requirements

May 21, 2012

Appfog
519 SW 3 rd Ave, Suite 801
Portland, OR 97204

Dear Chad Keck,

As soon as I learned of the Support Engineer & Product Specialist position at Appfog through Jeremy Voorhis, I felt excited. I felt excited because I believe I'm a perfect fit for this role. I will contribute my exceptional people skills and technical experience to this position. My ten years in customer service along with my growing experience in webdevelopment would be of great benefit to the Appfog support team.

At Camera World, I provide frontline troubleshooting support for our company photo ordering website. I help people understand photography, photographic equipment and computer applications. In this environment, I have developed the patience and diplomacy it takes to deliver services efficiently and manage customer expectations in high-pressure situations. I work with a broad range of customers with varied technical experience. I take the time to help everyone with the same care and enthusiasm and work with many diverse clients from around the world. I am perpetually learning and teaching new technologies and applications to novice and professional photographers alike.

I have been independently involved in media and animation, giving me a firm grasp of the technologies related to web, photography, video, and illustration. Those skills and experiences have evolved into to an interest in front-end web development. In 2010, I enrolled in the Continuing Education Graphic Design Program at the Pacific Northwest College of Art where I began to learn the basics of web design. I worked with a team of students to develop an open-source Drupal CMS solution intended for use by nonprofit organizations. While continuing to take classes, and utilize my skills in an applied manner, I took a position with the Oregon Museum of Science and Industry as the Web Support Volunteer where I have been helping convert older ColdFusion pages to PHP. My time spent learning HTML, CSS, and PHP has been truly exciting and I would like to continue to grow in these areas with your company.

Not only do I have the technical breadth you are seeking for this position, but I also have the patience and understanding to deliver information in a calm, professional manner. I look forward to speaking with you in the near future.

I may be reached at 503.236.8846 or by email at jasongiglio@gmail.com.

Thank you for your time and consideration.

Sincerely,

Jason Giglio
www.jasongiglio.com

Alison Wiley, xxxx SE xxxxxxx
Portland, OR 97215
axxx@opalcreek.org

To Mercy Corps,

I was delighted to read your current posting for a Development Associate. Please find my resume attached, and let me add a few details here on what I can bring to the Mercy Corps mission.

I have fourteen years combined experience in fundraising, telephone counseling, marketing and telephone-based sales. In the course of this I've been told I'm an excellent listener, quick to establish rapport, and have a warmly professional demeanor. A vice president emphasized how effective and appealing I was on the telephone.

One person I successfully cultivated over years remarked, "You always remember the last thing we talked about!" (Of course, I had documented our chats and then reviewed those notes right before my next contact with her.) I have spent most of my work life giving personalized attention, discerning where interest and passion lie, and taking sensible next steps to make good things happen. I am comfortable in asking people to do things, such as increasing their commitment. I am unalarmed at being told 'no'.

I'm a self-starter who also loves being part of a team. One supervisor told me I was unusually good at receiving feedback from her. Two others told me that coworkers found me an especially positive and encouraging presence. I have high standards for both the results I achieve and the relationship-building process I use to get there.

As a lifelong donor to humanitarian organizations, I am credible and sincere in conversations about giving. My interest in international aid and development is reflected in my husband's and my giving history, which includes Mercy Corps, Women to Women International and microloan programs in Rwanda and South America. I like the respectful way that Mercy Corps treats its donors, and I especially like the way it respects communities in need by working with them on the agendas that they themselves set.

I'll respect your valuable time by keeping this letter brief. I hope to interview with you soon to discuss how I could be of service to your mission.

Sincerely,

Alison Wiley

Daniel Wilson
Trust for Public Land
806 SW Broadway # 300
Portland, OR 97205

Dear Mr. Wilson:

I am excited to submit my application for the position of Project Associate at the Trust for Public Land's Oregon Field Office. For the past seven years, I have broadly explored environmental issues, and gained experience shaping environmental policy in government, journalism, and academic settings. Last year, I gave serious consideration to my career goal for the next ten years and decided to build on my environmental foundation to focus on a career in conservation.

In pursuit of this goal, I recently met with Chuck Sams to learn more about TPL's work. I am also applying my research skills and policy expertise as a volunteer assistant to the government relation's staff at The Nature Conservancy. My specific tasks in supporting the project manager researching sites, engaging property owners and other stakeholders, and preparing maps and informational material – have much in common with the Project Associate's duties at TPL.

I am firmly rooted in Oregon and familiar with its geography, politics, and culture. I care deeply about protecting its open spaces and can think of no organization so aligned with my goals as the Trust for Public Land. I admire TPL's tight focus on a pragmatic mission – to put high quality land in public ownership – and its entrepreneurial style. I'm especially drawn to TPL's vision of conserving land for people, from pristine ecosystems to urban brownfields.

I pursued my interest in making cities more livable as a research analyst at the Office of Sustainable Development (OSD). At OSD, I juggled multiple projects entailing research, project support, and coordination. My principal tasks included devising a blueprint for a policy and research division, through which OSD could influence the city's sustainability agenda by conceiving, independently funding, and partnering with the private sector to carry out demonstration projects. I balanced research and administrative support tasks to move projects forward.

As my resume indicates, I took a detour from my work in sustainability to pursue a doctorate in environmental history. After weighing the rewards of historical research against my desire to make a tangible contribution to the health of the environment, I packed up my research and analytical skills and brought them home to Oregon, with a newly clarified focus and the hopes of finding an entry position in a conservation organization. I'm confident that I've found the right position as Project Associate at TPL.

Sincerely,

Owen Wozniak

# Preparing for the Interview

An interview is an important performance without the option of a second chance. Even if you decide later that you don't want the job, at this juncture you have one goal: to win an offer. Being nervous is natural. The real issue is how to convert your nervous energy into productive action. Fortunately, there is a lot you can do to dramatically improve your performance. Preparation falls into three areas: research, strategy, and practice.

## Research

When you are offered an interview ask how many people will be interviewed, the names and positions of the interviewers, and how long the interview is expected to take. This will give you an idea if this is a screening interview (i.e. six candidates for 30 minutes) or a final interview (i.e., three candidates with the hiring manager for an hour).

The efficiency of the Web makes initial research easy and mandatory. If you don't study the company website before the interview, you send a message that you don't really care much about this job. A company website tells you what the employer wants people to think and feel about the organization. For example, "We are the technological leader in our field." To get another perspective, research the organization online, for example, *The Portland Business Journal* may show you what others have written about them.

If you know the names of the individuals who will be interviewing you, you can also google them and search for a LinkedIn profile. You might find professional articles that the person has written, presentations they have given, and/or if they belong to any LinkedIn groups. In addition to learning about them professionally, you might also get clues to initiate small talk that could create common ground quickly. For example, if you learn that your prospective manager is a judge for cat shows, and you love cats, you can mention your tabby.

Researching prospective employers is yet another place where having a strong network is an asset. You can email your team and ask if anyone knows anyone at the organization. This can give you access to information such as pet peeves or personal style of the supervisor. For example, one of my clients used her network to learn that the IT manager who would supervise her was very bottom-line oriented. Therefore, she was able to practice PAR (problem, action, results) statements that gave examples of her bottom-line outcomes in clear quantitative terms. Refer to **Telling a Story in PAR (Problem, Action, Results) Format.**

## Strategy

After you understand as much as you can about the perceived needs of the employer, determine which of your strengths should be accentuated in the interview. Vicki calls her approach "Three by Two." First, choose three strengths that you want to convey during the interview. These strengths should align closely with what you believe is important to the employer for this position. Then, develop two examples (PAR statements) for each strength.

Plan an approach on how to handle your weaknesses and any questions that you fear. The general rule is to minimize the amount of time spent on your weaknesses in the interview as you answer any questions about them. Model politicians who respond quickly to questions and move back on topic. In your case, your three strengths are "on topic."

Prepare to respond to the common question: "Tell us about your weaknesses." Just choose one. Three approaches that generally will not harm your candidacy are:

- Choose something obvious to the employer. For example, "You note that you prefer someone who speaks Spanish for this position and I do not speak Spanish." Then, you could continue with an example of your sensitivity to Hispanic culture.

- Or, if you feel that you are coming across as shy or introverted in the interview, you might say, "A weakness is that people do not always initially see the vibrancy of my ideas. That is because my interpersonal style is to listen first and then express my ideas after I understand the feelings and ideas of others."
- Choose something that has been a weakness in the past and explain how you have clearly improved. "I used to be shy in front of audiences and avoided public speaking. Last year I took a speech class and gained a lot of confidence. Now I am proud to say that I speak at public meetings several times a month and my presentations get rave reviews."
- Choose something that you honestly believe can be both a strength and a weakness. For example, "I am very serious about deadlines, and as a project manager, I frequently check in on progress. Some individuals have taken this to mean that I do not trust them. I have learned to minimize this reaction by telling all the team members at the start that these check-ins are part of standard procedure. Then they do not take it personally."

We always encourage people to present themselves as completely enthusiastic about a position and initially to bite their tongues about reservations. Reservations can be brought up after being offered a position. You have much more power in your relationship with the employer when they have decided that you are the best person to meet their needs. After they see you as part of the solution to their problems, they will be more motivated to consider possible adaptations to address your reservations. You can request a meeting after you have been offered a position, in which you can frankly address your concerns. Fortunately, the custom is that job offers are not rescinded during the negotiation process, even if there are some points of contention. In sum, in the formal interview they decide *if they want you*; in this second meeting you make a final decision *if you want them.*

**Practice**
Practice! Practice! Practice! This is the key to the successful interview. Identify the most important skills and character traits you have to offer that match each of the employer's needs. Identify the points that you want to get across in the interview, irrespective of the specific questions asked.

Practicing in front of people will convert a good strategy into a strong performance: a strong presentation of your strengths. Every job seeker who has rehearsed with Vicki, either in an individual session or in a small-group interview clinic, has visibly grown in competence and confidence. One participant who competed well for a marketing communication position at Tri-met said, "Because I was well prepared, I could relax. This allowed me to use humor to warm the relationship with the interviewers." She won the offer!

# Common Interview Questions

Current behavioral questions are in vogue, which means that questions often begin with "Tell me about a time" or "give me an example." Practice answering the following common questions:

- Why are you interested in this position?
- Where do you expect to be in three years?
- Describe a time that you were part of a team and your role as a team member.
- Describe a conflict you had on a job and how you resolved it.
- What have been your most important accomplishments?
- What are your strengths? Give an example of your strengths in action.
- What are your weaknesses?
- Give us an example of a time when you faced a difficult challenge?
- Why should we hire you?

**Questions You Ask the Employer**

At the end of most interviews you will be asked, "Do you have any questions that you would like to ask us?" You should prepare a list of five to ten questions in advance. You usually won't ask more than three or four, but because several of your questions may be covered during the course of the interview, you don't want to run out.

There are three interrelated goals that you want to meet when you ask your questions. First, you genuinely want to learn more about the organization and the position. That will help you decide if you want to accept an offer if one is extended. Second, you want to ask intelligent questions that show that you have done your research into the position and/or organization. Third, you want to demonstrate your outstanding listening skills.

It is human nature for people to bond with those who listen and express interest in their ideas and concerns. This ability to listen can be demonstrated verbally and non-verbally through body posture and facial expressions. The technique of *reflective* or *active listening* can be quite effective in building rapport. The listener reflects back key elements of the feeling and content of the interviewer's message. Examples that might be appropriate in an interview situation include:

- You sound concerned about the stresses caused by an outdated computer system. I'm interested in hearing more about this.
- Am I hearing you correctly that one of your biggest concerns is the reduction in the number of donors due to the downturn of the economy?

The following questions demonstrate your desire to understand the concerns and perspective of the people who are selecting a new employee:

- How do you see the organization changing over the next few years? I've had a chance to review the strategic plan on your website. Do you see it as realistic and on track?
- What are the goals of this department and how would the open position make a contribution?
- What would the top priority be for me to accomplish in the first six months if I am selected for this position?
- I read that you have been very successful at _____? What do you think accounts for this success?
- I read that New Seasons has been opening new stores at a rapid pace. What do you think accounts for this success in a down economy?
- I know that Marylhurst is a leader in providing access for adults returning to school, including the use of computer-based distance learning. What accounts for your leadership in this arena?
- I've heard that Ecotrust is running workshops for conventional companies that install heating units. How have they responded to your workshops?

# Telling a Story in PAR (Problem, Action, Results) Format

The purpose of telling a story during the interview is to illustrate your skills and accomplishments with a vivid example. An effective story begins by quickly identifying the **problem** (P) you faced in your professional activities. It then tells of the **action** (A) you took to resolve the problem. It concludes with the **results** (R) you achieved for the organization.

## First, review your accomplishments

To identify possible accomplishments to use as a basis for a PAR story, consider these questions. Are you proud to have:

- Developed something (A product? A procedure? A news release? A video?)
- Reduced costs or improved efficiency?
- Improved morale and teamwork?
- Surpassed an accepted standard for quality or quantity of performance?
- Gained new customers? Retained old customers?
- Improved operations to increase productivity or reduce stress?
- Received informal recognition or formal awards?

## Problem (P)

State the problem or situation *before* you talk about the action(s) you took to improve the situation. Your research of each potential employer will help you identify the types of problems that this company faces that are similar to problems you have addressed in the past. You may start explaining the problem in ways similar to the descriptions below.

- There was a lot of inter-departmental conflict and disorganization in the areas of _____.
- Most of the youth served by the NE Council for Drug and Alcohol were African American while only one of the 15 counselors was African American.
- The number of donors was ___ percent lower than anticipated.
- Expenses were too high, running ___ percent over budget.
- People in the community were not aware of the availability of curbside recycling.
- Clients regularly complained about _____.
- Deadlines were missed on _____.

## Actions (A)

Describe what you did individually and/or your role in actions taken by a team. Begin with action verbs such as improved, initiated, resolved, created, facilitated, sold, or wrote. Give enough details of what you said and did so your interviewer can "see" you in action. You may also comment on why you took this particular action. Actions often illustrate the skills identified on the resume. You can start describing your actions in the following ways:

- I interviewed members to create a survey to measure customer satisfaction.
- I initiated a call campaign of past members.
- I created a spreadsheet to compare costs and services of different promotional activities.
- I led a retreat where we revisited and recommitted to our vision and mission.
- I advertised in the *Scanner* and used my connections in NE Portland churches to recruit new African American counselors.
- I spearheaded a campaign that included a multi-media, multi-lingual outreach using direct mail, speeches and advertising.

**Results (R)**

Results are the positive outcomes directly resulting from your actions. They provide an *after* picture to contrast to the *before* picture presented in the problem. Private companies and many nonprofits are driven by the bottom line, so results are often impressive if you increased profits or decreased cost. You may have had an indirect impact on profits or costs by increasing efficiency, attracting more customers, reducing customer attrition, or introducing new services or programs.

Some positions lend themselves to measurable results or an estimation of measurable results. Your results can include one or several positive outcomes like the examples below:

- By calling inactive members, I increased membership by 22 percent.
- By running an effective campaign, I helped elect Green Party Candidate Sharon Ball.
- By training new employees more effectively, the number of complaints was reduced by twenty percent.
- The retreat increased morale so that only one staff member left during the year, compared to four during the previous year.
- We added three new African American counselors to the staff.

Nonprofits, government, and education are often impressed with results related to the organization's mission, standards, or performance. Examples:

- As a result of introducing a new program, the reading scores of students in my third-grade class surpassed those of other third-grade students in the district.
- Because my weekly meetings improved morale so significantly, my supervisor rated me as "exceeds expectations" on all aspects of my communication skills, including my ability to resolve conflict.
- Because of my outreach efforts, we doubled the Hispanic community's involvement in parks and recreation programs.

**Putting the Parts Together**

You can draft your PARS by putting the three parts together and then adding the detail. See the following examples of putting the three parts together.

- Most of the youth served by the NE Council for Drug and Alcohol were African American, while only one of the 15 counselors was African American (P). I advertised in the *Scanner* and used my connections in NE Portland churches (A) to recruit three new African American counselors (R).
- The Montana Arts Council had poor communication with its donors, its customers, and the public (P). I created an electronic newsletter and permission-based email system (A). As a result, the number of donors increased by 22 percent (R).
- The City of San Jose hired my company, Peynet Public Relations, to persuade residents to participate in an expanded curbside recycling program (P). I created a comprehensive multi-media, multi-lingual outreach campaign using direct mail, publicity, a speaker's bureau, school assemblies, and advertising (A). The recycling volume tripled, exceeding the goal of doubling (R).

# Interviewing for the "Older" Candidate

Thank goodness, if you are "older," you have had years to get wily and clever so that you can address every one of the subconscious concerns of a younger manager without the topic of age ever crossing a lip.

If your research indicates that you will be supervised by a Generation X or Generation Y person, carry out a cross-cultural study prior to the interview. What do they wear? What vocabulary do they use? What do they read? Or better yet, what TV shows do they watch? With this preparation, you won't be as likely to use a word that fossilizes you. For example, if someone in the interview mentions a BlackBerry don't mention how much you love picking them in the summer! Or, you can ascribe a good joke you learned from "Mork and Mindy" to the tall guy whose hair stood on end in "Seinfeld." And if you forget his name, don't cover up with a reference to having a "senior moment."

A second way to attack covert age prejudice is to tell stories with cleverly embedded messages. Example: the interviewer asks, "Can you give me an example of a challenge you faced?"

Your response: "I was leading a team of writers and graphic designers on the creation of a newsletter to raise funds for the library. I had sent the plans to my manager and she had signed off. However, on Friday, when the team was well underway, she returned from a national conference with the news that the best donors are now in the 35-to-45-year-old set rather than their blue-haired grandparents. I worked over the weekend and on Monday morning presented my manager with three new edgy looks, one I adapted from the logo on "Sex in the City." She was delighted and had plenty of time to pick up her child from Montessori right on time."

(Note: make the boss the same gender as your prospective boss or, if that is not possible, make the boss kind of unisex).

In two minutes, you have landed darts into two puffed-up legends: the IPBPO (Iron-Poor Blood Poop-Out) legend and the ODNTA (Old Dog, New Trick Aversion) legend. You have also demonstrated that you are respectful to your younger "superiors."

You will seem more "out of date" if you are not current on the technology they use. For example, if you're a whiz on Lotus 1-2-3 or Quark, don't mention it. Get current, and let your future employer know that you are competent with the technical skills required. One older interviewee was asked about her background with technology. When she began by saying, "When I started, back when there were punch cards," she was inadvertently labeling herself as a dinosaur.

My final advice for your interview is to present yourself as smart, but not smarter than the interviewer. You can achieve this by communicating as if you come from the Midwest. It has been proven that Midwesterners leave a longer polite pause after someone stops speaking, nearly twice as long as the New Yorker's speeding-bullet response. The Midwestern approach gives the speaker the impression that you are terribly interested in their pearls of wisdom and are pausing to see if they wish to tell you more. As a finale, when the interviewer asks you a closing question like "Do you have any questions for us, Gertrude?" this is an invitation to build mutual feelings of ease across the generational divide. You can say: "Justin, I was impressed with your analysis of the budget. Can you tell me more about your thinking so I can know how I can help you reach your goal?"

If all of this contorting and posturing is just too painful, you may decide "What the heck! They either want the real me or they don't." This can be a risky approach unless you have a sure source of income on the near horizon.

# Interviewing for the "Overqualified" Candidate

The challenges of the "over-aged" job seeker and the "overqualified" job seeker are very similar. Even the younger "overqualified" candidate can present somewhat of a threat to the manager. As with the "older" candidate, a hiring manager may harbor the unexpressed prejudice that the candidate will:

- Get bored and leave soon.
- Criticize the way things are done based on their greater expertise.
- Be resistant to supervision.
- Still be looking for a better-paying position and leave soon.
- Steal some of the accolades that the hiring manager covets.
- Expect more raises and perks.

Once again, the management concludes that it is better for the company, in the long run, to hire someone of more modest capabilities. Vicki confesses that she was once a young manager with a wobbly ego. The finalists for the Assistant Director position were Clare, a very tall, poised, and exacting professional from Chicago, or Heidi, a petite, quiet woman from Burns, Oregon. She decided on Heidi, even though her expertise was more modest and she had misspelled "liaison" in her cover letter. She had the typical worries about hiring Clare. She later regretted the cost of her insecurity since she had to work harder and do more damage control than if she had had the confidence to hire someone with more expertise than her.

**Tips for the Overqualified Candidate**
Fears about longevity, boredom, and a possible reversal of roles between the supervisor and employee are at the heart of discrimination for both the "over-aged" and "overqualified." You can use some of the same tactics as the older candidate. The recommendations and examples above will help you present yourself as responsive to supervision and smart, yet not threatening.

It is particularly important to offset the fear that you will be a short-timer. Because there is no law against it, the interviewer may even ask you a direct question about the job's ability to satisfy you for long. You may be asked, "Why would you want this position, given that the compensation and challenges are lower than your previous positions?" There are several answers that are wrong, although they may be true: e.g., "I need a root canal done and this company has great dental benefits." Or, "It is a great stepping stone. I figure that once I am inside as a proofreader you will see my brilliance, and I will become the marketing director next year."

Better responses include:
- I have been reflecting for the last year on what is most important to me in my career. I have decided that the top two criteria are working with a team and helping the environment. Although my old position had some positive aspects, this one meets my criteria much, much better.
- I am concerned about the direction of the country. I want to commit myself to an organization and position that shares my passion for social justice.

# What Should I Wear?

Author Alison Lurie says, "Clothes never stop talking." There is a clear message that you want your clothes to convey in an interview. Whether you wear jeans or a tailored suit, the message needs to be "I fit in. I am from your clan." When Vicki worked for a creative staffing agency where they placed people in edgy ad agencies, a man came in for an interview wearing a navy three-piece suit. They sent him to a bank instead.

It is helpful to take the perspective of the people hiring you. It does not mean that they are superficial if how you're dressed matters to them. They are trying to figure out from this brief encounter if you will be a good fit for their team. People are probably hard-wired to feel more comfortable with people who look and act like them. They intuit, rightly or wrongly, that values and work style will also be compatible.

Let me give you a story of how clothes can misspeak. Vicki had a client who came from a fine old Portland family. She dressed attractively in clothing from shops like Norm Thompson, wore tasteful gold jewelry, and had well-manicured red fingernails. She went to an interview for a fund-raising position for which she was very well qualified. She dressed in a style similar to the donors whom she would be approaching as part of her job. When she arrived at the interview, she noted that the three interviewers had silver ethnic jewelry and looked as if their clothes were a mix from REI and Goodwill. The cool reception that she got, including the subsequent rejection, conveyed, "We do not see you as fitting in with our culture."

The general rule of thumb is to dress slightly more professionally than the person/people interviewing you. To dress one level up, you first need to find out what people generally wear in the work setting, you may need to visit their site or use your network. One client noted that employees on the company's website were in shirts without ties and used this clue to dress accordingly.
For men, there is a pyramid of workplace attire, from jeans to suits.
- If he will be wearing jeans, you can safely wear Dockers and a dress shirt without a tie.
- If he will be wearing Dockers and a dress shirt without a tie, you can wear Dockers with a collared shirt and a jacket.
- If he will be wearing dress slacks with a button up shirt and a jacket without a tie, you can wear the same with a tie.
- If he is wearing a button up shirt, slacks, a jacket, and a tie, it is a pretty conventional business environment, and you can wear a suit with a button up shirt and a conservative tie. If the one suit that you have is pretty old, browse through Men's Wearhouse to see if your lapels, pants length, etc. are totally passé or retro, i.e. back in mode again.

Women have more choices of clothing combinations: i.e., those that men have as well as skirts and dresses. This makes it more difficult to create a parallel pyramid with specifics for women, but the same principle applies. There is no clear rule regarding pants, and pant-suits (a la Hillary) are generally fine. In Portland, you are generally safe with a neat skirt, blouse, and jacket.

The most important guideline is to look like you fit in the organization. Peruse the photographs on LinkedIn, particularly the managers, to find out the company's level of formality or informality. Sometimes it's even fun to drop by the organization to get a feel for the people and their culture. In creative environments, people often have fun with their clothing and may even sport a tattoo or two.

# Interview "Thank You" Letter

Thank you letters should be sent within a few days after the interview. They can be sent either by email or letter/art card. The decision should be based on the culture of the organization. A nature shot would be perfect for an interview with the Sierra Club, but not for an edgy technology start up. Reiterate your enthusiasm for the position, referring to specific comments that intrigued you. If you feel that you have not fully answered a question during the interview, you can provide some follow up information along with your thank you.

Below is an excellent example of a "thank you" letter for an interview that Alison Wiley had had with ODOT for the State of Oregon. In effect, the letter continues the professional conversation and stresses what she can bring to the table if she is selected for the position—which she was! It would be unusual to receive the kind of personal response she received, but this example gives you an idea of how such a well-done thank you letter can impress the desired employer.

Michael,

I really appreciated meeting with you and the rest of the interview panel yesterday.

Later in the afternoon I was at a reception for Focus the Nation, where I renewed my acquaintanceship with two dynamic state legislators, Greg Macpherson and Ben Cannon. In these chats I drew on what you had told me about Governor Kulongoski's desire to make transportation a prime focus in the 2009 legislature.

I learned that Greg is running for attorney general, and that if he wins that position he will be able to form proposals that go to the legislature as well as have a strong hand in implementing legislation that gets passed. He seems to hold a good value for transportation options.

If I get the opportunity to work with you, I would be sure to cultivate relationships like these in order to advance our department's transportation agendas.

Thank you again for yesterday's interview and for considering me for the position of Transportation Options Program Manager.

Sincerely,

Alison Wiley

Hi Alison,

Thanks for the kind words. It was my pleasure to answer your questions and provide guidance. In reality, I would have done the same for anyone that took the initiative to ask me for my input. You, however, were the only applicant to do so...and it really showed in the interviews yesterday.

I'm not at liberty to divulge anything more, as you can understand. But it was a pleasure to have had a hand in interviewing you for an important position and I wish you all the best!

Have a great weekend,
Dan

# References

Unless you are specifically requested to do so, don't include the names and contact information of references along with your resume. It can be to your advantage to wait until the potential employer asks for your references because after you know that you are getting an interview you can prep your references in a tactful way. Let's assume that most of your references feel good about you and want to assist you in reaching your career goals. If they know that you are applying to positions in general, their comments are likely to be quite general. They may focus on your great sense of aesthetics when the employer is deciding based on your technical competencies. In contrast, if the reference is aware of a specific job for which you are applying, their comments can be much more targeted to the major strengths you have identified on your resume and in your interview. For example, you may have stressed your teamwork and ability to take initiative. Such claims are naturally seen as much more credible if they are also mentioned by your references.

How can you influence your references to say what you want them to without being too directive? First, let them know in advance some of the specifics of the job and the organization and why you are enthusiastic about the position. Second, you can tactfully remind them of some of the pertinent projects that you did when you were working with them. In most cases, they will be happy to have some assistance so that they may be better prepared.

Here is a paraphrase of the conversation Vicki had with Janet Gifford when she applied for a position as a part-time coordinator of the Career Resource Center at Portland Community College.

Vicki: Hi, Janet. Will you please be one of my references for the position as a coordinator in the Career Resource Center at PCC?

Janet: I'd be glad to.

Vicki: I appreciate that. I have specifically asked you for a few reasons; first, because you reviewed my evaluations when I taught Career and Life Planning for Linfield College: and second, because this job is going to emphasize working with students of all ages and ethnic groups. I remember when we worked together to help XXX, the African-American student with a history of uneven academic success.

Janet: Oh yes, I remember seeing XXX and his father beaming when he finally made it to commencement after so many years. And you were so patient with him.

Vicki: I do miss working directly with a more diverse group of students. My private practice is wonderful, but I would like to complement it by working in a team environment. I would also get to teach career and planning skills similar to those that you hired me to teach at Linfield.

Janet: When do you expect I might receive a call?

Vicki: Within the next few days. Oh, and would you mind calling me if/when they call you? I am so enthusiastic about this—I want to know right away if they are moving forward with my candidacy.

Janet: Will do. Good luck!

# Bad or "Iffy" References

If you have been fired or asked to resign from your last job in the field, you will naturally have concerns about what your reference will say. First, we want you to know that you are in fabulous company. In our career practices we meet many wonderful, competent, and vital people who have been fired. John Fischer, a successful career changer, shared with Vicki a wonderful quote that he had heard during his rocky transition out of the ministry: "I wouldn't trust a person who hadn't been fired at least once in his or her life!" Vicki belongs to this club herself. And we both know wonderful people who had clashes on the job. So we speak from the heart on this topic as we offer you both strategies and optimism.

First, try to learn what your references will and will not say about you. It is particularly important to know how they will respond to the questions: "Why did he or she leave the position?" and/or "Would you rehire this person?" Our hunch is that these questions are only asked 30 percent of the time, but you don't want to lose sleep wondering if these responses could destroy your candidacy. Many large employers only verify dates of employment and will not comment on performance; you may be able to call their HR department and ask them their policy on references.

When Vicki was on the way to being released from a mental health crisis line where she was employed a few years ago, she took a direct approach. First, she asked the V.P. of HR their policy on references. She was pleased to know that she was given the option of permitting only a verification of employment. Alternately, she could approve responses to traditional reference questions on the quality of her work. Of course, she only wanted to opt for the latter if the comments would be affirming. Vicki posed a hypothetical question, "If I applied for a position that did not call for detailed and accurate record-keeping (my weakness), would you be able to convey primarily positive accounts of my skills and performance?" The response appeared to be genuinely positive. They were happy that Vicki was not leaving the position expressing hostility, and she was happy that the reference would not be damaging.

If your parting relationship was hostile, you may not want to take the direct approach. Another option (the sneaky one) is to ask someone you know and trust to pose as an employer and call the reference.

If you do not feel reasonably confident in the quality of the reference, take great effort to circumvent a conversation between this individual and your potential employer. This is most problematic if the damaging reference is your most recent supervisor. The absence of this individual may raise a red flag for your future employer. Clients have successfully used one or more of the following strategies to address this challenge:

- Told the prospective employer (truthfully) that the employer policy is not to release qualitative references so you have substituted the name of someone who is allowed to comment on your performance.
- Secured a short-term contract job in the field from a supportive colleague so that the most recent reference would be from a different individual.
- Used a supportive member of the board in place of the supervisor.
- Explained to the prospective employer the nature of the conflict and gave the names of three other people in the organization so that they can get a fuller perspective.
- Directed the prospective employer to a large pool of positive references on LinkedIn.

These actions may be quite emotionally demanding because they are prone to re-ignite the anger, sadness, and/or disappointment that you feel around the unhappy ending. Activate your self-care tools, from talks with supportive friends to massage therapy, when you need to make contact.

# Post-Assessment Job Search Plan Checklist:
## Finding the Job

Post-Assessment Date_____

❏ **Target your resume(s) to your career objective(s).**

❏ **Identify and review Internet job sites most likely to post appropriate job openings.**

❏ **Bookmark and periodically review Websites for desirable employers.**

1._____   6._____

2._____   7._____

3._____   8._____

4._____   9._____

5._____   10._____

❏ **Analyze job postings for required/desired technical skills; build *one or two* of these.**

_____   _____

❏ **Re-contact (phone/email/mail) people in your network who are most likely to hear about job openings.**

_____   _____

_____   _____

_____   _____

❏ **Carry out strategic volunteering or an internship to build the skills and/or contacts that fit your career objective(s).**

❏ **Become active in professional organizations/groups that can provide job leads that match your career objective(s).**

_____

❏ **Develop an interview strategy and practice PAR (problem, action, results) stories.**

❏ **Customize your cover letter and resume for each position to which you apply.**

❏ **Research the organization prior to each interview.**

# Gifts to Give Yourself Before Starting Your New Job

Soon you are going to have a new and fresh set of challenges, those that come with any vital job. So, take some time to enjoy some of the following before you begin:

- Take a new path in Forest Park
- Bake bread
- Ask yourself a Question; listen quietly
- Smell a flower
- Walk or take the bus and be glad
- Encourage a young person
- Finish up a project
- Take a different road home
- Exercise your creativity
- Disengage from your doubts of your creative limits
- Pick up litter in your neighborhood
- Let someone do you a favor
- Have a good cry
- Listen to the dawn
- Allow yourself yet another mistake
- Go for a swim
- Don't do something—just sit there
- Drop a quarter where someone will find it
- Champion a cause
- Forget an old grudge
- Try a new food
- Frame a beloved picture
- Help a struggling career changer
- Say "yes"
- Say "thanks" to all who helped you on your journey
- _____
- _____
- _____

*Making a difference is not an accident or casual occurrence
of the times. People choose to make a difference.*
— Maya Angelou

# Accepting the Job
## phase IV

# Phase IV: Accepting the Job

The final stage, **Accepting the Job**, involves two distinct sequential activities: **Negotiating** and **Accepting the Position**. The most difficult part for most Creatives and people who want to make a difference is negotiating for the optimal salary and other work conditions. The negotiating process is a particularly strange one for idealists who are excited about working collaboratively towards a shared vision with the new employer. In reality, during this brief phase you and your employer have different priorities and roles. Yours is to advocate for your own financial and professional needs; your employer's is to advocate for budget constraints in the organization.

Another reason that you may find this process uncomfortable is your commitment to honest and open communication, and conversely, your aversion to the game-like aspects of negotiating. For example, the first time a prospective employer says, "The most we can offer is $42,000," probably means "We *hope* that you will accept the offer of $42,000." You can't actually know if this is literally true unless you request $45,000 and they counter with $43,500.

When you are offered a position you may be very happy, even very hungry. Being invited into an organization you like may be so welcome and so overdue that you respond prematurely with a single-syllable answer: YES.

We advise you to breathe for a moment to consider negotiating the best possible compensation and conditions for your employment. You can convey great enthusiasm about being offered the position and ask for a follow-up meeting to discuss details before finalizing. We've never heard of an offer being rescinded when a client requests such a conversation to negotiate some aspects of the job. One reason that a woman's salary can lag behind a male counterpart's is her hesitancy to negotiate, which can lead to disparate starting salaries.

The employer has now decided that you are the best person for the position, and it is your turn to decide if the position, from terms of employment to compensation, will work for you. At this juncture, you have much more power to impact your future employment than you will have after you are an employee: i.e., formal policies are more uniformly applied to employees than to candidates.

Once the terms of employment have been offered and finalized, you will usually be happy to **Accept the Position**. However, this is also your last opportunity to say "No." Usually, you will have decided to back out at an earlier time if the job does not meet your needs. However, if you find that you have increasing nightmares or migraines, you do have one final option. You should return to your self-assessment to see if this position really does meet most of your criteria.

Can you find peace regarding what you were seeking in an employer and the realities of this specific offer? Bev, for example, wanted a job that a) did not hurt her ailing knees; b) was accessible by public transportation; c) was in a positive team environment; d) was in higher education; and e) was not full-time so she could continue to do her artwork. The position she was offered at the Portland State University Foundation met all of her criteria with the exception of being full-time. She had to do some soul-searching about how she could keep her life as an artist alive. With a mixture of happiness and sadness, she said "Yes" to the position and postponed some of her creative needs. Similarly, you need to make peace with your compromises so you can enter the position with a heart ready to greet the fresh challenges of the new job.

If you are unsure about accepting a position, review your initial **Self-Assessment Profile** to see how well the position matches your interests, values, skills, and what you wanted from the employer. With the help of several clients, Vicki developed a formula of six criteria that all start with the letter "P" (Purpose, Pay, Place, People, Pleasure, and Positioning), and it is outlined on the next page.

# Mind Your "P"s
## Is this job right for you?

**Put a check mark in front of all conditions that apply:**

\_\_\_\_ **Purpose**. The *purpose* of the organization matches your values.

\_\_\_\_ **Pay**. The *pay* and benefits are good or very good.

\_\_\_\_ **Place**. The drive time and quality of the location make it a good *place*.

\_\_\_\_ **People**. You like the *people* you will work with.

\_\_\_\_ **Positioning**. You will gain the experience, skills, and/or meet the people to *position* yourself to compete for your ideal job.

\_\_\_\_ **Pleasure**. You expect to experience *pleasure* in your daily activities.

_____**Total # of check marks**

Warning: A score of 3 or less may lead to short-term employment or long-term stress.

# How to Negotiate

In all stages of negotiation, you should be positive, assertive, and support your request with factual research. Here's how it works:

**Job Expectations:** During the interview, you may have wisely refrained from bringing up some of your concerns for fear that you might appear unenthusiastic or uncertain about your abilities. After an offer is extended, you can be more frank about your concerns and ask for greater clarity to implied agreements. For example, you might want to convey your confidence about three of the four desirable technical competencies but will need additional training on the fourth. You want to arrive at an understanding about expectations that leaves you feeling honest and poised for success.

**Salary:** A salary or salary range may have been posted with the initial job description. At the point that you are invited to an interview, you should begin research so that you know your market worth. (See the **Salary Research** and **Salary Survey** sections.) If the offer made is lower than your expectations, you can make a counter-offer backed up with your research. For example, one of Vicki's clients was offered a position in an environmental organization doing grant writing. Her research led her to believe $39,000 was a fair annual salary. She was keenly disappointed when the employer offered $32,000. The employer gave the rationale that another employee who had been working for two years in another job would be resentful if this client received a higher salary.

Following Vicki's guidance, the job candidate's response was to ask for a day to review the offer. She reviewed her research data and called the next day and told the prospective employer: "Based on my four years of experience in the field, my Master degree, and the expectation that I will raise considerable funds, the salary offer is low." She then provided data demonstrating that the offer was at the lowest end of expectations for someone with her job title. She asserted that the other employee did not have all of these qualifications. She told her prospective employer that her research showed she was worth $39,000 to the organization and referenced the source. Then came the hardest part—she had to hold her breath for another two long days when, at last, she was offered $37,000 and funds to attend a desirable national conference. She concluded, "It's too bad that it's a game, but in the end it was worth it. Now, I can go to my first day with genuine enthusiasm."

**Terms of Employment:** A myriad of items can fall under this umbrella. Many clients have been successful in negotiating the following requests before accepting a position. Of course, it wouldn't be wise to ask for more than a few.
- I have a prearranged vacation planned in October, which is six months before I would normally be eligible. The tickets are not refundable. May I go?
- To effectively meet your expectations, I would need three new computers in the office. Would that be possible?
- I need to arrive at 8:30 in the morning rather than 8:00 to take my daughter to daycare. Can that be arranged?
- Can I have a performance review in six months and a raise if I meet your expectations?
- Can I attend the national conference like my counterparts at _____?

The negotiation process normally lasts from a day to a week, although psychologically it may seem much longer. Your job during this period is to stay in balance using time-honored stress reduction techniques: remembering to breathe, dispelling nervous energy with friends, taking walks, etc.

# Salary Research

Strengthen your ability to negotiate by comparing the position you are being offered with that usually paid for a similar position. Begin by reviewing one of the big salary Websites such as Salary.com or Jobstar.org along with one or two more specialized sites. It is essential to quote the source of the data to your prospective employer. Many professional associations also sponsor salary scales pertinent to jobs in their field.

*"I LOVED www.salary.com. So helpful, and such quality, intuitive presentation. Definitely a thumbs up. I like how the site presents things very pictorially, and graphically. The site is definitely visually engaging and accommodating. I like how you can select different jobs that have overlap, you can then compare them side by side, and I like how when you go into salary, you can view some graphs, to provide you with data, and they have the different tabs you can look at that inform you of other useful information, such as 'similar jobs,' 'statistics,' and 'job openings.'"*
–Laura Huston

Another strategy is to research similar jobs that are currently posted. You can go into a large national job site such as www.Monster.com or www.Indeed.com. If you cannot find a similar job listed locally, you can do a national search. Often when you locate a similar job in another part of the country you'll need to adjust for regional differences in salaries. Also, nonprofit salaries tend to run about 25 percent to 33 percent lower than their counterparts in the private arena.

If you cannot find the exact same job title, search for similar or related job titles. For instance, a communications coordinator may be the equivalent of a coordinator of public relations. A vocational counselor is similar to a job developer; a graphic designer is similar to a commercial graphic designer; and a buyer is the equivalent of a procurement specialist. You can also approach your search by scanning the salaries of positions within particular categories like development, human resources, or counseling.

This is also a time to call on your trusted network in the field to ask their opinions. If you are hesitant about revealing the exact figure of the offer, you may want to use a range. For example: "Hi Claudia. I am so appreciative of all of your help in my job search, and I am now finally in the home stretch and have been offered a position as an environmental educator for Audubon. My research has indicated that the position ought to pay within the range of _____ and the offer is lower. What is your sense of a fair salary?"

This is also a time to be bolstered by friends and family who really believe in you, your capabilities, and the financial worth of your professional contribution. They will tell you, "Honey, you are clearly a $75,000 woman and any less would be a bald injustice."

# Salary Surveys

**America's Career InfoNet** (www.acinet.org/). Wage and occupational outlook information for your selected state and occupation.

**Business 2.0** (www.business2.com). Online and magazine subscription service that gives you the latest intelligence on business, technology, innovation, and more.

**Compensation and Benefits Reports** (http://salary-surveys.erieri.com). From Abbott, Langer & Associates. Helpful to download the demo version of Findpay.

**Data Masters Computer Industry Salary Survey** (2000) (www.datamasters.com/).

**Employment Cost Trends** (www.bls.gov/ncs/ect/ectfaq.htm). From the Bureau of Labor Statistics.

**Human Resource Management Compensation Survey** (2002). By SHRM and William M. Mercer, Inc. (www.shrm.org/). Many reports are available for purchase.

**JDA Professional Services. Inc.** (www.jdapsi.com/). Informational Technology Salary Data.

**JobStar Salary Guides** (www.jobstar.org/tools/salary/index.cfm). Service of California's Bay Area Public Libraries. Includes links to more than120 salary studies. Information on this site most helpful and more accessible than many of the others.

**Martin Fletcher** (www.martinfletcher.com/). Health care salary data.

**MIS Compensation Study Summary** (www.psrinc.com/salary.htm). From PSR Consultants.

**National Compensation Survey** (www.bls.gov/ncs/home.htm). US Bureau of Labor Statistics National Compensation Survey.

**Occupational Outlook Handbook** (www.bls.gov/emp/home.htm). From the Bureau of Labor Statistics.

**Payscale** (www.payscale.com/). Contains summary salary and compensation reports, international survey data and a helpful salary tool that takes about five minutes to complete.

**Riley Guide** (www.rileyguide.com/). Salary Guides & Guidance.

**River Network Salary Survey** (http://www.rivernetwork.org/forms/2011-salary-survey) A 2011 salary survey of jobs in conservation and sustainability.

**Economic Research Institute** (http://www.erieri.com/). On-line U.S., Canada and international wage and salary plus cost-of-living information.

**Salary Expert** (www.salaryexpert.com/). A source for accurate compensation information.

**Salary.com** (www.salary.com/) Salary Wizard feature computes salaries by occupation and location.

# Conclusion: Saying Yes

After reading and working through this handbook, we assume you are much clearer about your goal and have a strategy to reach it. However, you may not yet have found your "job worth having." There is no normal timetable. The career changers you met in the **Introduction** and throughout this handbook took between a few months and a few years to find a job worth having. We can all take heart from their successes:

**Susan Gilson** got out from behind the desk where she used to wrangle with budget and policy decisions. She is fulfilling her need to spend time with seniors whom she helps in her position as **Director** of **Loaves and Fishes Senior Center** downtown.

**Alison Wiley** found a job that matched her vision to help reduce carbon emissions. She landed the position as **Transportation Options Manager** for the **Oregon Department of Transportation (ODOT).**

**Owen Wozniak,** now **Project Manager** at the **Trust for Public Land's Oregon State Office,** gets to do his part to protect the green spaces he loves. He reports that he loves his job, but it was "hard to give up lots of free time in the wilderness, riding bikes, and hanging in coffee shops."

**Cyd Cannizzaro** got to "talk trash" all day when she accepted her dream job as **Recycling Specialist** with the **City of Beaverton**'s *Recycle at Work* program.

**Jennifer Bloeser** is now **Marine Planning Business Manager** for **EcoTrust**.

**Salvador Del Cid** got more weekends at home and more job satisfaction in his new career as the **Sustainability/Communications Events and Outreach Assistant** at **Metro.**

**Laura Belson** converted her volunteer work at the **Metropolitan Alliance for Common Good** into a half-time paid position.

**Lynn Welch** now has more stability as a **Senior Copywriter** at **The Standard.**

**Carla Ingrando** was offered the position as **Program Officer** at **Michigan Humanities Council** out of a field of over two hundred applicants.

**Nancy Kramer** is thriving in her position as **Executive Assistant** for the **Oregon Advocacy Commission** where she can delight in initiating and developing systems that run effectively and efficiently in an organization committed to respecting diversity.

**Kristine Mugot**'s volunteer work with NAMI, helping others with family members who are mentally ill, impressed the hiring manager at **Simplefill**. In her first serious job out of college, Kristine feels that her job at Simplefill is meaningful because it helps low income people gain access to medications.

# Appendix A—Resources for Cultural Creatives

## Books for Creatives

**Boldt, Laurence.** *Zen and the Art of Making a Living: A Practical Guide to Creative Career Design*. New York: Penguin, 1998. This 600-page resource guide for creative career changers integrates it all: from information about Zen and mythic archetypes to conventional materials for writing a resume. Boldt's premise is that everyone is an artist in his or her own life. The book contains thought-provoking exercises to help the reflective person discover work that will be deeply satisfying. The margins are full of designs and quotes from Zen masters, Joseph Campbell, William Blake and other spiritual, creative spirits.

**Eikleberry, Carol.** *The Career Guide for Creative and Unconventional People, 3rd Edition*. Ten Speed Press: Berkeley, CA: 2007. Eikleberry offers a realistic and novel approach to the unconventional person seeking career satisfaction. She lists more than 240 creative and unconventional job titles, most for social and creatives, including entrepreneurial options.

**Lloyd, Carol.** *Creating a Life Worth Living: A Practical Course in Career Design for Artists, Innovators, and Others Aspiring to a Creative Life*. New York: Harper Collins, 1997. Lloyd provides practical advice to those who choose the proverbial unpractical career goals—to make a living as writers, artists, filmmakers, musicians and dancers. She takes the reader from clarification of the dream through techniques for structuring each day.

**Lobenstine, Margaret.** *The Renaissance Soul: Life Design for People with Too Many Passions to Pick Just One*. New York: Broadway, 2006. Have you been stymied by too many interests? How do you pick just one when your interests are so numerous and so diverse? Career and life coach, Margaret Lobenstine, validates and encourages the Renaissance Souls of the world, offering tools for meshing numerous interests with a fulfilling career.

**Rosenberg, Gigi.** *The Artist's Guide to Grant Writing*. Watson-Guptill (a division of Random House), 2010. This book is designed to transform readers from starving artists fumbling to get by into working artists who confidently tap into all the resources at their disposal. Written in an engaging and down-to-earth tone, this comprehensive guide includes time-tested strategies, anecdotes from successful grant writers, and tips from grant officers and fundraising specialists. Sign up for her newsletter at her website (http://gigirosenberg.com/) for ongoing support.

# Websites for Creatives

## Job Postings

- **Craigslist** ([www.craigslist.org](http://www.craigslist.org)) the legendary San Francisco Bay Area-based Website, also has an ample Portland section. You will find here the most complete list of creative jobs in the area. Craigslist discussion forums provide a venue to ask for free feedback: So, how long did it take you to get QuickBooks going for your freelance business? Does anyone know a good proofreader who will barter for a massage?
- **The Regional Arts and Culture Council** (RACC [www.racc.org](http://www.racc.org)) has done hours of work for you by culling local job postings (both employment and freelance) from a wide range of sources. These postings are in the "information services" section under "employment."
- **Jackie Mathys** ([www.jackiemathys.com](http://www.jackiemathys.com)) is a recruiter in Portland who places studio artists and managers with clients in design, advertising and corporate marketing. Job announcements are listed at the site as well.
- **Mac Prichard** of Portland State University's School of Social Work moderates a listserv for job postings in communications, public affairs and politics. Send your full name and email address to [lori@prichardcommunications.com](mailto:lori@prichardcommunications.com) to join 500+ others in Salem, Eugene and Portland metro who post and/or receive job listings.

## Other Web Resources

- [www.veronikanoize.com](http://www.veronikanoize.com). Veronika (Ronnie) Noize is fun, funny, and knows marketing inside and out. Ronnie's Website is rich with practical tools for marketing that are applicable to freelancers in all areas. She regularly speaks in Portland and Vancouver and also offers telecourses. Veronika is an extrovert who "walks her talk" and has a thriving coaching business.
- [www.allfreelancework.com/newsletter](http://www.allfreelancework.com/newsletter). This is a free online newsletter and project board for freelancers in all fields that includes a directory to other online freelance resources. Article samples are: "Creating a Home Office on a Budget" and "Keeping Your Business's Finances on Track."
- [www.kathienelson.com](http://www.kathienelson.com). Kathie Nelson, a local networking guru, has helpful networking tips on her Website and e-newsletter.
- **Self-Employed Creative Professionals** (SECP, at [www.secppdx.com](http://www.secppdx.com)) provides resources for writers, graphic designers, multimedia professionals, etc. You can subscribe to the monthly newsletter through the Website.
- **Meetups** are ad hoc informal groups that bring people with similar interests together. You can attend once or on an ongoing basis. Most are at no cost or for a nominal fee, and are generally small gatherings. Groups include Portland Photographic Explorers, the Portland Web Design Meetup Group, and the NW Creatives Social Club. **Meetup** groups can be found at [http://www.meetup.com/](http://www.meetup.com/).

# Professional Associations for Creatives

**AIGA Portland, the professional association for design,** (http://aigaportland.org/) was founded in 1914 as the American Institute of Graphic Arts. It's the oldest and largest professional membership organization for design. AIGA's mission is to advance designing as a professional craft, strategic tool and vital cultural force. They have "Career Tools," which is a quarterly breakfast series, and you can sign up for their weekly email bulletin.

**Creative Mornings** (http://www.creativemornings.com/) is a monthly breakfast lecture and discussion series for Creatives. With lectures happening all over the world, the Portland chapter even films the talks so you can go back and watch them on Vimeo. Topics include local resources like ADX who provides a workspace and incubator community for artists, design theory talks, and design, culture and craft showcase and tips.

**Graphic Artists Guild** (GAG, https://www.graphicartistsguild.org) welcomes graphic artists of every profession (illustrators, graphic designers, cartoonists, computer artists, photographers) to join the Guild. The Website includes links to job banks and other job resources for Creatives.

**Oregon Columbia International Association of Business Communicators** (OCIABC, http://www.ociabc.org) serves writers who are employed in businesses with responsibilities including media relations, employee relations and communication, development, graphic design, media production, advertising, marketing, public affairs, program management and many others.

**Oregon Media Production Association** (OMPA, www.ompa.org) is an association of professionals working in film, video and news media. The association also has an active newsletter, meetings and a comprehensive directory of local resources in the field.

**Public Relations Society of America** (PRSA, www.prsa-portland.org) has a rich array of professional development activities at both the national and local levels. The society has a broad definition of public relations professionals, so many programs are relevant to all creatives. The atmosphere is welcoming and many programs are free.

**Self-Employed Creative Professionals** (SECP, www.secppdx.com) provides monthly meetings, generally Wednesday evenings, for writers, graphic designers, multimedia professionals, etc. Topics have included marketing materials, the psychology of working alone, making effective presentations and networking. You can subscribe to the monthly newsletter through the Website.

**Society for Marketing Professional Services/Oregon Chapter** (www.smpsoregon.org/) hosts luncheons and seminars. Its mission is "to enhance the marketing and management ability of its members and those who market professional A/E/C (Architecture, Engineering, Construction) services to secure profitable work for their firms through education, networking and resources.

**Software Association of Oregon** (SAO, www.sao.org) is very active in providing educational resources and networking for all careers in technology, ranging from Web designers to informational architects. The association publishes a useful industry directory and a salary survey.

**Girls in Tech** (GIT, http://girlsintech.net/) is a networking enterprise for women in technology. GIT offers a variety of resources and tools for women to supplement and further enhance their professional careers and aspirations in technology. Local monthly meetings are attended by 20 or more people of both genders and all ages.

# Appendix B—Resources for Careers in Sustainability

## Explore Local Green Resources

Use the following list to broaden your exploration of local individuals, books, and organizations dedicated to sustainability. Once you have a clear niche, you might use several of these resources to stay current in your part of the green world.

***AXIS Performance Advisors*** (www.axisperformance.com/). AXIS Performance Advisors is a management consulting firm specializing in the implementation of sustainable business practices. Primary Consultants: Darcy Hitchcock and Marsha Willard, Portland, OR.

***Business Guide to Sustainability: Practical Strategies and Tools for Organizations***, by Darcy Hitchcock and Marsha Willard. Earthscan, 2006. This no-nonsense guide to how to green your office or business offers practical strategies that apply equally to businesses, not-for-profits, and government offices.

***Portland Business Journal.*** This weekly business journal covers news from the four-county region, and now prints a quarterly insert called "Sustainable Oregon."

***Green Posting*** (www.greenposting.org) a local green directory. People learn about what makes a business green leaning and to write reviews based on personal experience regarding each company's sustainable attributes. It provides green business articles, event information, farmers market locations, tips, job postings, a glossary of sustainable terms –a one-stop site for residents to be part of Portland's sustainable community.

***Northwest Eco Building Guild*** (http://www.ecobuilding.org/gp) is a Web-based directory designed to connect the region's most innovative green building products and service providers with the growing number of consumers and professionals in the Pacific Northwest who want to employ green building practices and use environmentally sensitive technologies.

***Sustainable Industries*** (www.sustainableindustries.com/jobs). *Sustainable Industries* magazine lists green employment options for the Northwest, and includes a handful of job postings for Portland. This trade publication aimed at serving readers already on the inside of sustainability-oriented businesses also gives job seekers a great deal by reading it. It features local businesses committed to sustainability, focusing on four core industry sectors: Agriculture & Natural Resources, Energy, Green Building and Recycled Markets.

***ReDirect Guide: Guide to Healthful & Sustainable Businesses*** (http://redirectguide.com/) This free progressive yellow pages, found in many locations throughout Portland, lists and advertises hundreds of mostly small, approachable businesses and self-employed professionals. The sustainable-minded job seeker can find many desirable workplaces and potential employers in this guide.

***"Sustainable Life" section of Portland Tribune*** (www.portlandtribune.com/sustainable/index.php) This weekly installment of the Portland Tribune, published every Tuesday, with stories about individuals, groups and companies who are working towards creating a sustainable quality of life in the Portland region.

***SustainableOregon.net*** (http://www.sustainableoregon.com/) communicates developments in Oregon state government and connects you with local agencies, organizations and businesses taking leadership roles in sustainable development.

***City of Portland Bureau of Planning and Sustainability*** (www.portlandonline.com). The bureau's mission is to provide leadership and to contribute practical solutions to ensure a prosperous community where people and nature thrive, now and in the future. This website provides lots of resources to keep the green job seeker informed.

# Websites for Local Sustainability Job Postings

There is no one local website that captures all of the postings for jobs in sustainability. So we suggest that you first check out the sites listed below to see which three have the postings most relevant to your goals. Then you can focus on regularly checking those three sites. In addition to reviewing these general job sites, don't forget to periodically check the websites for your favorite, potential employers.

**\*CNRG** (www.cnrg-portland.org). Subscribers to this Listserv receive daily e-mail notification of job openings, classes, events and other information related to community involvement and the nonprofit sector.

**\*Craigslist** (portland.craigslist.org). The Nonprofit and Creative job sections have a significant number of postings. Try searching all jobs with terms like "sustainability," "environment," and "conservation."

**\*PNW Job Seekers** (groups.yahoo.com/group/pnwJobSeekers). This listserv was established to share information about Portland area job opportunities in natural resource conservation and environmental education. To subscribe, visit the link above or send a blank e-mail message to: pnwJobSeekers-subscribe@yahoogroups.com.

**\*Green Drinks** (www.pdxgreendrinks.org). Portland's chapter of Green Drinks meets monthly and posts local job openings in sustainability.

**Earth Share Oregon** (earthshare-oregon.org). This federation of nonprofit environmental organizations promotes environmental education and charitable giving through workplace campaigns. There are no listings for paid jobs, but lots of volunteer opportunities.

**Groundwire** (http://groundwire.org/about) engages the public to work to solve social and environmental challenges.

**Cascadia** (cascadiagbc.org/resources/cascadia-job-board). Pioneering innovative green building initiatives, Cascadia is the Pacific Northwest's regional U.S. Green Building Council Chapter. Posts green building-related jobs.

**City of Portland Bureau of Planning and Sustainability** (http://www.portlandonline.com/bps/) Click on the "Events, News & Opportunities" tab. This website is designed to be a clearinghouse for jobs, sustainability tours, advisory groups, and sustainability classes.

**Sustainable Industries** (http://www.sustainablebrands.com/)You'll find a regularly updated list of green jobs in the jobs section of the site.

\*Those with an asterisk generally have the largest number of job postings in sustainability.

---

**Green Jobs Network** (http://www.greenjobs.com/). Although it's a national site, we want to call special attention to this hub for sustainable and socially responsible jobs. The Green Jobs Network typically has an extensive listing of Oregon jobs aggregated from other sites, and offers a green job board (http://www.greenjobsearch.org/), green job e-mail list (http://www.greenjoblist.com/), blog on green collar jobs (http://www.greencollarblog.org/), and listings of green career books (http://www.greenjobs.net/green-career-books/), green job fairs (http://www.greenjobs.net/green-job-fairs/), green job boards (http://www.greenjobs.net/green-job-boards/), solar jobs (http://www.greenjobs.net/solar-jobs/), and jobs at environmental non-profits (http://www.greenjobs.net/green-non-profit-jobs/).

# National Websites: Job Postings and Career Information in Sustainability

Note: Some sites require key word searches. Try "green" "renewable" "environmental"

- **Care2.com** (jobs.care2.com/a/all-jobs/list). Very large site dedicated to healthy and sustainable living. Try "jobs" + other key word in the Job Finder.

- **Clean Edge Jobs** (jobs.cleanedge.com). A good place to check out the range of job titles in clean energy, including some Oregon options.

- **CleanTechRecruits** (www.cleantechrecruits.com) Specializes in renewable energy jobs. View clean energy jobs including Wind, Solar, Hydro, Biomass, and Geothermal.

- **Eco.org** (www.eco.org) Focuses on environmental career planning and internships for students and graduates. Includes tips and resources with primers on "Ten career skills all environmental professionals need" and "Learn about ecosystems management."

- **Ecobusiness Links** (www.ecobusinesslinks.com/environmental_jobs.htm) Chock full of links to green job boards. Categories include Environmental, Environmental-Specific Industries, Promotion of Sustainable Job Creation, Regional Green Job Listings, Biofuel, Clean Energy, Environmental Employers, and Internships.

- **Ejobs** (www.ejobs.org). Useful for its comprehensive list of environmental organizations, environmentally linked businesses, and environment-related government agencies. The job listings are not broken down by state.

- **Green Dream Jobs** (www.sustainablebusiness.com/index.cfm/go/greendreamjobs.main). One of the most comprehensive sites allowing you to search by city, state, and career level.

- **GreenBiz.com** (jobs.greenbiz.com) features news, technical assistance, discussion forums, and job listings for sustainable businesses. The job postings also include nonprofits, as they overlap substantially with Green Dream Jobs.

- **Greenjobs** (www.greenjobs.com/public/index.aspx#). This site "brings recruiters and job seekers together in the renewable energies industry." Includes blog about green collar jobs.

- **Idealist** (www.idealist.org). This is a project within Action Without Borders, a nonprofit created with the intention of building a better world by connecting people, resources, and organizations to find practical solutions to social and environmental problems. This website is a job board link through Sustainable Communities Network.

- **North American Association of Environmental Educators** (eelink.net/pages/EE+Jobs). The primary emphasis of this site is environmental education. It also links to other job sites, including a few already listed here, and has its own database at eelink.net/pages/EE+Jobs+Database.

- **Sustain Lane Green Collar Jobs** (www.sustainlane.com/green-jobs). People-owned site has lots a Portland job focus, including ranking Portland and #1 city for sustainability.

- **Treehugger** (jobs.treehugger.com/?campaign=th_nav_jobs). A one-stop media outlet focused on sustainability. Blogs, articles, video on design, architecture, transportation, nutrition, culture, fashion, politics, and business. Posts listing in the U.S. and abroad in public, private, and nonprofit sectors.

# Green Occupations
### Contributed by Jim Cassio ([www.cassio.com](www.cassio.com))

In response to climate change and other concerns, our society is going green and that includes the workplace. Many employers are creating new green jobs and changing their existing jobs in terms of how the work is done. Others are starting up new businesses built on a foundation of green values. Although we don't know the exact number, it is clear that number of green jobs in the United States is growing. It is also clear that green jobs now represent a wide variety of occupational choices that didn't exist just 2–3 years ago. Green jobs can now be found in every corner of the workplace and economy. It's even reasonable to think that, someday, the majority of jobs in the U.S. will be green – or at least have a green tint!

The list that follows shows the industries and their sectors where most green jobs can be found:

### Advertising & Public Relations Services Industry (Green)
All sectors

## Agriculture & Food Industry
Green sectors include:
- Green/Natural/Organic Food Restaurants
- Makers of Natural/Organic Food Products
- Sellers of Prepared Natural/Organic Food
- Sustainable/Organic Farms
- Sustainable/Organic Nurseries/Greenhouses
- Sustainable Aquaculture Farms/Fish Hatcheries

## Alternative Fuel Vehicles Industry
Green sectors include:
- Advanced Technology Vehicle Manufacturers (electric, hybrids, fuel cell, hydrogen)
- Alternative Fuel Vehicle Manufacturers
- Alternative Fuel Producers/Distributors
- Alternative Fuel Vehicle Repairers (technicians, first–responders)
- Alternative Fuel Vehicle Sales/Service
- Battery Manufacturers

## Bicycle Industry
Green sectors include:
- Bicycle Courier & Cargo Services
- Bicycle Manufacturing
- Bicycle Sales & Service

## Biotech/Life Sciences Industry
Green sectors include:
- Blue Biotechnology (marine and aquatic applications)
- Green Biotechnology (agricultural applications)
- Red Biotechnology (medical applications)
- White Biotechnology (industrial applications)
- Bioeconomy (investments and economic output)

## Building Industry (Green/Sustainable)
Green sectors include:
- Architectural Services
- Building Materials
- Building/Construction/Specialty Trade Contractors

- Furniture/Cabinet Makers (using environmentally certified/recycled wood)
- Salvage & Deconstruction Services

## Cleaning & Janitorial Services Industry (Green Cleaning)

All sectors

## Clothing & Accessories Industry (Organic/Natural/Recycled Material)

Green sectors include:
- Design
- Manufacturing
- Wholesale
- Retail

## Ecotourism Industry

All sectors

## Engineering Services Industry (Green)

Green sectors include:
- Chemical
- Civil
- Construction Management Services
- Environmental
- Land Planning
- Manufacturing/Production
- Surveying
- Transportation

## Environmental Health & Safety Services Industry (Consulting)

All sectors

## Environmental & Hazardous Materials (HazMat) Services Industry

Green sectors include:
- Environmental Consulting Services
- Hazardous Materials (HazMat) Services
- Environmental Engineering Services – see Engineering Services Industry

## Geography & GIS Services Industry

All sectors

## Government

Green sectors include:
- Federal – e.g. Army Corps of Engineers; Bureau of Land Management (BLM); Centers for Disease Control and Prevention (CDC); Department of Energy; Environmental Protection Agency; Fish and Wildlife Service; Forest Service; Geological Survey (USGS); National Oceanic and Atmospheric Administration (NOAA); National Park Service; Natural Resources Conservation Service (NRCS)
- State – e.g. Agriculture and Food Safety; Coastal Zone Management; Community and Economic Development; Emergency Services; Energy; Fisheries and Wildlife Protection; Parks and Recreation; Planning; Pollution Control and Prevention; Public Health; Water Resources
- Local (cities, towns, counties, special districts) – e.g. Air Quality Management; Conservation/Park Land Management; Electricity; Green Building; Green Business; Public Transportation; Recycling; Regional Planning; Waste Management; Water and Wastewater Treatment

**Investment Services Industry (Sustainable/Socially Responsible Investing/SRI)**

All sectors

**Journalism & Publishing Industry (Green/Sustainable)**

All sectors

**Legal Services Industry (Environmental and Land Use Law)**

All sectors

**Landscaping & Habitat Restoration Services Industry (Green)**

Green sectors include:
- Arborist/Tree Services
- Gardening/Landscape Maintenance Services
- Habitat Restoration Services
- Landscape Architectural Services
- Landscape Contractors

**Natural Sciences Consulting Services**

Specialties include:
- Atmospheric and Space Scientists
- Biochemists, Biophysicists, and Toxicologists
- Chemists and Forensic Toxicologists
- Environmental Scientists
- Epidemiologists
- Foresters and Forest Pathologists
- Geoscientists, Environmental Geologists, Hydrogeologists, and Marine Geologists
- Hydrologists and Water Resources Managers
- Microbiologists and Environmental Health Microbiologists
- Physicists and Health Physicists
- Soil and Plant Scientists
- Soil and Water Conservationists
- Zoologists, Wildlife Biologists, and Marine Biologists

**Nonprofit Organizations (Green/Environmental)**

All environmental sectors

**Printing Industry (Green/Sustainable)**

All sectors

**Recycling Industry (Green)**

Green sectors include:
- Electronics (cell phones, computers)
- Glass
- Metal & Plastics
- Paper
- Textiles

**Renewable Energy Industry**

Green sectors include:
- Biomass
- Solar Systems Manufacturing
- Solar Systems Sales, Installation and Service
- Wind Turbines Manufacturing
- Wind Turbines Sales, Installation and Service

**Utilities Industry**

Green sectors include:
- Electric Power Generation, Transmission & Distribution
- Natural Gas Distribution
- Water, Sewage & Other Systems

**Other – Misc. Retail (Green/Sustainable/Organic Products)**

Green sectors include:
- Crafts/Artwork Made by Third–World Artisans
- Gardening Supplies
- Recycled, Reclaimed and Earth–Friendly Products
- Outdoor Apparel/Equipment
- Scooters

**Top 20 Green Job Titles during a recession***

- Executive Director, Nonprofit
- Project Leader/Manager
- Sustainability Program Director/Manager
- Sales/Business Development Associate or Manager
- Marketing Manager/Coordinator
- Community Crew Leaders/Supervisors, Conservation Associations
- Business/Data Analyst
- Research Analyst/Manager
- Environmental Educator/Naturalist
- Account Executive/Manager, Sales
- Professor (various academic fields)
- Sustainability Analyst/Consultant
- Operations Manager
- Wind Energy Engineer
- Administrative Assistant
- Trainer, Training Specialist or Training Coordinator
- Electrical/Design Engineer
- Green Architect
- Green Building Project Manager
- Solar Process Engineer/Process Integration Engineer

*Green Dream Jobs of www.sustainablebusiness.com and Jim Cassio, green careers author and workforce consultant

# Appendix C—Resources for Social Justice

## Websites and Books for Social Justice

There are hundreds of social service and social justice agencies and advocacy groups in Oregon. Here's a sampling of key organizations whose websites lead you to more information and contacts in your field of interest. Some are statewide organizations while others are local service providers.

### Oregon Non-profits

- **Non-profit Association of Oregon** (http://www.nonprofitoregon.org/) is the leading agency providing technical assistance and training to Oregon nonprofits.
- **Oregon Business Journal's 100 Best Non-profits** to work for in Oregon (http://www.oregonbusiness.com/articles/104-october-2011/5920-100-best-nonprofits) is an excellent report on the variety/resilience/contributions of Oregon's non-profits.
- **Oregon Non-profit Sector Report 2011** (http://www.nonprofitoregon.org/sites/default/files/uploads/file/ONSR.pdf) is an excellent report on the variety/resilience/contributions of Oregon's non-profits.
- **www.Idealist.org** This organization and website provide excellent resources, tips and job leads for folks who want to make a difference. It's a national organization with offices in Portland. The website includes self assessment tools designed to help you select goals, find out about the nonprofit world, and link to current job openings as well.
- **CNRG** (http://www.cnrg-portland.org/) The Community Nonprofit Resource Group is a "must join" electronic community for nonprofit job seekers. When you sign up for their notices (we suggest the digest, so you get only 2-3 emails per week) you'll find dozens of Portland-area jobs, internships and volunteer opportunities posted.

### Legal and Human Rights

- **American Friends Service Committee** (http://afsc.org/office/portland-or) is the local arm of a national peace and activism organization founded by Quakers.
- **Legal Aid Services of Oregon** (http://www.lawhelp.org/program/694/index.cfm) provides free civil legal services for low-income individuals.
- **Oregon Law Center** (http://www.oregonlawcenter.org/) is a firm that advocates for the rights of low-income communities.
- **Basic Rights Oregon** (http://www.basicrights.org/) is a gay rights organization.
- **Human Rights Campaign** (http://www.hrc.org/states/oregon) is a local chapter of national gay rights organization.

### Poverty/Human Services

- **Multnomah County Community Services** (http://web.multco.us/dchs-community-services) provides a listing of county services for families, seniors and people with disabilities.
- **Oregon Food Bank** (http://www.oregonfoodbank.org/Our-Work?c=129844745617546417) is a statewide agency providing food and advocacy for low income communities.
- **Human Services Coalition** (http://www.oregonhsco.org/) is a group of nonprofits that advocates on human services and rights.
- **Oregon Microenterprise Network (OMEN)** http://www.oregon-microbiz.org/) is a network of agencies that provide small business development services that focus on low-income individuals.

### Women's Issues

- **Oregon Coalition Against Rape and Domestic Violence** (http://www.ocadsv.com/) is a statewide advocacy and support agency for Oregon's domestic violence programs.

- **Community College Transitions Programs** (http://mhcc.edu/StudentServices.aspx?id=499) are community college-based programs that help women prepare for academic and career success; some programs serve men as well.

### Mental Health
- **Mental Health Association of Portland** (http://www.mentalhealthportland.org/) is an advocacy organization for people with mental illness.
- **Association of Oregon Community Health Programs** (http://www.aocweb.org/aoc/aocmhp/AboutUs/tabid/275/Default.aspx) advocates for mental health services.

### Youth
- **Children First for Oregon** (http://www.cffo.org/) researches and advocates on children's issues.
- **Children's Trust Fund of Oregon** (http://ctfo.org/) funds programs to prevent child abuse.
- **Homeless Youth Continuum** (http://web.multco.us/sun) is a network of Portland area youth-serving agencies.

### Elders
- **Campaign for Oregon seniors and people with Disabilities** (http://www.oregonspromise.org/2009/09/17/advocacy-coalition-for-seniors-and-people-with-disabilities/) advocates for seniors and people with disabilities.
- **Oregon Association of Area Agencies on Ageing and Disabilities** (http://www.o4ad.org/resources1.html) provides advocacy and services for seniors and people with disabilities.

### Health
- **Community Health Advocates of Oregon** (http://www.chao-oregon.org/) is a community health advocacy agency
- **Multnomah County Community Capacitation Center** (http://web.multco.us/health/community-capacitation-center) provides community health education programs.
- **Multnomah County Health and Human Services** (http://web.multco.us/health-human-services) is the county health services agency.
- **Oregon Health Sciences University** (http://www.ohsu.edu/xd/about/services/human-resources/) has a broad range of healthcare training and service jobs.

### Minority/Immigrant Rights
- **Center for Intercultural Organizing** (http://www.interculturalorganizing.org/) is a nonprofit that trains and advocates for immigrant rights.
- **Latino Network** (http://www.latnet.org/) is a network advocating for and serving Latino community needs.
- **Coalition of Communities of Color** (http://www.coalitioncommunitiescolor.org/) is a research and advocacy group representing Portland area communities of color.

### International Relief and Service
- **Mercy Corps Northwest** (http://www.mercycorpsnw.org/) is an international organization that provides medical and development services.

### Books
**Cryer, Shelly.** *The Nonprofite Career Guide: How to Land a Job That Makes a Difference.* 2008.
**Land, Stephanie.** *The Idealist.org Handbook to Building a Better World: How to Turn Your Good Intentions into Actions that Make a Difference.* 2009.

# Appendix D—Resources for Make-a-Difference Types
## Books for People Who Want to Make a Difference

The purpose of the early stages of **Career Exploration** is to learn about a broad spectrum of options that match your values, skills and interests. The following books and websites give you an overview of a variety of career options. In the later stages of **Career Exploration**, you will want to use resources more targeted to your top career possibilities. For example, if you are considering a career in development, you should read *Careers in Fundraising* by Lila Wagner and ask people attending the Willamette Valley Development Officers meetings which journals and books they find useful. A risk in using any of these books is that trends change faster than the publishing industry. For example, books were just starting to proclaim the huge need for Webmasters after the bubble had already burst. In addition, these books are written for national audiences and may not reflect trends in Oregon. Therefore, double-check what you find in books with online resources. Discuss your findings with local professionals in your desired field through informational interviews and by attending professional organization meetings.

**Broad Exploration of Job Titles**

- **Cryer, Shelley.** *The Nonprofit Career Guide: How to Land a Job That Makes a Difference.* Fieldstone Alliance Nashville, TN, 2008. This excellent book provides an in-depth look at nonprofit jobs in specific sectors and provides practical tools and tips for preparing for and landing nonprofit jobs.
- **Everett, Melissa.** *Making a Living While Making a Difference: Conscious Careers for an Era of Interdependence.* New Society Publishers: Gabriola Island, Canada, 2007. The substantially revised third edition acknowledges that while the path to finding a life's work that is satisfying, sustainable and financially feasible is not easy, there are simple steps to follow. She gives an empowering ten-step program.
- **Everett, Melissa.** *Making a Living While Making a Difference: The Expanded Guide to Creating Careers with a Conscience.* New Society Publishers: Gabriola Island, Canada, 1999. Everett speaks to people committed to creating a better planet through their work. She aims to rouse people to think creatively and entrepreneurially about the true work to be done to move toward environmental sustainability and economic justice. The volume is 80 percent inspiration and 20 percent practical advice.
- **Idealist.** (www.idealist.org). A site dedicated to helping idealists network. Here you can research jobs, organizations, volunteer opportunities, internships, events, programs, resources and even people. For those of us interested in the arts, sustainability, alternative education, and community, it's easy to use and internationally based.
- **Nemko, Marty.** *Cool Careers for Dummies.* Hungry Minds: New York, 2007. Resources from the government and those drawn from government research are out of date before they are even printed. Recent editions barely mention the range of environmental and creative/technical jobs that emerged in the late nineties. In contrast, Nemko gives less carefully researched but more current insight into newly emerging uncommon careers. In the early exploration phase, take an hour in a comfy chair at Borders or the coffee shop at Powell's to review Nemko's yellow pages in *Cool Careers For Dummies* to see if any new career titles catch your eye.

# Websites for People Who Want to Make a Difference

This section focuses on careers in nonprofit, education and health care. Careers in sustainability are covered in a separate section.

**Portland/Metro Area Websites: General**

- www.cnrg-portland.org. This is an excellent resource for nonprofit job seekers. Subscribers to this listserv receive daily notification by email of job openings, classes, events and other issues of interest to people seeking alternative careers.
- www.craigslist.com. A large proportion of jobs posted elsewhere show up on Craigslist within a few days. However, it is frustrating that many jobs do not identify the employer.
- www.easystreet.com/services/nplist.html. This is not a job site but an excellent resource nonetheless. It's one of the best single collections of links to the Websites of Portland Metro area nonprofits.
- www.Indeed.com. This comprehensive site seems to review and compile listings from other major traditional job sites, like Monster.com. I recommend trying it for a few weeks and seeing if you can save time by dropping Jobdango, Monster, etc.

**Portland/Metro Area: Development**

- www.wvdo-or.org. Willamette Valley Development Officers sponsors this site that has the most comprehensive local listing of jobs in development, including event planning, fundraising and grant writing.

**Portland/Metro Area: Government**

- www.portlandonline.com/omf/index.cfm?c=26588 City of Portland jobs.
- www.portofportland.com Port of Portland jobs.
- www.co.multnomah.or.us/jobs Multnomah County jobs.
- http://www.oregonmetro.gov/index.cfm/go/by.web/id=24255 Metro Region jobs.
- www.oregonjobs.org State of Oregon jobs.

**National Jobsites: General**

The following all serve as clearinghouses for national nonprofit job information. All of them allow users to narrow their search criteria to jobs from one specific state, so it's pretty easy to go through them and check what's available in Oregon right now.

- www.idealist.org. This is one of the first Web job sites to focus exclusively on nonprofits. Today it lists more than 8,000 organizations, publications, nonprofits and community organizational interests in its database of 18,000 nonprofit and community organizations in 130 countries. Despite its vast scope, you can customize it so that it will send you only those postings from Oregon.
- www.nonprofit.about.com. About.com's Nonprofit Charitable Orgs is a massive clearinghouse of information about nonprofits. It's not exclusively geared toward job seekers. There are, however, many useful links such as "One Stop Resource for Job Seekers," "Local Nonprofit Connection," and help to start your own nonprofit. There are many useful links under the section "Work in a Nonprofit" also.
- www.accessjobs.org. Click "Jobs" to get an extensive list of links to all sorts of jobs, some of which are for nonprofit organizations.
- www.nonprofitcareer.com. The Nonprofit Career Network is a resource center for individuals seeking job and volunteer opportunities in nonprofit organizations.

- www.opportunitynocs.org. Opportunitynocs.org is a good resource for nonprofit jobs and career opportunities with a reasonable number of Oregon postings.
- www.groups.yahoo.com/group/NonprofitTechJobs. This is a list of jobs and internships in technology for all around the country. While there are not a lot of Oregon postings, it is a good place to research the types of technical skills generally in high demand in the nonprofits.

**General Information Sites**

- www.careers-in-marketing.com/nplinks.htm. This site features links to the Websites of several nonprofits. There is also useful information and links to resources on topics relevant to nonprofit career seekers, such as fundraising and management techniques.
- www.guidestar.org. Although there are no jobs listed here, it's a great resource for people who've narrowed their job search to the nonprofit sector. This is a database that lists every IRS-registered 501(c)(3) organization in the U.S.
- www.handsonportland.org (formerly Volunteerworks). This Website provides a searchable database of volunteer opportunities. Sponsored by Hands on Portland, the site links volunteers to a variety of service opportunities. It also helps nonprofit organizations, schools and governments harness volunteer power. You can select the type of organization or skills you want to use.
- www.marcsmiley.com. This is not a job site, but it has an excellent resource list for people who want to understand management and development in nonprofits. Marc Smiley is a consultant who has worked for energy, conservation and other nonprofits throughout the NW. His workshops are a great place to network and research current trends.

**Other Internet Resources for People Who Want to Make a Difference**
You may be interested in nonprofit jobs in fundraising, health or education. You may also want to research public employment, where job security, salaries and benefits may be higher and more predictable. We know that public employment has also been affected by this decade's recession, but there are still jobs, and likely public employment will be on the upswing again in future years.
**Here are sample Internet resources for you:**

**Portland-area public employers**
City of Portland (http://www.portlandonline.com/omf/index.cfm?c=54930)
Multnomah County (http://web.multco.us/jobs)
Clackamas County (http://www.clackamas.us/des/jobinfo.jsp)
Washington County (http://www.co.washington.or.us/Support_Services/HR/Employment/employment-opportunities.cfm)
Metro (http://www.oregonmetro.gov/index.cfm/go/by.web/id=24255) regional government
State of Oregon (http://www.oregonjobs.org/)

**Education**
Portland Public Schools (http://www.pps.k12.or.us/departments/hr/index.htm)
Portland Community College (http://www.pcc.edu/hr/employment/)
Clackamas Community College (http://wcmsprod.clackamas.edu/jobs/)
Mt Hoot Community College (https://jobs.mhcc.edu/applicants/jsp/shared/frameset/Frameset.jsp?time=1340041066943)
Portland State University (http://www.pdx.edu/hr/employment)
Education Northwest (http://educationnorthwest.org/) is a regional education research and consulting agency.

# Appendix E-Fundraising Resources

## Resources for Fundraising and Development Careers

Books and Articles

*Careers in Fundraising* by Lilya Wagner Ed.D., CFRE. NY: John Wiley & Sons, Inc: 2002. From The AFP/Wiley Fund Development Series. Whether you are new to the fundraising profession or a seasoned professional, this book is a must-have for your permanent library. Most chapters include excellent 'further information' sections featuring recommended printed materials and selected Internet resources. The book also features many testimonials and tips presented as sidebars. Individuals currently engaged in or considering a job search will especially appreciate the chapters which comprise "Part Five: Conducting the Job Search."

*Advancing in Your Fundraising Career (online article, Association of Fundraising Professionals)*

- *http://www.afpnet.org/ResourceCenter/ArticleDetail.cfm?ItemNumber=5805*

### Professional Associations

Association of Fundraising Professionals (AFP)

- http://www.afpnet.org/about/?navItemNumber=500

### National Websites

### Chronicle of Philanthropy Guide to Continuing Education

- http://philanthropy.com/section/Continuing-Education-Guide/195/

### The Center on Philanthropy at Indiana University

- http://www.philanthropy.iupui.edu/thefundraisingschool/

### AFP Code of Ethical Principles and Standards

- http://www.afpnet.org/files/ContentDocuments/CodeofEthics.pdf

### Local and Regional Resources

- APRA (Prospect Research)
  - http://www.aprahome.org/p/cm/ld/fid=182
- CASE - Council for Advancement and Support of Education
  - http://www.case.org/Career_Central/For_Job_Seekers.html
- Grant Professionals Association
  - http://grantprofessionals.org/job-center

### Educational Institutions (Oregon) Offering Nonprofit Degree and/or Certificate Programs

- Portland State University, Institute of Nonprofit Management - http://www.inpm.pdx.edu/
- University of Portland - http://business.up.edu/default.aspx?cid=10204&pid=457

### Professional Development Resources

### AFP Oregon & SW Washington (Association of Fundraising Professionals)

- http://afporegon.afpnet.org/

Copyright©2012 Brenda Ray Scott, CFRE and Adept Diva Consulting

**WVDO (Willamette Valley Development Officers (WVDO)**

- http://www.wvdo-or.org

**Credential**

- http://www.cfre.org/

The CFRE (Certified Fund Raising Executive) is the premier credential for professionals working in fundraising and development. There are 5,322 professionals with the CFRE designation throughout the world with 4,422 in the United States (as of the writing of this article). This credential is a must for professionals seeking to advance their standing – and their salaries – in fundraising and development.


**<u>Resources at the Multnomah County Library (Central in downtown Portland, Oregon)</u>**

- **Databases & Links**
  - *http://www.multcolib.org/ref/bus.html#Nonprofits*
  - *Click on the word nonprofit to go to links on the page.*

- **Fundraising References** (Government Documents Room)
  - *The Chronicle of Philanthropy*
  - *Grassroots Fundraising*
  - *The Foundation Databaook – Oregon and Washington*
  - *Other fundraising and grant seeking reference books*

- **Periodicals**
  - *The Business Journal (Portland)*
  - *Fast Company Magazine*
  - *Oregon Business Magazine*
  - *Stanford Social Innovation Review*

Copyright©2012 Brenda Ray Scott, CFRE and Adept Diva Consulting

# Appendix F—Community Resources

A database contains the most up-to-date resource directory for the Portland metro region and includes every resource you may be able to imagine is called 2-1-1 (http://211info.org/). We recommend that you go to this resource first because it is continuously updated and has a staffed resource referral program. If you prefer to speak to someone who knows the database, call during the day. Otherwise, search the database yourself online. Check out 2-1-1 for any resource you need, including housing, healthcare, counseling, clothing, childcare, legal services, and many other services.

For additional resource information, you may want to review the following websites. Because these directories may not be updated as frequently as 2-1-1, make sure you double check your information by contacting the resource directly.

- **Where to Turn Guide** (http://www.mhcc.edu/docs/HeadStart/WheretoTurn.pdf) is a document from Mt. Hood Community College that focuses on East Multnomah County resources, but includes many regional services as well.
- **Oregon Helps** (http://www.oregonhelps.org/) you to enter your information and will list government benefits for which you may qualify, including food stamps.
- **Rose City Resource** (http://www.rosecityresouce.org/) is a Portland area resource directory.
- A **Mental Health Resource** list is available on the Mt. Hood Community College website (http://mhcc.edu/StudentService.aspx?id=496) You do not have to be a student to utilize these resources.
- **Tax Credit** information is available through the Allsup website (http://www.allsup.com/personal-finance/manageing-your-taxes/tax-credits-for-lower-income-taxpayers.aspx).

# Appendix G—Funding for School

School funding falls into three general categories: state and federal financial aid, scholarships, and fellowship or assistantship programs. If you already have a bachelor degree, you will not qualify for free public aid. Your focus will be on student loans, scholarships and other programs.

**Federal financial aid** includes three types of aid for undergraduates:
- Grants based on income. Most states, including Oregon, have state grants as well. This is free money!
- Work Study gives you federal wages for part-time employment, typically on campus. These jobs can be leveraged in several ways: earn a small paycheck in between classes, gain job experience and good references, and feel a part of campus life rather than being a PCP (parking lot, class, parking lot) commuter.
- Loan programs offer some subsidized by the feds, others unsubsidized, which affects interest payments and grace periods. Almost everyone qualifies for some type of loan.

Apply for federal financial aid in January, or as early in the calendar year as you can. Early applicants are more likely to receive maximum aid packages for the next school year. You can apply at any time of the year for aid, including for a current term or year of school. For example, if you are just starting school in January 2012, you would apply for both the 2011-2012 year to cover your winter and spring costs, and for the 2012-2013 year, (which starts in July or September, depending on your school), so you are first in line for next year's aid. Aid is determined based on the previous calendar year's income. If your income has drastically changed between calendar years, you may be able to argue for a change in your "base year" and receive more aid.

Financial aid is awarded based on an unrealistic budget set by the federal government, which does not consider age and barely considers size of household. Age is only a factor if you are under 24, in which case you are stuck with using your parents' income, unless you are married or have kids. It doesn't matter that you haven't spoken to your parents in 10 years and that they have no ability or intention of paying for your college education. These funds are not intended to support an individual or a family, although many students do manage to live entirely on financial aid by taking out the maximum number of loans and paring their lifestyle costs. A large percentage of college students, particularly at community colleges and urban universities, work full or part-time while they are in school.

Those who already have a bachelor degree are out of luck for grants, unless you can prove your bachelor degree is terribly outdated and there are no jobs in your field. In which case, you may be able to finagle some limited aid for a technical certificate. If you already took out loans for your previous bachelor degree, you also may want to look into the federal limits on how much money you can take out total. They do cap it, and the amount may change. **Graduate students** can only get loans from the feds.

**Taxes and Paying Student Loans**
You may be able to deduct some of your educational costs, and/or enjoy tax credits based on your student status. Check the latest IRS regulations (http://www.irs.gov/pub/irs-pdf/p970.pdf). Also, student loan programs do provide some flexibility in payment for those who are unemployed or disabled. Loans may be temporarily suspended or set up for interest payment only.

There are also limited "forgiveness" programs which might allow you to reduce or eliminate your loan debt. You may also want to consider a year or two of service in the Peace Corps, Americorps, or VISTA, which end with monetary awards that can be used to pay off portions of student loans. Also, these experiences can build excellent job experience and references for your later job search or for school and scholarship applications. Check out Heather Jarvis's website (http://askheatherjarvis.com/tools) for detailed information on student loan options.

### Scholarships and Fellowships
**For undergraduates**, scholarships are abundant. Here's the basic approach:
- Look at your school or prospective schools and apply for their scholarships. Plan ahead.
- Tons of other scholarships are available at the local, regional and national level.
- See **How to Find, Organize and Win Scholarships** for information on how to locate and apply for scholarships in more detail.

**Graduate students** may find scholarships at their schools. However, they are limited in number so again, plan ahead.

### Tuition Waivers and Assistantships
Colleges and universities offer a variety of undergraduate and graduate tuition waiver or payment programs for students who work and/or volunteer. At community colleges and universities, for example, students may obtain a waiver of their tuition as members of student recruitment teams, as student government leaders, as athletes, or as student newspaper editors. Graduate students often obtain assistant positions in which they act as faculty aides or teaching assistants, with tuition covered or paid for them.

### Fellowships
Graduate students, and even some undergraduates, may obtain school funding by winning local or national fellowships. We recommend the school aid directories published by Reference Service Press, (http://www.rspfunding.com/index.html) which include volumes for women, people of color, and people with disabilities. These directories are a bit expensive, but may be worth the price if you find them helpful. The directories are often available as reference books at public libraries. The Multnomah County Library maintains several directories for review onsite.

# How to Find, Organize and Win Scholarships

**Who Gets Scholarships?**
There is no answer. Lots of people get scholarships, including very ordinary, regular people. No you don't have to be a genius and have a 4.0 GPA. You don't have to be an athlete or a beauty queen. You can be a small town boy who coached Little League and had the best 4-H heifer in his county and now wants to be a nurse. You can be a battered woman who left her husband and got a life and is now studying social work. You can be an immigrant from the Ukraine who sold honey on the streets and is now working towards an engineering degree. You can be a middle class person with a privileged background who has volunteered extensively working with troubled kids. You do need to write good scholarship essays and have good references. It helps to have a history of volunteer work. It is worth it for everybody who goes to school to apply for scholarships.

**Portland Area Scholarships**
All colleges and universities offer scholarships. Check out availability at PCC, MHCC and PSU:

- Portland Community College Foundation (http://www.pcc.edu/foundation/what-we-do/scholarships/) offers scholarships in the spring each year, as well as a smaller set of scholarships in the fall.
- Mt. Hood Community College (http://www.mhcc.edu/FinancialAid.aspx) offers scholarships fall, winter and spring, so you have three opportunities to apply.
- Portland State University (http://pdx.edu/finaid/scholarship) offers scholarships each spring for new and continuing students.

**The State and Region**
In Oregon we have tons of other sources as well, the best being the Oregon Student Assistance Commission (http://www.oregonstudentaid.gov/scholarships.aspx). OSAC administers a wide variety of scholarships, and you can apply for multiple scholarships with one set of essays and one application. Most wonderfully, OSAC administers the Ford Scholarship Program (http://www.getcollegefunds.org/ford-scholarships.aspx), which is an amazing gift to college students in Oregon. Are you 25 or older and just starting college? Are you a single parent? Or are you a sophomore with enough credits to transfer next fall? The Ford Scholarship will pay for a significant percentage of all your school expenses at an Oregon college of your choice, for several years until you get your degree. In some cases, students with high GPA's have also been awarded full funding for their master degree. You have to be competitive, but a lot of regular, hard working folks have received this scholarship. It's not just grades. It's background, obstacles overcome, community service performed, strong essays, and a good interview for the finalists.

Oregon scholarships on the MHCC site (http://mhcc.edu/StudentServices.aspx?id=468). There are also local scholarships for:

- GLBT students (http://www.equityfoundation.org/scholarships)
- Healthcare students (http://www.legacyhealth.org/body.cfm?id=524)
- Nursing students (http://www.linfield.edu/catalog/endowed-and-special-scholarships.html)
- Latino students (http://www.hmccoregon.com/scholarships/)

**National Scholarships**
Here's a listing of scholarship websites (http://mhcc.edu/StudentServices.aspx?id=483). This is where you must be strategic. Search by category to find scholarships specific to you. Don't pay for scholarship search services; they are a scam. Try http://www.fastweb.com/ some people like it, some don't. You have to deal with advertisements.
Here's just a tiny sampling of scholarships for women:

- National Scholarships for Women: (http://mhcc.edu/StudentServices.aspx?id=478)
- Women in Careers: http://mhcc.edu/StudentServices.aspx?id=479
- Women in Healthcare: http://mhcc.edu/StudentServices.aspx?id=480

## Appendix H—Career Services

# Vicki Lind, MS,
# Career Counselor and Marketing Coach
*"I help my clients articulate their core strengths, go out into the world, and prosper."*

**Career Counseling and Job Search Services**

*Career Assessment: What's Inside?*
For people who seek clarity about what they really want in a career. Clients clarify their key passions, values, skills, and what they want from their work. As an outcome, you will have a list of two to four career choices that match your interests, values, skills, and financial needs.

*Making a Career Decision: What's Out There?*
For people who are clear about their key passions, values, skills, and what they want from their work. You have identified a few options and need guidance in researching them and making a final commitment. This stage includes an analysis of job availability and compensation. Networking and informational interviews will be facilitated by Vicki putting you in contact with her prior clients whenever possible.

*Finding the Job: Making the Match.*
For people who have a clear career objective but are having trouble finding a job that matches their skills and values. As an outcome, you will have a strategic job search plan, a cheerleader, a network of professionals in your field, targeted resumes and cover letters, and effective interviewing skills.

**Marketing for Solo Professionals**

*Marketing Group for Creatives* is a group for experienced creative people in all fields – designers, writers, fine artists, performers, and marketing/PR professionals – that provides support, resources, and marketing plans for freelancers. It meets twice a month for two hours, is limited to 7 people, and costs $200 for five months.

*Marketing Group for Healers* is a group for healers in all fields – therapists, personal trainers, yoga teachers, naturopaths, and chiropractors – that provides support, resources, and marketing plans for practitioners. It meets twice a month for two hours, is limited to seven people, and costs $200 for five months.

**Workshops**

Scheduled as needed:

*Introduction to LinkedIn:* Two hour class to help you develop an engaging LinkedIn Profile as well as an introduction to more advanced features of networking through LinkedIn.

*Interview Clinic:* A two-part workshop to help you develop interviewing strategies, compelling stories about your accomplishments, and tactics for challenging questions.

More information may be found at www.vlind.com.

# Cynthia Dettman, JD, MSW
## Life and Career Coach

Cynthia offers affordable, sliding-scale individual and group career coaching services. She focuses on helping folks find satisfying jobs and careers that MAKE A DIFFERENCE, whether it's serving youth and women, the elderly, the environment, or bringing peace to the world. Cynthia is particularly interested in working with groups, having found that career changers often thrive with group networking and support.

Having worked for many years in both social service, legal service and community college settings, Cynthia's special skills includes:
- Supporting women in transition
- Leading career transition groups
- Offering culturally competent services to minorities and immigrants
- Helping adults plan and fund their college education (with special focus on scholarships)
- Locating both short term and long term training and education opportunities
- Encouraging networking into Portland's many "make a difference" communities

Cynthia maintains a private practice and also teaches at area community colleges in credit and non-credit programs. She frequently teaches at Mt Hood and Portland Community Colleges, offering a variety of career planning and college skills development classes.

Her website http://www.cynthiadettman.com/ includes current information on both her private and public services.